teach yourself...

FOURTH EDITION

Al Stevens

MIS: PRESS

A Subsidiary of
Henry Holt and Co., Inc.

First Edition—1995

Library of Congress Cataloging-in-Publication Data

```
Stevens, Al,
    Teach yourself--C++ / Al Stevens. --4th ed.
        p. cm.
    Includes index.
    ISBN 1-55828-406-0
    1. C++ (Computer program language)  I. Title.
QA76.73.C153S73  1994
005.13'3--dc20                              94-24954
                                CIP
```

Printed in the United States of America.

10 9 8 7 6 5 4 3

MIS:Press books are available at special discounts for bulk purchases for sales promotions, premiums, fund-raising, or educational use. Special editions or book excerpts can also be created to specification.

For details contact: Special Sales Director
                        MIS:Press
                        a subsidiary of Henry Holt and Company, Inc.
                        115 West 18th Street
                        New York, New York 10011

Editor-in-Chief: Paul Farrell

Managibg Editor: Cary Sullivan

Development Editor: Debra Williams Cauley

Technical/Copy Editor: Betsy Hardinger

Production Editor: Anthony Washington

Dedication

To Landon, Woody, and Landon Woodie (wherever she is).

Acknowledgments

Thanks are due to the companies and individuals mentioned here.
These vendors, who contributed C++ compiler products:

> Borland International
>
> Comeau Computing
>
> Microsoft Corporation
>
> Symantec Corporation
>
> The Free Software Foundation
>
> Watcom International Corporation
>
> MetaWare Incorporated

DJ and Pat Delorie, who developed and distribute DJGPP, an extended MS-DOS port of the GNU C++ compiler.

Alexander Stepanov, who coauthored the Standard Template Library, made it available, and provided guidance on its future and use.

P.J. Plauger, who developed the first implementation of the Standard C++ Library.

Bjarne Stroustrup, who created C++.

Table of Contents

PART 1
Traditional C++

Table of Contents

PART 1
Traditional C++

PART 2
Contemporary C++

PART 3
Future C++

Preface

This book is the fourth edition of *teach yourself C*++, a tutorial text with which C programmers teach themselves C++. The first edition was published in 1990, the second in 1991, and the third in 1993. Significant changes in the C++ language resulted in each edition. The ANSI/ISO C++ Standardization Committee is working toward a standard definition of C++, adding features to the language and changing others. The standardization activity is dynamic, and the Committee is not finished. In February 1994, it published a working paper for informal public review. Many of the language and class library additions and changes defined in the informal working paper have been implemented in PC compilers. Those implementations represent the contemporary C++ language, which is available for use by programmers. Since that time, more changes have been proposed and approved.

Readers of earlier editions of *teach yourself C*++ will observe that the book gets bigger with each new edition. This growth reflects the growth in the language. C++ is a much larger language than it was when I wrote the first edition.

As a result there are more things to learn, and this book adds chapters to cover new subjects. The third edition included an introductory chapter on object-oriented programming. I deleted that chapter in this edition to make room for coverage of new language features. Readers interested in object-oriented programming will find a similar chapter in *C++ Database Development*, 2nd Edition, 1994, MIS:Press.

This edition of *teach yourself C++* includes a C++ compiler system on the companion diskette that you can use to compile and run the exercises in most of the chapters. This feature places *teach yourself C++* into a trilogy of programming texts that consists of *Welcome to Programming* (1994, MIS:Press), *Al Stevens Teaches C* (1994, M&T Books), and this work. All three books provide language development environments for the student to use when running the exercises. The trilogy constitutes a complete programming course that teaches programming fundamentals with QBasic, the C language, and C++.

C++ is a superset of the C language and contains all the program constructs of C. The C++ language adds features to C that improve its syntax and expand its application through object-oriented programming extensions. *teach yourself C++* leads you through the C++ learning process with a series of exercises. Each exercise includes C++ source code that you can compile and execute. To get the maximum benefit from these lessons, you should load, compile, and run the exercises as you go along.

The exercises lead you through the subjects in a sequence that introduces simpler concepts first, using them in successive exercises as more complex subjects are developed. The exercises build upon preceding ones, and sometimes you modify programs from earlier exercises. Therefore, you should follow the exercises in the order in which they appear.

A complex subject such as a programming language often sends you into a learning loop. You cannot learn a lesson without knowing about a prerequisite lesson, which itself has the new lesson as a prerequisite. A case in point is the C++ *iostream* class. To understand it thoroughly, you must understand C++ classes and overloaded operators, both of which are advanced C++ topics. Yet to progress to those advanced topics, you must run exercises that use the keyboard and screen, and those devices are implemented in the *iostream* family of classes. You have to use the system-defined *cin* and *cout* objects with an unquestioning faith that what they do and how they do it will eventually make sense. Trust the book and be patient—everything eventually becomes clear. Stick with it, and you will be rewarded.

Because of this circular approach, the programmer who is already well versed in C++ might wonder about the organization of this book. Some exercises do not include code constructs that a seasoned C++ programmer would recognize as conventional, appropriate, or even necessary. These omissions are intentional and result from the learning sequence of *teach yourself C++*. Eventually the book covers those bases. Other omissions are due to the highly advanced nature of C++ and the kind of strange and exotic code that it permits. There are elements in C++, just as in C, that a tutorial work should spare the newcomer. Later, when you have the language well in hand, you can push it to its limits.

The exercise programs are small. They are not full-blown, useful programs that you take into the workplace, nor are they intended to be. Each exercise demonstrates a particular feature of C++. Perhaps some of the exercises could lead to useful software tools. That potential is itself a lesson. The strength of extensible languages is that they allow the programmer to build reusable software. You soon learn that C++ is extensible, far more so than C and most other traditional programming languages.

Most exercises in this book are complete programs in that they compile and link independently. A few exercises illustrate common programming errors and might not compile or run properly. Where this is true, the book and the comments in the code point it out. Some programs combine code from several exercises. In these cases, the dependent code always follows closely behind the code it needs. You will have no trouble keeping track of where you are if you follow the exercises in the order in which they appear.

A BRIEF HISTORY OF C++

The C++ programming language was designed and developed by Bjarne Stroustrup in the Computer Science Research Center at AT&T Bell Labs in Murray Hill, New Jersey. He began this work in about 1980 to answer a need for a simulation language with the features of object-oriented programming, then a relatively new programming paradigm. Rather than design a new language from the ground up, Dr. Stroustrup decided to add the features he wanted to the well-established C language, itself an earlier development from within the Center.

C was already implemented on several different architectures and supported portable program development, so Dr. Stroustrup made an historic decision: He elected to develop the C++ language system as a translator program that processes C++ source language into C source language. The translated C source language could then be compiled on any computer system that supports C. He called his translator program CFRONT, and many implementations of C++ have been ports of that same CFRONT program and its successors, the source code of which is available to language system developers under license from AT&T. The C++ language has been available outside AT&T since about 1985.

Over the years, C++ has continued through several versions. Dr. Stroustrup remains its staunchest advocate and is a strong contributing presence wherever C++ issues surface. The standardization of C was completed by a joint committee of the American National Standards Institute (ANSI) and the International Standards Organization (ISO) in 1989. A new joint ANSI/ISO committee—designated X3J16 within ANSI and WG11 within ISO and hereinafter called the *committee*—was formed in 1989 to tackle the formidable task of defining a standard for C++. Five years later that effort continues, and in February 1994 the committee published a working paper of a draft standard for informal public review.

C++, like C before it, is becoming the language of choice among programmers. Since the first edition of this book came out, C++ language systems have appeared in every environment and on most architectures where C once reigned supreme, adding testimony to the assertion of Dr. Stroustrup and others that C++ will ultimately replace C.

THE C++ LEGACY TO C PROGRAMMERS

Even if you have never seen a C++ program, you have been touched by it. Although C came before C++, many of the features in C saw their first light of day in the improvements that Dr. Stroustrup sought to add to the language when he defined his first superset. These features were widely admired, incorporated into various C compilers, and ultimately adopted by the ANSI/ISO C standardization committee.

Examples of the C++ improvements that are now standard in C are function prototypes, *void*, and the *const* type qualifier.

Even if you are using a C++ compiler, you can still build C programs. The full range of C language features and C standard-library functions is automatically a part of every C++ language system because C++, as originally designed, passes through to a C compiler. Learning C++ begins with the C that you already know.

THE THREE STATES OF C++

C++ is an evolving language with no published formal standard definition. It has, at any given time, three states, called here *traditional* C++, *contemporary* C++, and *future* C++. Traditional C++ is the language as it has existed in released AT&T versions and that all serious compilers support. Contemporary C++ consists of traditional C++ with new features approved by the committee but implemented only by a few compilers. Future C++ consists of the language under discussion in the committee with new features that are approved—for the interim, at least—but not yet implemented. There is a great deal of overlap with respect to which features are implemented by which compilers, and it is not necessarily true that any one compiler supports only one of the three states. Furthermore, new versions of compilers appear regularly. What is true today will have changed by the time this book gets into print and will change further during the life of this edition.

The three states of C++ will coexist until the committee has formally published an approved standard definition and all compilers comply. Because the committee has decided to innovate new language features and to change, remove, or deprecate old features, none of the three states can be considered sacrosanct until publication of the formal ANSI/ISO C++ Standard.* The organization of this book, discussed next, reflects the condition of the three states of the language as of the summer of 1994.

THE ORGANIZATION OF THIS BOOK

The best way for a C programmer to learn C++ is to take it in small steps, using the features in a sequence that introduces the C++ extensions one at a time. The organization of this book takes that approach within the framework of the three states of C++.

The book contains three parts, loosely reflecting the three states of C++. The exercises in Part I (Chapters 1–10) teach traditional C++ and compile and run with any implementation of C++ that supports AT&T version 3.0 or higher. Part II (Chapters 11–13) teaches contemporary C++. Chapter 11 is about templates,

---

* The committee's decision to innovate language is a departure from the tradition established by the C standardization committee to codify existing practice.

Chapter 12 is about exception handling, and Chapter 13 is about runtime type information and new-style casts. The exercises in Chapter 11 work only with compilers that have implemented templates, which, among MS-DOS compilers, include GNU C++, Borland C++, Comeau C++, MetaWare High C++, Microsoft C++, Watcom C++, and Symantec C++. The exercises in Chapter 12 work only with the Borland, MetaWare, and Watcom compilers, the only ones that support exception handling at this time. The exercises in Chapter 13 work only with the Borland and MetaWare compilers, which are the only current implementations of runtime type information and new-style casts. Part III (Chapters 14–15) discusses future C++. Chapter 14 is about namespaces and other additions and changes to the language approved by the committee but not yet implemented. Chapter 15 discusses additions to the Standard C++ class library.

A Glossary and Bibliography follow Chapter 15. The Glossary provides brief definitions of terms that are common to C++. The Bibliography lists the books and articles that contributed to the research that went into this book.

The Appendix discusses MS-DOS compilers and describes how you can use the GNU C++ compiler, which is included on the companion diskette. The compiler is an MS-DOS port of GNU C++, a compiler provided by the Free Software Foundation. The Appendix explains how to install and operate the GNU compiler and how, for a minimum cost, you can get the complete GNU C and C++ compiler systems including full source code.

Although I used MS-DOS-based compilers to develop and test the exercises, none of the exercises is specific to MS-DOS, the PC platform, or any particular compiler's nonstandard extensions to the language and libraries. The code in this book is generic C++, as close to the moving standard as possible.

Al Stevens
October 1994

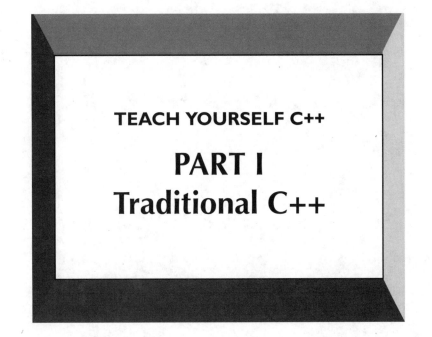

TEACH YOURSELF C++

PART I
Traditional C++

CHAPTER 1

C++ Basics

C++ is a superset of the C language with extensions and improvements. Extensions are new features in the language, whereas improvements are better ways of doing the things that C already does. You teach yourself C++ by first learning the improvements and extensions as enhancements to what you already know as a C programmer. Later, you apply this new knowledge as you learn the object-oriented features of C++. This chapter is the first step. You will learn about:

- ❖ The *iostream* class
- ❖ Comments
- ❖ Function prototypes
- ❖ Keywords

3

THE FIRST C++ PROGRAM

Exercise 1.1 is your first C++ program.

Exercise 1.1   *The Simplest C++ Program*

```
main()
{
}
```

Look familiar? It should. It's the smallest possible C program as well. Because C++ is a superset of the C language, you can use a C++ compiler to develop and compile C programs. The minimum program just shown does not do anything, of course. It contains no more than one function, which, as in C, must be named *main*. Exercise 1.2 is a program that does something.

Exercise 1.2   **Hello.cpp**

```
#include <iostream.h>
main()
{
    cout << "Hello, world";
}
```

This program is **hello.cpp**, the C++ equivalent to the **hello.c** program that introduced the world to the C language in Kernighan and Ritchie's *The C Programming Language*, traditionally referred to as K&R. But instead of **stdio.h**, this program includes **iostream.h**, and instead of a *printf* call, it uses an unfamiliar syntax with the undefined variable name *cout*, the bitwise shift left operator (<<), and—the only familiar part of the example—a literal string expression that greets the world. You might well wonder about the meaning of it all.

N O T E

The exercises in this book declare the *main* function with no return type, which implies that *main* returns an integer; yet the *main* functions in the exercises have no *return* statement and, therefore, return nothing. The C++ language specification says that the *main* function type is implementation-dependent. Traditionally, *main* returns an integer value, which the program returns to the system. If *main* returns no value, the compiler assumes a *void* return, and the system receives an undefined return value when the program terminates by a return from *main*. Most C++ textbooks declare *main* the same way this one does. Some C++ compilers issue the warning. The Symantec C++ compiler issues an error and refuses to compile programs with *main* functions that are declared to return something but that do not return anything. This compiler behavior is unconventional. If you are using the Symantec compiler and compiling the exercises one at a time, either add the *void* return type to all *main* functions or insert a statement at the end of the *main* function that returns a zero value.

INPUT/OUTPUT STREAMS

The **hello.cpp** program in Exercise 1.2 is your introduction to the powerful C++ facility called the *class*, a feature that lets a programmer define new data types and operators. A complete explanation of the class is premature in this chapter, but you should know that C++ compiler products use classes to implement an improved stream input/output system. That design has become a de facto standard in C++ programs and is a part of proposed Standard C++. You use these improved streams to read and display information throughout these lessons, and you need this early exposure to it.

The Standard Output Stream

The *cout* variable, seen in Exercise 1.2, is the C++ standard output stream, which writes to the console:

```
cout << "Hello, world";
```

Exercise 1.2 sends the "Hello, world" string to the standard output device stream, represented by the *cout* object. The << operator is the output operator. It points symbolically from what is being sent to where it is going. You can think of *cout*, *cin*, and *cerr* (described soon) as devices, in much the way you think of *stdout*, *stdin*, and *stderr* in C programs. In C++ stream input/output, *cout*, *cin*, and *cerr* are identifiers that name objects—instances—of classes. In this example, the string is being written to the *cout* object, which displays the string on the console.

Suppose you wanted to display the contents of an integer variable on the screen. In C you would use the *printf* function along with a format string that describes the parameters to *printf* as shown here:

```
printf("%d", amount);
```

In C++ you would use the *cout* object. Exercise 1.3 sends data values to the C++ stream output device directly—no format string is required.

Exercise 1.3   *The Standard Output Stream*

```
#include <iostream.h>
main()
{
    int amount = 123;
    cout << amount;
}
```

Exercise 1.3 displays an integer value on the console. Suppose you want to display the value as part of a sentence. By using the techniques that you learned in Exercise 1.3, you can display different data types by sending each of them in turn to the output stream. The *cout* stream can discern the format of the data type from the variable's identifier because the C++ compiler makes the association when it compiles your code. The discussions in Chapters 4 and 8 on function and operator overloading show how the compiler does this. For now you can accept it as a feature of the standard output stream in C++. Ready or not, you must now acquaint yourself with *iostream* input and output, because you need them to enter and display data values.

Exercise 1.4 sends a string, an integer, and a character constant to the output stream.

Exercise 1.4 *Multiple Data Types to the Standard Output Stream*

```
#include <iostream.h>
main()
{
    int amount = 123;
    cout << "The value of amount is ";
    cout << amount;
    cout << '.';
}
```

Exercise 1.4 displays the following message on the screen:

```
The value of amount is 123.
```

The exercise sends three different data types to *cout*: a string literal, the integer *amount* variable, and a character-constant '.'. This approach might send you scurrying back to the standard C language *printf* function, because the exercise used three statements where *printf* could have done it in one.

Exercise 1.5 sends multiple data types to the standard output stream in one line of code. The exercise displays the same value as that from Exercise 1.4.

Exercise 1.5 *Several Outputs in One Statement*

```
#include <iostream.h>
main()
{
    int amount = 123;
    cout << "The value of amount is " << amount << '.';
}
```

Exercise 1.5 connects several data types with the << operator. This behavior is a by-product of the *this* pointer (which is used in the definition of the *stream* classes and gets full treatment in Chapter 7). For now, accept the behavior and forge ahead.

Formatted Output

The ways that you have used *cout* so far do not apply the well-formatted displays of the C *printf* family of functions. Suppose you want to display the hexadecimal representation of a variable. The C *printf* function handles that nicely. How does C++ do it?

The *iostream* class system associates a set of *manipulators* with the output stream. These manipulators change the displayed numerical base for integer arguments. You insert the manipulators into the stream to make the change. The manipulators' symbolic values are *dec*, *oct*, and *hex*.

Exercise 1.6 uses manipulators to display an integer in three numerical base representations.

Exercise 1.6   *Formatting Numerical Data*

```
#include <iostream.h>
main()
{
    int amount = 123;
    cout << dec << amount << ' ' << oct << amount << ' '
        << hex << amount;
}
```

The exercise inserts the manipulators *dec*, *oct*, and *hex* into the stream to convert the value that follows—*amount*—into different numerical base representations.

Exercise 1.6 displays the following result:

```
123 173 7b
```

Each of the values shown is the decimal value 123 in a different base representation.

N O T E   The concept of sending manipulators to a device is alien to C programmers. In C, everything beyond the formatting string that you pass to printf gets displayed. In C++, each device is implemented as an object. The object reacts to the data you send it according to the types of the data. Manipulators are themselves objects of a unique type defined within the iostream class system. When you send a manipulator to a stream object, the object uses the value of the manipulator to modify the object's own behavior, in these cases the format of the data to be displayed.

The Standard Error Stream

The *cerr* object uses the same syntax as *cout*, except that *cerr*'s output goes to the standard error device. This technique allows you to display error messages on the console even when the program's user redirects the standard output device.

The Standard Input Stream

By using *cout* and *cerr* you can display all types of data on the screen. Next you must learn to read data into your programs. The *iostream* version of standard input is implemented with the *cin* object.

Exercise 1.7 uses *cin* to read an integer from the keyboard.

Exercise 1.7   *The Standard Input Stream*

```
#include <iostream.h>
main()
{
    int amount;
    cout << "Enter an amount...";
    cin >> amount;
    cout << "The amount you entered was " << amount;
}
```

Exercise 1.7 sends a string to *cout* to prompt you for input. The *cin* device writes the value that you enter into the *amount* integer variable. The exercise then displays the *amount* variable on *cout* to demonstrate that the *cin* operation worked.

Exercise 1.7 displays the following messages. (The first **123** is the value that you type into the program. It could be any other integer value.)

```
Enter an amount...123
The amount you entered was 123
```

Suppose that you use this program in a system with a 16-bit integer (as with some MS-DOS compilers). If you enter the value **65535**, the program displays **–1**. If you enter **65536**, the program displays **0**. These displays occur because the *amount* variable is a signed integer. Change the *amount* variable's type to an unsigned integer, and retry the program. For another experiment, see what happens when you enter a value that has decimal places.

Try entering alphabetic characters instead of numbers into Exercise 1.7. It doesn't work. The *cin* device is able to work with strings—character arrays, actually—as well as with numbers, but you must use the correct data type in the expression. To illustrate, Exercise 1.8 uses the *cin* device to read a string value from the keyboard into a character array.

Exercise 1.8 *Reading a String*

```
#include <iostream.h>
main()
{
    char name[20];
    cout << "Enter a name...";
    cin >> name;
    cout << "The name you entered was " << name;
}
```

Exercise 1.8 displays the following messages. (The name "Tyler" is used here for the name that you type into the program.)

```
    Enter a name...Tyler
    The name you entered was Tyler
```

Exercise 1.8 has a flaw. The character array is only 20 characters long. If you type too many characters, whatever follows the *name* array on the stack is over-written, and peculiar things happen. An *iostream* function named *get* solves this problem; you learn about *get* in Chapter 10. For now, the exercises assume that you do not type more characters than the declared character array can accept.

The *cin* and *cout* objects are not themselves a part of the compiled C++ language. The stream classes are not built-in data types, and the << and >> operators are not, in this context, built-in C++ operators. Input and output streams are implemented as C++ classes, and *cin* and *cout* are global instances of those classes. This implementation exists outside the C++ language implementation, just as the *printf* and *scanf* functions are implemented through functions in the C language and not as a part of the C language. But whereas C limits its extensibility to function and structure definitions, C++ allows you to define new data types and to associate custom operators with those data types. You learn how to do this later.

C++ COMMENTS

The exercises so far have contained no comments. C++ supports the standard C comment format. The /* character sequence begins a comment, and the */ sequence ends it. But C++ has another comment format. The C++ comment token is the double-slash (//) sequence. Wherever this sequence appears (other than inside a string literal), everything to the end of the current line is a comment.

Exercise 1.9 repeats Exercise 1.8 and adds comments to the program.

Exercise 1.9 *C++ Comments*

```
#include <iostream.h>
main()
{
    char name[20];              // declare a name string
    cout << "Enter a name...";  // request a name
    cin >> name;                // read the name
    // ------------ display the name
    cout << "The name you entered was " << name;
}
```

FUNCTION PROTOTYPES

Standard C supports function-declaration blocks that describe the function's storage class, return value, and parameters to the C compiler. This feature, called the function *prototype*, allows the compiler to check the function's definition and function calls with the prototype. C compilers do not require function prototypes. If you provide prototypes, all references to the functions must comply with the prototypes, but if you omit them, the best that you can get are warning messages.

C++ requires that all functions have prototypes. As with C, a prototype can stand alone as an independent declaration or it can be implied by the function header block in the function definition. If the function definition precedes any references to the function, no other prototype is required. To illustrate the C++ requirement for prototypes, Exercise 1.10 uses a function with no prototype to display the "Hello, world" message on the screen.

Exercise 1.10   *A Program without Function Prototypes*

```
// This program will not compile
#include <iostream.h>
main()
{
    display("Hello, world");
}
void display(char *s)
{
    cout << s;
}
```

Because the display function has no prototype, the program in Exercise 1.10 does not compile without error messages.

Exercise 1.11 adds a function prototype to the program in Exercise 1.10. This addition allows the program to compile without errors.

Exercise 1.11   *A Program with a Function Prototype*

```
#include <iostream.h>
void display(char *s);  // function prototype
main()
{
    display("Hello, world");
}
void display(char *s)
{
    cout << s;
}
```

Now, with a proper prototype, the program compiles and runs correctly. C++ also requires that the function definition declare the types of function parameters within the parentheses that follow the function's name, as shown here.

```
void func(int x, int y)  // C++ function
{
    // ....
}
```

Standard C accepts this format, too, but still permits the old K&R style where parameter declarations are listed immediately below the function name, as shown here.

```
func(x, y)  // K&R C function, invalid C++
int x;
int y;
{
    // ....
}
```

C++ uses stronger parameter type-checking than C and does not permit the older style.

The prototype and function-definition requirements are strict but necessary ones. They also represent exceptions to the general rule that a C++ compiler can compile a C program. If your C programs do not have function prototypes and new-style function-definition header blocks, then you must add those features before compiling the programs with a C++ compiler.

C++ KEYWORDS

When you port C programs to C++ you must be aware of all the C++ keywords—which have meaning to the language and which you must not use as identifiers. Older C programs might use one or more of them, and you must change these usages before you compile the program with a C++ compiler. C++ reserves the Standard C keywords and adds some of its own. Table 1.1 lists the Standard C keywords. Table 1.2 lists the the common keywords that C++ adds.

Table 1.1   *Standard C Keywords*

asm	double	long	typedef
auto	else	register	union
break	enum	return	unsigned
case	extern	short	void
char	float	signed	volatile
const	for	sizeof	wchar_t
continue	goto	static	while
default	if	struct	
do	int	switch	

Table 1.2   *Common C++ Keywords*

bool	friend	protected	true
catch	inline	public	try
class	mutable	reinterpret_cast	typeid
const_cast	namespace	static_cast	using
delete	new	template	virtual
dynamic_cast	operator	this	
false	private	throw	

C++ includes other keywords that cannot be identifiers. These keywords are alternatives to the Standard C trigraphs for international keyboards that do not have the special characters used in English to express some operators. The committee added these keywords so that international programs would be more readable. This book does not use these keywords in any exercises. Table 1.3 lists them so that you know to avoid using them as identifiers. Chapter 14 discusses them in more detail.

Table 1.3   *International C++ Keywords*

and	*bitor*	*or*	*xor_eq*
and_eq	*compl*	*or_eq*	*not_eq*
bitand	*not*	*xor*	

SUMMARY

This chapter gave you your first exposure to the C++ language. It identified some of the language extensions and introduced C++ input/output streams so that you can use them in the exercises that follow. Chapter 2 discusses more of the improvements that C++ brings to the C language.

CHAPTER 2

C++ Extensions to C

Programmers often describe C++ as an improved C, because C++ offers better ways to write code within the structure of the C language. You learned about C++ comments, the first of those improvements, in Chapter 1. Many programmers prefer the C++ double-slash comment style to traditional C comments.

This chapter introduces several other improvements that C++ brings to the language. These improvements enhance your use of C and prepare you for the more advanced object-oriented properties of C++. You will learn about:

- ❖ Default function arguments
- ❖ Variable declaration placement
- ❖ Scope resolution operator
- ❖ *inline* functions
- ❖ *const* variables and functions

17

- ❖ *enum* as a type
- ❖ Linkage-specifications
- ❖ Anonymous unions
- ❖ Unnamed function parameters
- ❖ Constructor notation for intrinsic types

DEFAULT FUNCTION ARGUMENTS

A C++ function prototype can declare that one or more of the function's parameters have default values. When a call to the function omits the corresponding arguments, the compiler inserts the default values where it expects to see the arguments.

You can declare default values for arguments in a C++ function prototype in the following way:

```
void myfunc(int = 5, double = 1.23);
```

The expressions declare default values for the arguments. The C++ compiler substitutes the default values if you omit the arguments when you call the function. You can call the function by using any of the following ways:

```
myfunc(12, 3.45); // overrides both defaults
myfunc(3);        // effectively func(3, 1.23);
myfunc();         // effectively func(5, 1.23);
```

To omit the first parameter in these examples, you must omit the second one; however, you can omit the second parameter by itself. This rule applies to any number of parameters. You cannot omit a parameter unless you omit the parameters to its right.

Exercise 2.1 shows the use of default parameters.

Exercise 2.1 *A Function with Default Parameters*

```
#include <iostream.h>
void show(int = 1, float = 2.3, long = 4);
main()
{
    show();                 // all three parameters default
    show(5);                // provide 1st parameter
    show(6, 7.8);           // provide 1st two
    show(9, 10.11, 12L);    // provide all three parameters
}
void show(int first, float second, long third)
{
    cout << "\nfirst = "  << first;
    cout << ", second = " << second;
    cout << ", third = "  << third;
}
```

Exercise 2.1 displays the following result:

```
    first = 1, second = 2.3, third   = 4
    first = 5, second = 2.3, third   = 4
    first = 6, second = 7.8, third   = 4
    first = 9, second = 10.11, third = 12
```

The first call to the *show* function in Exercise 2.1 allows the C++ compiler to provide the default values for the parameters just as the prototype specifies them. The second call provides the first parameter and allows the compiler to provide the other two. The third call provides the first two and allows the compiler to provide the last. The fourth call provides all three parameters, and none of the defaults is used.

VARIABLE DECLARATION PLACEMENT

In C, local variables are declared at the beginning of the block in which they come into scope. All variable declarations in a block must occur ahead of any statements. C++ removes that restriction. You can declare a variable anywhere in the block before you reference it. This feature lets you put a variable's declaration closer to the code that uses it. When the variable's declaration is close to its use, its purpose and behavior can be easier to understand.

Exercise 2.2 places the declaration of a variable close to its first reference.

Exercise 2.2 *Relocating a Variable Declaration*

```
#include <iostream.h>
main()
{
    cout << "Enter a number: ";
    int n;
    cin >> n;
    cout << "The number is: " << n;
}
```

Exercise 2.2 displays the following messages on the screen. The **234** is the number you enter.

```
Enter a number: 234
The number is: 234
```

The freedom to declare a variable anywhere in a block makes possible expressions such as the following:

```
for(int ctr = 0; ctr < MAXCTR; ctr++)
    // ...
```

Exercise 2.3 declares a variable inside a *for* statement's expression list.

Exercise 2.3 *Variable Declaration Placement*

```
#include <iostream.h>
main()
{
    for (int lineno = 0; lineno < 5; lineno++)
        cout << "\nThis is line number: " << lineno;
}
```

Exercise 2.3 produces the following output:

```
This is line number: 0
This is line number: 1
This is line number: 2
This is line number: 3
This is line number: 4
```

Observe the scope of the *lineno* variable. The variable is in scope for the current block and all blocks subordinate to it. The variable's scope, however, begins where the declaration appears. C++ statements that appear before the declaration cannot refer to the variable even though they might appear in the same block as the variable's declaration.

N O T E

Future C++ permits the declaration of a variable from within the conditional expression of an *if* statement. Chapter 14 discusses this change.

THE SCOPE RESOLUTION OPERATOR

In C, if a local variable and a global variable have the same name, all references to that name while the local variable is in scope refer to the local variable. Local variable names in C take precedence over global variable names. You must be aware of and program for this characteristic of C. You cannot refer to a global variable when a local variable has the same identifier. You would need to change the name of one of the two.

C++ offers a better approach. To tell the compiler that you want to refer to a global variable rather than the local one with the same name, use the :: scope resolution operator. The global scope resolution operator—which is coded as a prefix to the variable's name (for example, ::*varname*)—lets you explicitly reference a global variable from a scope where a local variable has the same name.

Exercise 2.4 is an example of the scope resolution operator.

Exercise 2.4   *Global Scope Resolution Operator*

```
#include <iostream.h>
int amount = 123;       // a global variable
main()
{
    int amount = 456;   // a local variable

    cout << ::amount;   // display the global variable
    cout << ' ';
    cout << amount;     // display the local variable
}
```

The exercise has two variables named *amount*. The first is global and contains the value 123. The second is local to the *main* function.

The first *cout* statement displays **123**, the contents of the global *amount* variable because that reference to the variable name uses the :: global scope resolution operator. The second *cout* statement displays **456**, the contents of the local *amount* variable because that reference to the variable name has no global scope resolution operator and defaults to the local variable.

Exercise 2.4 displays the following output:

```
123 456
```

inline FUNCTIONS

You can tell the C++ compiler that a function is *inline*, which compiles a new copy of the function each time it is called. The *inline* function execution eliminates the function-call overhead of traditional functions. You should use *inline* functions only when the functions are small or when there are relatively few calls to them.

Exercise 2.5 uses the *inline* keyword to make a small function into an *inline* function.

Exercise 2.5   *An* **inline** *Function*

```
#include <iostream.h>
#include <stdlib.h>
inline void error_message(char *s)
{
    cout << '\a' << '\n' << s;
    exit(1);
}
main()
{
    error_message("You called?");
}
```

Exercise 2.5 sounds the computer's audible alarm and displays the message **"You called?"** on the screen.

Observe that the exercise declares the *inline* function ahead of the call to it. The C++ draft standard does not define where an *inline* function must be declared as such and under what conditions the compiler may choose to ignore the *inline* declaration except to say that the compiler may do so. Because of this ambiguity in the language specification, compiler builders have leeway in how they interpret the requirements. You could desire and declare an *inline* function (for performance reasons, perhaps) and have the compiler overrule you without saying so. To be safe, always declare *inline* functions ahead of all calls to them. If an *inline* function is to assume the appearance of an *extern* global function—if it is to be called by code in several source files--put its declaration in a header file.

Using *inline* supports two idioms. First, it offers an improved macro facility, which is discussed next. Second, it permits you to break a large function with many nested levels of statement blocks into several smaller *inline* functions. This usage improves a program's readability without introducing unnecessary function-call overhead.

Functions declared *inline* are similar to *#define* macros with these exceptions: An *inline* function is subject to the same C++ type-checking as normal functions; *inline* functions are not subject to macro side effects. For example, consider this macro:

```
#define min(a,b) (a < b ? a : b)
```

The *min* macro has potential side effects. Suppose you called it this way:

```
int c = min(a++,b++);
```

The macro expansion, shown next, invokes undesirable side effects in that the lesser of the *a* and *b* variables is incremented twice.

```
int c = a++ < b++ ? a++ : b++;
```

inline function calls, which the compiler treats as normal function calls, do not have such side effects.

THE *const* QUALIFIER

The *const* qualifier adds the constant property to variables, pointers, and function parameters.

const Variables

C++, like C, supports the *const* type qualifier. The *const* qualifier specifies that a variable is read-only, except during initialization. Except through initialization, a program cannot write a value into a *const* variable. C++ carries the *const* idea one step further and treats such variables as if they were true constant expressions. Wherever you can use a constant expression, you can use a variable that has the *const* type qualifier.

Exercise 2.6 is an example of how you can use the *const* qualifier.

Exercise 2.6 *The* ***const*** *Variable Qualifier*

```
#include <iostream.h>
main()
{
    const int size = 5;
    char cs[size];

    cout << "The size of cs is " << sizeof cs;
}
```

Exercise 2.6 displays the following message:

```
The size of cs is 5
```

There are limitations to this usage. You cannot initialize the *const* variable with anything other than a constant expression; therefore, you cannot use the syntax to derive dynamically dimensioned arrays. There are other ways to do that, and Chapter 3 explains them.

const Pointers

You can qualify a pointer with *const* in one of two ways. The first usage specifies that the pointer may not be modified by the program, and it looks like this:

```
char *const cp = MyString;  // cannot modify cp
```

The *cp* pointer is constant. The program may not modify it. Therefore, the declaration must initialize the pointer to give it a value.

A second usage specifies that the program may not dereference the pointer to modify the object being pointed to. That usage looks like this:

```
const int *ip;  // cannot modify what ip points to
```

Combining the two usages to define a constant pointer to a constant object looks like this:

```
const int *const ip =;  // cannot modify either
```

const Function *Parameters*

The prototype and declaration block for a function can specify that a pointer parameter—or what it points to—is *const*. This usage looks like this:

```
void bar(const char *cp); // what cp points to is const
```

The *bar* function may not modify the character or character array that the *cp* pointer parameter points to.

It follows that you cannot pass a pointer to a *const* variable as an argument to a function's parameter that is a pointer to a non-*const* variable. The function would otherwise assume that it can modify the object through the pointer, and the compiler does not permit the usage. This situation is shown here:

```
void foobar(char *cp);    // cp -> non-const
const char *ccp = "123";
foobar(ccp);              // illegal: ccp -> const
```

const Return Values

A function can return a pointer to *const*, as shown here:

```
const char *foo()
{
     return "foo";
}
```

The caller of *foo* cannot use the return pointer to modify what the pointer points to. The caller cannot assign the return value to a pointer to a non-*const*. The caller cannot pass the return value to a function that is expecting a pointer to non-*const*. The caller cannot assign another value to the object that the return value points to. These restrictions are shown here:

```
const char *foo();       // foo returns pointer to const
char *cp = foo();        // illegal: cp -> non-const
strcpy(foo(), "bar");    // illegal: *foo() is const
const int *bar()         // bar returns pointer to const
*bar() = 123;            // llegal: *bar() is const
```

const Member Functions

Other uses of *const* are to qualify class and structure member functions to ensure that they do not attempt to change any of the object's data members and to qualify references in function parameters. Chapters 6 and 7 discuss these usages.

enum AS A TYPE

The *enum* in C++ is the same as *enum* in C with one exception: All declarations of instances of a C *enum* must include the *enum* keyword. A C++ *enum* becomes a data type when you define it; therefore, once defined, it is known by its identifier alone—the same as any other type—and declarations may use the identifier name alone.

Exercise 2.7 demonstrates how a C++ program can reference an *enum* object by using the type identifier without the *enum* qualifier.

*Exercise 2.7   **enum** as a Data Type*

```
#include <iostream.h>
enum ignition_parts {
    distributor, cap, points, plug, condenser,
    coil, wires, done
};
main()
{
    ignition_parts ip;
    do    {
    cout << "\nEnter part number (0-6, 7 to quit): ";
    cin >> (int) ip;
    switch ( ip )    {
        case distributor: cout << "Distributor";
                          break;
        case cap:        cout << "Distributor cap";
                          break;
        case points:     cout << "Ignition points";
                          break;
        case plug:       cout << "Spark plug";
                          break;
        case condenser:  cout << "Condenser";
                          break;
        case coil:       cout << "Ignition coil";
                          break;
        case wires:      cout << "Coil, plug wires";
                          break;
        case done:       break;
        default:         cout << "Unknown part number";
                          break;
        }
    } while (ip != done);
}
```

Exercise 2.7 displays these messages. You type one of the digits 0–7 followed by the **Enter** key after each of the prompts.

```
Enter part number (0-6, 7 to quit): 0
Distributor
Enter part number (0-6, 7 to quit): 1
Distributor cap
Enter part number (0-6, 7 to quit): 2
Ignition points
Enter part number (0-6, 7 to quit): 3
Spark plug
Enter part number (0-6, 7 to quit): 4
Condenser
Enter part number (0-6, 7 to quit): 5
Ignition coil
Enter part number (0-6, 7 to quit): 6
Coil, plug wires
Enter part number (0-6, 7 to quit): 7
```

This exercise translates a part number into its name. The *enum* associates the numbers 0 to 6 with identifiers that associate with the names of the parts. Observe that the declaration of the data item *ip* uses only the *enum* name, *ignition_parts*, and does not use the *enum* keyword itself. Because *ignition_parts* is a new data type, you do not need to further qualify it with the *enum* keyword.

Exercise 2.7 illustrates another difference between the C *enum* and the C++ *enum*. Observe that the program reads from *cin* into the *int* variable *p*. Then it casts *p* to an *ignition_parts* type and assigns it to *ip*. The *cin* object does not know how to read data into the new *ignition_parts* data type. In C, *enum*s and *int*s are interchangeable. Wherever you can use one, you can use the other. Not so in C++. Each *enum* is a distinct type subject to the strong type-checking of C++.

The cast in Exercise 2.7 uses traditional C++ notation. Contemporary C++ introduces a new style notation for casting. Chapter 13 discusses this new casting convention.

N O T E

LINKAGE-SPECIFICATIONS

This next feature is not so much a C++ improvement to C as a way that the two languages coexist. It is discussed here because later exercises use it.

A *linkage-specification* is the technique that C++ employs to make functions that were compiled by a C compiler accessible to a C++ program. There are differences in the way the two languages build external names. If you are calling functions that were compiled by a C compiler, you must tell that to the C++ compiler.

C++ uses a different linkage system to support *type-safe linkage*, a feature that ensures that calls to functions in separately compiled source modules match the definitions of the functions with respect to parameter types. The C method is not as safe because it depends on every module using the same prototype, and you can intentionally or inadvertently override that assumption.

The C++ compiler modifies each function's name with suffixes that identify the parameter types. Use of these so-called mangled names allows duplicate function names to exist across separately compiled source files and allows the linker to properly resolve calls to the functions. The mangled names also transcend the use of prototypes to ensure that the functions match their calls. You cannot override the C++ type-checking simply by using different prototypes for the same function, although you can in C.

The C compiler does not mangle function names. An object file generated by a C compiler does not have mangled names for external objects. Unless you tell the C++ compiler otherwise, it assumes that external identifiers are subject to C++ name mangling. Therefore, you must tell the C++ compiler when a function has been (or must be) compiled with C linkage conventions.

Exercise 2.8 uses the linkage-specification to tell the C++ compiler that the functions in a header file are compiled by a C compiler.

Exercise 2.8 *Linkage-specifications*

```
#include <iostream.h>
extern "C"    {      // the linkage-specification
#include "stdlib.h"  // tells C++ that functions in the
}                     // library were compiled with C
main()
{
    cout << rand();   // call a C function
}
```

Exercise 2.8 displays a value on the screen. The *extern "C"* statement says that everything within the scope of the brace-surrounded block—in this case, everything in the header file—is compiled by a C compiler. If you do not use the braces, the linkage-specification deals only with the statement that immediately follows the C string.

Usually you put the linkage-specification in the header file that contains the prototypes for the C programs. Language environments that support both languages often manage the translation for you by hiding the linkage specification in the standard header files for the C functions. So, for the most part, you can be unaware of the difference between C functions and C++ functions. The exercises in this book assume that such files as **stdlib.h** and **string.h** include the appropriate linkage-specification. Contemporary C++ programming environments include C compilers and take care of the linkage-specifications in the Standard C header files.

There are times when you need to use linkage-specifications outside the realm of Standard C header files. If you have a large library of custom C functions to include in your C++ system and if you do not want to take the time and trouble to port them to C++ (perhaps you do not have the source code), then you must use a linkage-specification. If, within a C linkage-specification, you have some C++ prototypes, you can code a nested C++ linkage-specification.

Occasionally you need to tell the C++ compiler to compile a function in the C++ program with C linkages. You would do this if the function were called from an external function compiled with C linkages (a function from your C library, for example).

Exercise 2.9 is an example of a C++ program that calls a function that is compiled with a C compiler and has C linkages. The C++ program includes a function that is called from the C program and must be compiled with C linkages.

Exercise 2.9a   *The C++ Source*

```
#include <iostream.h>
// --------- array of string pointers to be sorted
static const char *brothers[] = {
    "Frederick William",
    "Joseph Jensen",
    "Harry Alan",
    "Walter Ellsworth",
    "Julian Paul"
};
// ------ prototype of functions compiled in C
extern "C" void SortCharArray(const char **);
```

continued

Exercise 2.9a   *The C++ Source (continued)*

```
// ------ C++ function to be called from the C program
extern "C"    {
  int SizeArray(void)
  {
      return sizeof brothers / sizeof (char*);
  }
}
main()
{
    // ---------- sort the pointers
    SortCharArray(brothers);
    // ---------- display the brothers in sorted order
    int size = SizeArray();
    for (int i = 0; i < size; i++)
        cout << '\n' << brothers[i];
}
```

Exersise 2.9b *The C Source*

```
/* C program for linkage-specifications */
/*
 * A C program compiled with a C compiler to demonstrate
 * C linkage to a C++ program
 */
#include <string.h>
#include <stdlib.h>
static int comp(const void *a, const void *b);
int SizeArray(void); /* The C++ function */

void SortCharArray(const char **List)
{
    qsort(List, SizeArray(), sizeof(char *), comp);
}
```

continued

Exercise 2.9b *The C Source (continued)*

```
/* ----- the compare function for qsort ---- */
static int comp(const void *a, const void *b)
{
    return strcmp(*(char **)a, *(char **)b);
}
```

Exercise 2.9a displays these messages:

```
Frederick William
Harry Alan
Joseph Jensen
Julian Paul
Walter Ellsworth
```

Exercise 2.9 consists of two source files: a C++ program (2.9a) and a C function (2.9b). The C function sorts an array of character pointers but does not know the length of the array. It must, therefore, call a function—whose name must be *SizeArray* and which must be provided by the caller—to determine the length of the array. The C++ program declares two C linkages—one for the *SortCharArray* C function that the C++ program calls, and one for its own *SizeArray* function that the C function calls.

Without the linkage-specifications, the C++ compiler mangles the names of the C++ function and the C++ program's call to the C function. The linker cannot resolve the C++ program's call to the *SortCharArray* C function or the C function's call to the *SizeArray* C++ function.

N O T E

In the real world, you would take other measures to give the length of the array to the C function. You could null-terminate the array, and the C function could determine the array length on its own. You could pass the length of the array as an argument to the C function. You could pass the address of a function in the C++ program, which would then not need to be compiled with C linkages. Perhaps you are not in control of the C program, not having its source code, and you are stuck with whatever conventions the C programmer used. Perhaps the C function is already so widely used that you cannot change it.

Languages other than C and C++ can be supported by linkage-specifications, and their string values are implementation-dependent.

ANONYMOUS *UNIONS*

A C++ program can define an unnamed *union* anywhere it can have a variable. You might use this feature to save space, or you might use it to intentionally redefine a variable.

Exercise 2.10 illustrates the use of the anonymous *union*.

Exercise 2.10 *Anonymous **unions***

```
#include <iostream.h>
main()
{
    union    {
        int quantity_todate;
        int quantity_balance;
    };
    cout << "Enter quantity to date: ";
    cin >> quantity_todate;
    cout << "Enter quantity sold: ";
    int quantity_sold;
    cin >> quantity_sold;
    quantity_todate -= quantity_sold;
    cout << "Quantity balance = " << quantity_balance;
}
```

The program in Exercise 2.10 allows the two variables *quantity_todate* and *quantity_balance* to share the same space. After it subtracts *quantity_sold* from *quantity_todate*, *quantity_balance* contains the result shown by the program's output.

```
Enter quantity to date: 100
Enter quantity sold: 75
Quantity balance = 25
```

This feature eliminates a lot of *union* name prefixes in places where the only purpose for the *union* name is to support the *union*.

You must declare a global anonymous *union* as *static*.

UNNAMED FUNCTION PARAMETERS

You can declare a C function with one or more parameters that the function does not use. This circumstance often occurs when several functions are called through a generic function pointer. Some of the functions do not use all the parameters named in the function pointer declaration. Following is an example of such a function.

```
int func(int x, int y)
{
    return x * 2;
}
```

Although this usage is correct and common, most C and C++ compilers complain that you failed to use the parameter named *y*. C++, however, allows you to declare functions with unnamed parameters to indicate to the compiler that the parameter exists and that the callers pass an argument for the parameter, but that the called function does not use it. Following is the C++ function coded with an unnamed second parameter.

```
int func(int x, int)
{
    return x * 2;
}
```

CONSTRUCTOR NOTATION FOR INTRINSIC DATA TYPES

C++ allows you to initialize objects of the intrinsic data types, such as *int, long, double*, and so on, by using the notation of a class constructor. You learn about class constructors in Chapter 7. The following statements are valid initialized variable declarations in C++.

```
int qty(123);
double spec(5.378);
```

The two statements just shown have the same effect as these traditional C declaration initialization statements:

```
int qty = 123;
double spec = 5.378;
```

SUMMARY

What you have learned so far have been ways that C++ improves the C language. Each subsequent chapter is more of the same, but the improvements that follow set C++ apart as its own language rather than just an improved C. You can use these new features in ways unrelated to the object-oriented paradigm, or you can totally immerse yourself in the paradigm and use C++ as your object-oriented development environment.

CHAPTER 3

C++ Memory Allocation

This chapter is about the *free store*, the C++ mechanism that supports dynamic memory allocations. Classic C calls the free store the *heap*. They are the same thing, although the C++ implementation provides improved mechanisms for memory management. You will learn about:

- ❖ The *new* and *delete* operators
- ❖ Allocating dynamic arrays
- ❖ Dealing with out-of-memory conditions
- ❖ Installing custom *new* and *delete* operators

C programmers use the *malloc, calloc, realloc,* and *free* functions to allocate memory from and return it to the heap. C++ uses the *new* and *delete* operators to manage dynamic memory on the C++ free store. These operators associate memory allocation with how you use the memory. In the C++ lexicon, free store means heap, and *new* and *delete* are similar to *malloc* and *free*.

THE *new* AND *delete* OPERATORS

The *new* operator, when used with the name of a pointer to a data type, structure, or array, allocates memory for the item and assigns the address of that memory to the pointer.

The *delete* operator returns the memory pointed to by the named pointer variable to the free store.

Exercise 3.1 is your first use of the *new* and *delete* operators.

Exercise 3.1 *The C++ Free Store: The **new** and **delete** Operators*

```
#include <iostream.h>
struct Date {          // a date structure
    int month;
    int day;
    int year;
};
main()
{
    Date *birthday = new Date;  // get memory for a date
    birthday->month = 6;        // assign a value to the date
    birthday->day = 24;
    birthday->year = 1940;
    cout << "I was born on "    // display the date
        << birthday->month << '/'
        << birthday->day   << '/'
        << birthday->year;
    delete birthday;   // return memory to the free store
}
```

Exercise 3.1 displays this message:

```
I was born on 6/24/1940
```

The structure in this exercise defines a date. The program uses the *new* operator to allocate memory for an instance of the structure. Then the program initializes the new structure with a date. After displaying the contents of the structure, the program disposes of it by using the *delete* operator.

N O T E

> The declaration of the *birthday* pointer in Exercise 3.1 does not include the *struct* keyword. This omission appears to be an error, but it is not. You learn more about this C++ improvement in Chapter 5.

Allocating a Fixed-Dimension Array

The advantages of *new* and *delete* over the C functions *malloc* and *free* are not obvious in Exercise 3.1. They appear to be the same. However, *new* and *delete* provide a more readable syntax for memory allocation. Later, when you learn about classes and their constructors and destructors, you encounter even more advantages of the *new* and *delete* operators.

Exercise 3.2 shows how you can use *new* and *delete* to acquire and dispose of memory for an array.

**Exercise 3.2 new *and* delete *with an Array*

```
#include <iostream.h>
main()
{
    int *birthday = new int[3];   // get memory for a date array
    birthday[0] = 6;              // assign a value to the date
    birthday[1] = 24;
    birthday[2] = 1940;
    cout << "I was born on "      // display the date
        << birthday[0] << '/'
        << birthday[1] << '/'
        << birthday[2];
    delete[] birthday;     // return memory to the free store
}
```

Exercise 3.2 displays the same message as Exercise 3.1.

Allocating Dynamic Arrays

Exercise 3.2 shows how the *new* operator accepts a data type with an array dimension. The dimension in the exercise is a constant 3, representing the number of integers in the date. You can, however, supply a variable dimension, and the *new* operator allocates the correct amount of memory.

Exercise 3.3 shows the use of a variably dimensioned array as allocated by the *new* operator.

Exercise 3.3 *The C++ Free Store:* ***new*** *with a Dynamic Array*

```
#include <iostream.h>
#include <stdlib.h>
main()
{
    cout << "Enter the array size: ";
    int size;
    cin >> size;                   // get the array size
    int *array = new int[size];    // allocate an array
    for (int i = 0; i < size; i++) // load the array
        array[i] = rand();         // with random numbers
    for (i = 0; i < size; i++)     // display the array
        cout << '\n' << array[i];
    delete[] array; // return the array to the free store
}
```

When running this exercise, you first type in the size of the array. The *new* operator uses that value to establish the size of the memory buffer to be allocated. It multiplies the *size* value times the size of the array type, which is *int* in this example. The program builds the array by using the *new* operator, fills it with random numbers, displays each of the elements in the array, and deletes the array by using the *delete* operator.

Observe that the *delete* operator in Exercise 3.3 is followed by a pair of brackets. This notation tells the compiler that the memory being deleted is an array. In this example, the notation has no effect. Programmers use it by convention and to stay in the habit of using the notation for all deletes of dynamically allocated arrays. It has consequences when the array contains objects of user-defined class types. You learn about that in Chapter 7.

N O T E

The two *for* statements in Exercise 3.3 illustrate a usage where future C++ might fail to compile programs written in traditional C++. The second *for* statement uses the *i* variable declared within the first *for* statement. Under future C++, if the proposed change is approved, the first *i* variable goes out of scope at the bottom of the *for* statement. The second *for* statement would have to declare its own *i* variable. See Chapter 14.

Exercise 3.3 displays the messages shown below. (The **5** is the number you would enter. The five other numbers are random numbers generated by the Standard C *rand* function and are implementation-dependent.)

```
Enter the array size: 5
346
130
10982
1090
11656
```

Exercise 3.4 offers another variation on the dynamically dimensioned array through the *new* operator. The exercise uses a function call to compute the dimension. The purpose is to read a number of variable-length strings from the user, sort them, and display them in a left-justified column.

Exercise 3.4 *The C++ Free Store: More Dynamic Array Allocation*

```
#include <iostream.h>
#include <stdlib.h>
#include <string.h>
// ---------- compare function to sort array of pointers
int comp(const void *a, const void *b)
{
    return strcmp(*(char **)a, *(char **)b);
}
main()
{
    cout << "How many names at most? ";
    int maxnames;
    cin >> maxnames;
    char **names = new char *[maxnames];
    char *name = new char[80];
    for (int namect = 0; namect < maxnames; namect++)    {
        cout << "Enter a name ('end' if done before "
                << maxnames << " names): ";
        cin >> name;
        if (strcmp(name, "end") == 0)
            break;
        names[namect] = new char[strlen(name)+1];
        strcpy(names[namect], name);
    }
    qsort(names, namect, sizeof(char *), comp);
    for (int i = 0; i < namect; i++)
        cout << names[i] << '\n';
    for (i = 0; i < namect; i++)
        delete[] names[i];
    delete[] name;
    delete[] names;
}
```

Exercise 3.4 begins by asking you to enter the maximum number of names. From this value, the program allocates an array of character pointers. Then you begin entering names. For each name, the program allocates a new array with its address in the names array. When you enter the name **end** or after you have entered as many names as you said you would, the program displays all of them.

Exercise 3.4 displays the messages shown below. (The **6** is the number of names you intend to enter. The **Bill**, **Sam**, **Paul**, **Jim**, **Chick**, and **Spuff** entries are the names you enter. The sorted list of the same names follows the entries.)

```
How many names at most? 6
Enter a name ('end' if done before 6 names): Bill
Enter a name ('end' if done before 6 names): Sam
Enter a name ('end' if done before 6 names): Paul
Enter a name ('end' if done before 6 names): Jim
Enter a name ('end' if done before 6 names): Chick
Enter a name ('end' if done before 6 names): Spuff
Bill
Chick
Jim
Paul
Sam
Spuff
```

WHEN THE STORE IS EXHAUSTED

So far these exercises have not considered the question of what to do if the free store is out of memory when you use the *new* operator. Instead, they assume that the store is never exhausted. Clearly, this is not a real-world approach. The C *malloc* function returns a null pointer under that condition, and C programs that call *malloc* usually test for the null return and do something meaningful about it.

The *set_new_handler* Function

You could take the same approach with C++ by simply testing each use of the *new* operator for a null return; *new* returns a null pointer if there is no memory to allocate. There is a better way, however. C++ includes an internal *new_handler* function pointer. Normally, that pointer is null, and when *new* runs out of memory, *new* returns a null value. But if the pointer contains a non-null value, *new* assumes that the value is the address to call when memory is exhausted. C++ includes a function named *set_new_handler* that lets you assign the address of an out-of-memory handler function to the internal *new_handler* function pointer.

Exhausting the Free Store

If the *new* operator finds itself out of free store space, it calls the function pointed to by *new_handler*. Exercise 3.5 is a rather ill-behaved program that attempts to consume all of the free store. The program illustrates a *new* handler function that terminates the program when the free store is exhausted.

*Exercise 3.5   The **set_new_handler** Function*

```
#include <iostream.h>
#include <stdlib.h>
#include <new.h>
static void all_gone()
{
    cerr << "\n\aThe free store is empty\n";
    exit(1);
}
main()
{
    set_new_handler(all_gone);
    long total = 0;
    while (1)    {
        char *gobble = new char[10000];
        total += 10000;
        cout << "Got 10000 for a total of " << total << '\n';
    }
}
```

This exercise goes into a loop, consuming free store and displaying messages about it. When the store is empty, the *new* operator turns things over to the *all_gone* function, which sends an error message to *cerr* and exits.

Exercise 3.5 displays the following messages:

```
Got 10000 for a total of 10000
Got 10000 for a total of 20000
Got 10000 for a total of 30000
Got 10000 for a total of 40000
Got 10000 for a total of 50000
Got 10000 for a total of 60000
The free store is empty
```

NOTE

The Microsoft C++ compiler implements *set_new_handler* in an unconventional manner, and Exercise 3.5 does not work with that compiler. Refer to the Microsoft documentation for a description of its implementation of *set_new_handler*.

Going for More Store

If your *new* handler function returns to its caller, the *new* operator tries again to allocate the required memory. This permits a programmer to do something about free store exhaustion. What you do depends on how your free store works. The default *new* and *delete* operators take their memory from the heap. Heap management is an implementation-dependent operation, and anything you might do to increase the memory available to the default *new* operator would not be portable to other systems, perhaps not even to other C++ compilers on the same system.

ROLLING YOUR OWN *new* AND *delete* OPERATORS

The default *new* and *delete* operators are general-purpose enough to suffice for most programming situations. There maybe times, however, when your program wants more control over what happens when the *new* operator executes. For example, the default *new* operator does not initialize the memory that is allocated. Perhaps you want to set all of the space to zeros. To do this, you build your own *new* operator.

N O T E

You are about to learn how to install your own dynamic memory manager into your C++ environment. This ability implies a certain amount of responsibility. Overloading the global *new* and *delete* operators puts your functions in the position of allocating and freeing dynamic memory for all global uses of the free store, including *new* and *delete* calls from within the compiler's library functions and startup code. Although C++ provides this powerful overloading facility, most programmers do not find it necessary to replace the global *new* and *delete* functions provided by the compiler.

Exercise 3.6 is an example of a custom-built *new* operator that initializes memory to zeros before returning.

Exercise 3.6   *Home-brew **new** and **delete***

```
#include <iostream.h>
#include <stdlib.h>
// ------------ overloaded new operator
void *operator new(size_t size)
{
    void *rtn = calloc(1, size);
    return rtn;
}
// ----------- overloaded delete operator
void operator delete(void *type)
{
    free(type);
}
main()
{
    // ------ allocate a zero-filled array
    int *ip = new int[10];
    // ------ display the array
    for (int i = 0; i < 10; i++)
        cout << ' ' << ip[i];
    // ----- release the memory
    delete[] ip;
}
```

Exercise 3.6 displays this message of zero values:

0 0 0 0 0 0 0 0 0 0

This exercise is an early look at operator overloading, a powerful feature of C++. The *new* and *delete* keywords are implemented in C++ as operators, and you can redefine their meaning within the context of how they are called—by writing operator functions that replace them. Chapter 8 is dedicated to the subject of overloaded operators for the C++ classes that you develop.

The overloaded *new* operator in Exercise 3.6 uses the Standard C *calloc* function to get memory. That function allocates memory and sets it to zero, so your work is done for you.

N O T E

Previous editions of this book included exercises that overloaded the *new* operator with multiple parameters. The draft ANSI working paper of February 1994 is vague about this behavior, and contemporary C++ compilers implement it differently. For these reasons I chose to remove the exercises until the subject is cleared up.

SUMMARY

This chapter dealt with the basics of the C++ free store and the *new* and *delete* operators. You learn more about these aspects of C++ in later chapters, where their advanced features contribute to C++ class construction.

During your excursion into *new* and *delete*, you received an introduction to overloaded operators. Overloading is one of the more powerful facilities in C++. You can overload operators, and you can overload functions. Chapter 4 deals with the overloading of functions.

CHAPTER 4

Overloaded Functions

This chapter is about function overloading, the C++ technique that allows you to give more than one function the same name. You will learn about:

❖ Overloading to change functionality

❖ Overloading to accommodate different data formats

You can reuse a function name in a C program if you want the new function and if the old one is not in scope. The two functions cannot, however, share the same scope. If you want to have two similar C functions with slightly different operations on different parameter types, you must write two different C functions. The standard C *strcpy* and *strncpy* functions are examples.

C++ has a better way. It allows you to reuse a function name in the same scope, but with different parameter types. Both versions of the function are then available at the same time. This feature is called *function overloading*. In function overloading, you redefine a function in a way that makes multiple versions of the same function name available to the same program.

OVERLOADING FOR DIFFERENT OPERATIONS

Sometimes you overload a function because it performs a generic task but there are different permutations of what it does. The standard C *strcpy* and *strncpy* functions are examples. Both functions copy strings, but they do so in slightly different ways. The *strcpy* function simply copies a string from the source to the destination. The *strncpy* function copies a string but stops copying when the source string terminates or after the function copies a specified number of characters. These functions are likely candidates to be members of an overloaded function family.

Exercise 4.1 replaces the standard C *strcpy* and *strncpy* functions with the single function named *string_copy*.

Exercise 4.1   Overloading Functions for Different Operations

```
#include <iostream.h>
void string_copy(char *dest, const char *src)
{
    while((*dest++ = *src++) != '\0')
        ;
}
void string_copy(char *dest, const char *src, int len)
{
    while (len && (*dest++ = *src++) != '\0')
        -len;
    while (len-)
        *dest++ = '\0';
}
static char misspiggie[20], kermit[20];
```

continued

Exercise 4.1   *Overloading Functions for Different Operations (continued)*

```
void main()
{
    string_copy(misspiggie, "Miss Piggie");
    string_copy(kermit,
        "Kermit the file transfer protocol", 6);
    cout << kermit << " and " << misspiggie;
}
```

Exercise 4.1 displays this message:

```
Kermit and Miss Piggie
```

There are two functions named *string_copy* in this program. What sets them apart is their different parameter lists. The first of the two *string_copy* functions has destination and source character pointers as parameters. The second function has the pointers and an integer length as well. The C++ compiler recognizes that these are two distinct functions by virtue of these differences in their parameter lists.

OVERLOADING FOR DIFFERENT FORMATS

Exercise 4.1 showed how you might overload a function to get a different algorithm on similar data. Another reason to overload a function is to get the same result from data values that can be represented in different formats. Standard C has different ways of representing the date and time. You will find more ways in UNIX, and still others in MS-DOS.

Exercise 4.2 shows how you can send two of the standard C formats to the overloaded *display_time* functions.

Exercise 4.2   *Overloaded Functions for Different Data Formats*

```
#include <iostream.h>
#include <time.h>
void display_time(const struct tm *tim)
{
    cout << "1. It is now " << asctime(tim);
}
void display_time(time_t *tim)
{
    cout << "2. It is now " << ctime(tim);
}
void main()
{
    time_t tim = time((time_t *)NULL);
    struct tm *ltim = localtime(&tim);

    display_time(ltim);
    display_time(&tim);
}
```

Exercise 4.2 uses the Standard C data formats *time_t* and *struct tm*. It gets the value of the current date and time into them with the Standard C *time* and *localtime* functions. Then it calls its own overloaded *display_time* function for each of the formats.

Exercise 4.2 displays the following results:

```
1. It is now Wed May 12 12:05:20 1993
2. It is now Wed May 12 12:05:20 1993
```

Dates and times are good ways to experiment with overloaded functions. There are many ways to represent them internally, many ways that different systems report them to a program, and many ways to display them. In addition to all these formats, there are many common date and time algorithms. A comprehensive date and time package would be a solid addition to any programmer's tool collection.

SUMMARY

Function overloading is one of the facets of C++ that supports the object-oriented programming view of things. As this chapter shows, you can also use function overloading in your traditional programming environment to design and develop programs that are more readable.

CHAPTER 5

C++ Structures

This chapter describes how C++ enhances a programmer's use of structures. You will learn about:

- ❖ Structures as data types
- ❖ Structures with function members
- ❖ Access specifiers
- ❖ Unions

C++ structures are similar to C structures, but C++ structures have more features. This chapter describes the characteristics of the C++ structure that distinguishes it from C in a way that brings the programmer closer to the object-oriented paradigm.

STRUCTURES AS DATA TYPES

When you define a structure in C++, you have designed a new data type and added it to the language within the scope of the structure declaration. In C, however, every declaration of an instance of a defined structure must include the *struct* keyword, as in the following example:

```
/* --- defining a C structure --- */
struct Date {int month,day,year;};
/* --- declaring a C structure --- */
struct Date today;
```

In C++, a structure is its own data type and can be known by its own name without the *struct* keyword.

Exercise 5.1 shows the various ways you can use a structure's name in C++.

Exercise 5.1 *The Structure as a Data Type*

```
#include <iostream.h>
// ------   structure = data type
struct Date {
    int month;
    int day;
    int year;
};
static void display(Date);           // a date parameter
main()
{
    static Date birthday = {10,12,1962}; // a date
    Date dates[10];                      // an array of dates
    Date *dp = dates;                    // a pointer to a date
```

continued

Exercise 5.1   *The Structure as a Data Type (continued)*

```
    for (int i = 0; i < 10; i++)     {
        *(dp + i) = birthday;
        dates[i].year += i;
        cout << "\nOn ";
        display(dates[i]);
        cout << " Sharon was ";
        if (i > 0)
            cout << i;
        else
            cout << "born";
    }
}
static void display(Date dt)
{
    static char *mon[] = {
        "January","February","March","April","May","June",
        "July","August","September","October","November",
        "December"};
    cout << mon[dt.month-1] << ' ' << dt.day << ", "
        << dt.year;
}
```

Exercise 5.1 defines a Date structure with a member for each of the elements *day, month,* and *year.* The *main* function contains an instance of the structure, an array of the structure, and a pointer to the structure. The program includes a prototype of a function that accepts the structure as a parameter. Yet the keyword *struct* does not appear in any of these objects because *Date* became a data type when the structure was defined.

Exercise 5.1 displays the following messages:

```
On October 12, 1962 Sharon was born
On October 12, 1963 Sharon was 1
On October 12, 1964 Sharon was 2
On October 12, 1965 Sharon was 3
```

```
On October 12, 1966 Sharon was 4
On October 12, 1967 Sharon was 5
On October 12, 1968 Sharon was 6
On October 12, 1969 Sharon was 7
On October 12, 1970 Sharon was 8
On October 12, 1971 Sharon was 9
```

STRUCTURES WITH FUNCTIONS

A structure is an aggregate of data types. Grouping the different members forms a record of sorts with different fields. The structure can contain *integers, floats, arrays, pointers, typedefs, unions,* and other data types. In other words, any valid data type can be a member of a structure. This convention is consistent with the C definition of a structure. C++ adds another type of member to the structure. In C++, structures can include functions.

A Glimpse at Object-Oriented Programming

Take a moment to consider the implications of what you just learned. By adding functions to structures, you add the ability for a structure to include algorithms that are bound to, and work with, the other structure members. You closely associate the algorithms with the data they process; this is called *encapsulation,* and it is one of the fundamental concepts of the object-oriented paradigm.

Adding Functions to Structures

Exercise 5.2 is a program that adds a function to the *Date* structure in Exercise 5.1. The function's name is *display,* and its purpose is to display the contents of an instance of the *Date* structure.

Exercise 5.2 *Structures with Functions*

```
#include <iostream.h>
// ------ structure with a function
struct Date {
    int month, day, year;
```

continued

Exercise 5.2   *Structures with Functions (continued)*

```
    void display(void);      // a function to display the date
};
void Date::display()
{
    static char *mon[] = {
        "January","February","March","April","May","June",
        "July","August","September","October","November",
        "December"};
    cout << mon[month-1] << ' ' << day << ", " << year;
}
main()
{
    static Date birthday = {4, 6, 1961};
    cout << "Alan's date of birth was ";
    birthday.display();
}
```

Exercise 5.2 codes the display function's declaration as *Date::display*. This notation tells the C++ compiler that the *display* function exists to support instances of the *Date* structure. In fact, the only way to call this *display* function is as a member of a declared *Date*.

The *main* function declares a *Date* named *birthday* and initializes it with a value. Then the *main* function calls the *Date::display* function by identifying it as a member of the *birthday* structure using the following notation:

```
    birthday.display();
```

The *Date::display* function displays the following date format:

```
Alan's date of birth was April 6, 1961
```

The *Date::display* function can reference members of the structure with which it is associated directly without naming an instance of the structure, because the function it is a member of the structure.

MULTIPLE INSTANCES OF THE SAME STRUCTURE

As you might expect, you can declare more than one instance of the same structure, and the member function associates itself with the data in the particular structure for which you call it.

Exercise 5.3 uses the *Date* structure in two places.

Exercise 5.3 *Multiple Instances of a Structure with a Function*

```
#include <iostream.h>
// ------  structure with a function
struct Date {
    int month, day, year;
    void display(void);   // a function to display the date
};
void Date::display()
{
    static char *mon[] = {
        "January","February","March","April","May","June",
        "July","August","September","October","November",
        "December"};
    cout << mon[month-1] << ' ' << day << ", " << year;
}
main()
{
    static Date alans_birthday = {4, 6, 1961};
    cout << "\nAlan's date of birth was ";
    alans_birthday.display();

    static Date wendys_birthday = {4, 28, 1965};
    cout << "\nWendy's date of birth was ";
    wendys_birthday.display();
}
```

The program declares two *Date* structures and uses the *display* function to display the following messages:

```
Alan's date of birth was April 6, 1961
Wendy's date of birth was April 28, 1965
```

OVERLOADED STRUCTURE FUNCTIONS

You can have different structure definitions that use the same function name. This is another form of the function overloading that you learned about in Chapter 4.

Exercise 5.4 is an example of two structures that each use a function named *display*.

Exercise 5.4   *Two Structures with the Same Function Name*

```cpp
#include <iostream.h>
#include <stdio.h>
#include <time.h>
// ------  date structure with a function
struct Date {
    int month, day, year;
    void display(void);        // a function to display the date
};
void Date::display()
{
    static char *mon[] = {
        "January","February","March","April","May","June",
        "July","August","September","October","November",
        "December"};
    cout << mon[month] << ' ' << day << ", " << year;
}
```

continued

Exercise 5.4   *Two Structures with the Same Function Name (continued)*

```
// ------ time structure with a function
struct Time {
    int hour, minute, second;
    void display(void);   // a function to display the clock
};
void Time::display()
{
    char tmsg[15];
    sprintf(tmsg, "%d:%02d:%02d %s",
        (hour > 12 ? hour - 12 : (hour == 0 ? 12 : hour)),
        minute, second,
        hour < 12 ? "am" : "pm");
    cout << tmsg;
}
main()
{
    // -------- get the current time from the OS
    time_t curtime = time((time_t *)NULL);
    struct tm tim = *localtime(&curtime);
    // --------- clock and date structures
    Time now;
    Date today;
    // --------- initialize the structures
    now.hour = tim.tm_hour;
    now.minute = tim.tm_min;
    now.second = tim.tm_sec;
    today.month = tim.tm_mon;
    today.day = tim.tm_mday;
    today.year = tim.tm_year+1900;
```

continued

Exercise 5.4   *Two Structures with the Same Function Name* *(continued)*

```
    // ---------- display the date and time
    cout << "At the tone it will be ";
    now.display();
    cout << " on ";
    today.display();
    cout << '\a';
}
```

The program in Exercise 5.4 has a *Date* structure and a *Time* structure. Both structures have functions named *display*. The *display* function associated with the *Date* structure displays the date; the *display* function associated with the *Time* structure displays the time.

Exercise 5.4 sounds the audible alarm and displays the following message.

```
At the tone it will be 6:19:12 pm on October 12, 1994
```

The date and time in the display will be the current ones when you run the program.

ACCESS SPECIFIERS

By default, the members of a structure are visible to all the functions within the scope of the structure object. You can limit this access with three *access specifiers* in the structure's definition. The *Date* structure in the earlier exercises might be modified with the *private* and *public* access specifiers, as shown here.

```
struct Date {
private:
    int month, day, year;
public:
    void display(void);
};
```

All members following the *private* access specifier are accessible only to the member functions within the structure definition. All members following the *public* access specifier are accessible to any function that is within the scope of the structure. If you omit the access specifiers, everything is *public*. You can use an access specifier more than once in the same structure definition.

N O T E

A third access specifier, protected, is the same as the private access specifier unless the structure is a part of a class hierarchy, a subject that Chapter 9 addresses.

When you define a structure with the *private* access specifier, the structure begins to take on the properties of a class, and you should define it as such. You cannot, for example, initialize the structure shown above with a brace-separated list of integers because the data members are private to the class's member functions and are not visible to the rest of the program. You would need to define a *constructor* function, and perhaps a *destructor* function, to handle the structure's initialization when it comes into scope and destruction when it goes out of scope. These subjects take on meaning when you learn about C++ classes in Chapter 7.

UNIONS

C++ unions are similar to C unions in that the data members share the same memory, and only one of the members can contain a value at any one time. (You learned about C++ anonymous unions in Chapter 2.) C++ unions share some of the enhancements that C++ structures have. A union can have function members, but it cannot be a part of a class hierarchy the way structures can. You will learn about classes in Chapter 7 and class hierarchies in Chapter 9. A union can have constructor and destructor functions (Chapter 7), but it cannot have any virtual functions (Chapter 9).

Unions can have private and public members. You will learn more about the private and public access specifiers in Chapter 7.

SUMMARY

This chapter has moved you closer to object-oriented programming. Structures that become data types and that have functions associated with them resemble closely the C++ class, which is the basic unit of the object-oriented paradigm. Chapter 6 digresses to discuss the C++ reference, an important alternative to pointer notation.

CHAPTER 6

References

This chapter is about the C++ reference. You will learn about:

- ❖ What you can and cannot do with a reference
- ❖ The alias nature of a reference variable
- ❖ How and when to initialize a reference
- ❖ Passing references to functions
- ❖ Returning references from functions

A *reference* variable is an alias or synonym for another variable. It is most often used for passing parameters and returning values by reference rather than by value. The reference lets you pass and return large data structures without the overhead of copying them.

The reference is also a way to avoid pointer dereferencing syntax in your code.

If you are like most C programmers, the pointer gave you the most trouble when you first learned C. Veteran C programmers can still get bogged down trying to comprehend some of the complex operations allowed by C pointers and pointers-to-pointers. The C++ reference variable can give you the same kind of trouble until you understand it, and it has some of its own wrinkles as well. Its syntax and usage, however, prevent many of the pointer pitfalls that trap C programmers.

Following is a list of things to remember when you deal with references. You learn about each of these items in the paragraphs and exercises in this chapter.

- ❖ A reference is an alias for an actual variable.
- ❖ A reference must be initialized and cannot be changed.
- ❖ References work well with user-defined data types.
- ❖ You can pass references to functions.
- ❖ You can return references from functions.
- ❖ A function that returns a reference can appear on either side of an assignment.
- ❖ The only thing you can do to the reference variable itself is initialize it.

THE REFERENCE IS AN ALIAS

A C++ reference is an alias for another variable. When you declare a reference variable, you give it a value that you may not change for the life of the reference. The & operator identifies a reference variable as in the following example:

```
int actualint;
int& otherint = actualint;
```

These statements declare an integer, named *actualint,* that has another name, *otherint.* Now all references to either name have the same effect.

Exercise 6.1 illustrates how a reference and the data item it refers to appear to be one and the same.

Exercise 6.1   *The Reference*

```
#include <iostream.h>
main()
{
    int actualint = 123;
    int& otherint = actualint;

    cout << '\n' << actualint;
    cout << '\n' << otherint;
    otherint++;
    cout << '\n' << actualint;
    cout << '\n' << otherint;
    actualint++;
    cout << '\n' << actualint;
    cout << '\n' << otherint;
}
```

Exercise 6.1 shows that operations on *otherint* act upon *actualint*. The exercise displays the following output, and it shows that whatever you do to *otherint*, you do to *actualint*, and vice versa:

```
123
123
124
124
125
125
```

The alias metaphor is almost perfect. A reference is neither a copy of nor a pointer to the thing to which it refers. Instead, it is another name that the compiler recognizes for the thing to which it refers.

Exercise 6.2 demonstrates the alias metaphor by displaying the addresses of both identifiers. When you run the exercise, you see that they both have the same address.

Exercise 6.2 *Addresses of References*

```
#include <iostream.h>
main()
{
    int actualint = 123;
    int& otherint = actualint;

    cout << &actualint << ' ' << &otherint;
}
```

Exercise 6.2 displays something similar to the following message.

```
0x3b96fff4 0x3b96fff4
```

N O T E

The format and values of these addresses depend on where your run-time system locates the variables, and the format of the hexadecimal address in your compiler. The point here is not what the addresses are, but that they are the same.

Although the reference variable is described as an alias, it is a data item unto itself and not the same as the true alias that you get by using the preprocessor's *#define* statement. Although a reference apparently delivers the behavior of a defined alias, it is treated as a separate variable. References that are function parameters refer to different variables throughout the program's execution; their alias property changes from use to use.

INITIALIZING A REFERENCE

A reference is of no use unless it refers to something. Unlike a pointer, a reference is not a variable that you can manipulate. It is, as you learned in the first two exercises in this chapter, an alias for something real. Therefore, it is only natural that you must initialize a reference (explicitly give the reference something to refer to) when you declare it unless one of the following statements is true:

1. It is declared with *extern*, in which case it would have been initialized elsewhere.

2. It is a member of a class, in which case the class's constructor function initializes the reference.

3. It is a parameter in a function declaration, in which case its value is established by the caller's argument when the function is called.

4. It is declared as the return type of a function, in which case its value is established when the function returns something.

As you work through the exercises in this and later chapters, observe all uses of references to see that each one matches one of these criteria.

REFERENCES TO USER-DEFINED DATA TYPES

Many programmers use references primarily to refer to structure and class objects and avoid references to the standard C++ data types. References are not as useful when they refer to *ints*, *longs*, and the like. An advantage of references is that they reduce the overhead involved in passing and returning parameters to and from functions. This advantage does not exist for references to the smaller data types, because passing the original data type is as efficient as passing a reference.

REFERENCES AS FUNCTION PARAMETERS

References are often used as function parameters. There is little need to build a reference that exists only in the view of the variable that it refers to. You might as well use the original name of the variable. The exercises in this chapter until now have used references in that way, but the purpose of those exercises was to show you the behavior of references, not necessarily to show the best way to use them.

References as function parameters offer three advantages:

1. They eliminate the overhead associated with passing large data structures as parameters and with returning large data structures from functions.

2. They eliminate the pointer dereferencing notation used in functions to which you pass references as arguments.

3. Like pointers, they can allow the called function to operate on and possibly modify the caller's copy of the data.

These advantages are illustrated in the next set of exercises.

Reference Parameters to Eliminate Copies

By using a reference as a function parameter, you avoid the overhead of passing large structures to functions, in much the same way you do when you pass pointers to functions.

Exercise 6.3 illustrates the difference between passing a structure and passing a reference to a structure.

Exercise 6.3 *Reference Parameters Reduce Overhead*

```cpp
#include <iostream.h>
// ---------- a big structure
struct bigone    {
    int serno;
    char text[1000];    // a lot of chars
} bo = { 123, "This is a BIG structure"};
// -- two functions that have the structure as a parameter
void slowfunc(bigone p1);        // call by value
void fastfunc(bigone& p1);       // call by reference
main()
{
    slowfunc(bo);    // this will take a while
    fastfunc(bo);    // this will be a snap
}
// ---- a call-by-value function
void slowfunc(bigone p1)
{
    cout << '\n' << p1.serno;
    cout << '\n' << p1.text;
}
// ---- a call by reference function
void fastfunc(bigone& p1)
{
    cout << '\n' << p1.serno;
    cout << '\n' << p1.text;
}
```

Exercise 6.3 displays these messages:

```
123
This is a BIG structure
123
This is a BIG structure
```

Unfortunately, nothing in the exercise jumps out at you to prove the point. The only apparent difference is the use of the & reference operator in the function's prototype and parameter declaration. But the differences are real.

First, suppose that the character array in the *bigone* structure was 20,000 bytes instead of 1,000. The program could fail on the first function call because C++ passes parameters on the stack, and the stack might not be big enough. You would need to use a compiler option to specify a bigger stack just to support this one function call. By passing a reference to the function, you don't have to worry about it.

Second, by passing the big structure by reference, you eliminate the processing overhead required to copy the structure into the called function's parameter. This overhead becomes more significant when you get into complex class design with copy constructor functions (Chapter 7).

References to Eliminate Pointer Notation

By using a reference in the called function instead of using a pointer, you avoid the pointer dereferencing operators that can make pointer usage difficult to read.

Exercise 6.4 illustrates the difference between reference notation and pointer notation.

Exercise 6.4   *Reference Parameters Eliminate Pointer Notation*

```
#include <iostream.h>
// ---------- a big structure
struct bigone    {
    int serno;
    char text[1000];    // a lot of chars
} bo = { 123, "This is a BIG structure"};
// -- two functions that have the structure as a parameter
void ptrfunc(bigone *p1);        // call by pointer
void reffunc(bigone& p1);        // call by reference
```

continued

Exercise 6.4 *Reference Parameters Eliminate Pointer Notation (continued)*

```
main()
{
    ptrfunc(&bo);    // pass the address
    reffunc(bo);     // pass the reference
}
// ---- a pointer function
void ptrfunc(bigone *p1)
{   cout << '\n' << p1->serno;        // pointer notation
    cout << '\n' << p1->text;
}
// ---- a call by reference function
void reffunc(bigone& p1)
{
    cout << '\n' << p1.serno;         // reference notation
    cout << '\n' << p1.text;
}
```

Exercise 6.4 displays the same messages as Exercise 6.3.

You might argue that there is little about the pointer notation in Exercise 6.4 to make it less readable than the reference notation. The perceived advantage is one of personal choice. The differences are more dramatic in a function with a lot of pointer dereferencing.

Call-by-reference

When one function passes a reference as an argument to another function, the called function is working on the caller's copy of the parameter, not a local copy (as it does when you pass the variable itself). This behavior is known as *call-by-reference*. Passing the parameter's value to a private copy in the called function is known as *call-by-value*.

If the called function changes a referenced parameter, it is changing the caller's copy.

Exercise 6.5 shows how reference parameters allow a swapper function to swap the parameters of the caller.

Exercise 6.5 *Call-by-Reference*

```
#include <iostream.h>
// ------ simple date class
struct Date {
    int da, mo, yr;
    void display(void);
};
void Date::display()
{
    cout << da << '/' << mo << '/' << yr;
}
void swapper(Date&, Date&);
void display(Date&, Date&);
main()
{
    static Date now  = {23,2,90};    // two dates
    static Date then = {10,9,60};
    display(now, then);         // display the dates
    swapper(now, then);         // swap them
    display(now, then);         // display them swapped
}
// ----- this function swaps the caller's dates
void swapper(Date& dt1, Date& dt2)
{
    Date save;
    save = dt1;
    dt1 = dt2;
    dt2 = save;
}
void display(Date& now, Date& then)
{
    cout << "\n Now:  ";
    now.display();
    cout << "\n Then: ";
    then.display();
}
```

In Exercise 6.5, the first two dates are initialized with different values as local variables in the *main* function. The *swapper* function swaps those two dates. It accepts two *Date* references and swaps them by using simple assignment statements. Because the parameters are references, the swapping occurs to the *main* function's copy of the structures.

Exercise 6.5 displays the following date formats:

```
Now:   23/2/90
Then:  10/9/60
Now:   10/9/60
Then:  23/2/90
```

const Reference Parameters

Consider Exercise 6.5 again. The call to *swapper* gives no indication that it uses references. The compiler knows to use references because that is how the function is prototyped and declared. But the programmer who writes *main* might not know that.

Given the purpose of the *swapper* function, it should be obvious that it uses references. If it did not, it would swap its own copies of the parameters, accomplishing nothing. But it might not be obvious that other functions could change a caller's copy of a parameter. If the prototype is in a header file and the function is in an object library or a separately compiled source module, the reader gets no clue from the code about what is going to happen when the function gets called.

In cases in which the called function is going to modify the caller's copy of the variable, you can use either non-*const* pointers or non-*const* references. But when the function is not going to modify the caller's copy, you can use a *const* reference (or pointer). A function that has a *const* reference as a parameter cannot modify the referenced object even when the object itself is non-*const*. This notation is shown here:

```
void foo(const Date& dt); // foo cannot modify dt
```

This practice assures the caller that the variable is unchanged when the function returns. The protection extends fully. The *foo* function cannot pass the *dt* reference to a lower function that might modify the referenced variable.

Always use the *const* qualifier for pointer and reference parameters when the function you are designing is not going to change the referenced argument.

Pointer vs. Reference Parameters

When should you use a pointer as a function parameter and when should you use a reference? Here is a good rule to follow: If the argument variable must exist, use a reference. If the argument variable might exist, use a pointer. You can pass a null address value as an argument to a pointer parameter to indicate that the argument does not exist. There is no such thing as a null reference.

RETURNING A REFERENCE

You have seen how you can pass a reference to a function as a parameter. You can also return a reference from a function. When a function returns a reference, the function call can exist in any context where a reference can exist, including being on the receiving side of an assignment.

Exercise 6.6 calls a function to select from an array of dates.

Exercise 6.6   *Returning a Reference from a Function*

```
#include <iostream.h>
#include <stdlib.h>
// ---------- a date structure
struct Date {
    int mo, da, yr;
};
```

continued

Exercise 6.6   *Returning a Reference from a Function (continued)*

```
// -------- an array of dates
Date birthdays[] = {
    {12, 17, 37},
    {10, 31, 38},
    { 6, 24, 40},
    {11, 23, 42},
    { 8,  5, 44},
};
// ----- a function to retrieve a date
Date& getdate(int n)
{
    return birthdays[n-1];
}
main(int argc, char *argv[])
{
    if (argc > 1)    {
        Date& bd = getdate(atoi(argv[1]));
        cout << bd.mo << '/' << bd.da << '/' << bd.yr;
    }
}
```

Exercise 6.6 displays a different date depending on the command line option, which must be 1–5. Following are the messages displayed on a PC. The first line of each pair is the MS-DOS command line prompt and the program command you enter. The second line is the date that the exercise displays.

```
C>ex06008 1
12/17/37
C>ex06008 2
10/31/38
C>ex06008 3
6/24/40
C>ex06008 4
11/23/42
C>ex06008 5
8/5/44
```

You must not return a reference to an automatic variable. The code in the following example is incorrect:

```
Date& getdate(void)
{
    Date dt = {6, 24, 40};
    return dt;   // bad-reference to auto variable
}
```

The problem is that the *dt* variable goes out of scope when the function returns. You would, therefore, be returning a reference to a variable that no longer exists, and the calling program would be referring to a *Date* object that does not exist. Some C++ compilers issue a warning when they see code that returns references to automatic variables. Ignore the warning and you will get unpredictable results. Sometimes the program appears to work because the stack location where the automatic variable existed is intact when the reference is used. A program that appears to work in some cases can fail in others because of device or multitasking interrupts that use the stack.

When you call a function that returns a variable, you do not necessarily know whether the function returns a whole variable or a reference unless you look at the function's prototype. The compiler makes the determination and generates appropriate code in either case.

THINGS YOU CANNOT DO WITH REFERENCES

There is a tendency among C++ programmers who are making the transition from C to think of references as pointer forms rather than aliases. Here is the list of things that you cannot do to references.

- ❖ Point to them
- ❖ Have an array of them
- ❖ Take the address of one
- ❖ Compare them
- ❖ Assign to them
- ❖ Do arithmetic to them
- ❖ Change what they refer to

When you try to do one of these things, you might think you are getting away with it because the compiler does not complain. Chances are, the operation you are trying to apply to the reference is being applied to what the reference refers to. If you try to increment a reference, for example, you increment what it refers to if its data type accepts the increment operator. If you take the address of a reference, you are really taking the address of what the reference refers to.

All you can do to the reference itself is initialize it. Everything else is done to what the reference refers to, not to the reference.

SUMMARY

The reference is a handy way to optimize your program by eliminating the overhead associated with moving large structures around in memory. You will use the reference variable extensively after you learn to build C++ classes in the next chapter. Later, when you learn about operator overloading, you will see even more uses for the reference.

CHAPTER 7

C++ Classes

Before coming up with its present name, Dr. Stroustrup called C++ "C with classes." Classes support the way you use C++ for object-oriented programming, and they are the way you build new data types into the language. Not all extensible languages support object-oriented programming, but C++ does with its class mechanism. At first, you should think of classes as the means for extending C++ by designing and implementing new data types. Later you can extend this knowledge into your understanding of object-oriented programming. In this chapter you will learn about:

- ❖ Designing a class
- ❖ Data members
- ❖ Member functions
- ❖ Constructors and destructors

❖ Class conversion functions

❖ Friends

❖ References

❖ Assignment functions

❖ The *this* pointer

❖ Arrays of class objects

❖ Static class members

❖ The free store

❖ Copy constructors

DESIGNING A CLASS

Consider the intrinsic numerical data types that C and C++ use. There are several types of integer and floating-point numbers. These suffice for most of your numerical needs, but there are times when the basic types need to be expanded. In C, you would traditionally organize the basic types into a logical structure and write functions to manipulate that structure. With C++, you do the same thing, but you also bind together the data description and its algorithms and set them up as a new data type by defining a class. The class in C++ is a data type defined by the programmer. The class consists of a user-defined data structure, member functions, and, as you will learn in Chapter 8, custom operators.

Class Declaration

A class resembles the structure you learned about in Chapter 5. The class is distinguished from the C structure by its ability to hide some of its members from the rest of the program and its ability to associate functions with the class.

The C++ class differs from the C++ structure only in the defaults that each assumes with respect to access specifiers. Everything that you learned about structures in Chapter 5 applies to classes. Everything that you learn about classes in this chapter applies to and adds to what you learned about C++ structures.

Begin by considering a simple class design. Exercise 7.1 is an example of a class that describes the geometrical cube form.

N O T E

Before proceeding to Exercise 7.1, ask yourself why you might want to build a class that describes a cube. Perhaps you are writing a program that deals with cubic containers of one kind or another, and the cube is a basic unit that the program must deal with. Any data entity that your program might process is a candidate to be a class in C++. This begins to answer the question, "What are the objects?" This is the first question asked by every functional programmer who is considering object-oriented programming.

Exercise 7.1 introduces classes by declaring the *Cube* class.

Exercise 7.1   *The **Cube** Class*

```
#include <iostream.h>
// ------------ a Cube class
class Cube    {
private:
    int height, width, depth;    // private data members
public:
    Cube(int, int, int); // constructor function
    ~Cube();              // destructor function
    int volume(void);     // member function (compute volume)
};
// ---------- the constructor function
Cube::Cube(int ht, int wd, int dp)
{
    height = ht;
    width = wd;
    depth = dp;
}
// ---------- the destructor function
Cube::~Cube()
{
    // does nothing
}
```

continued

Exercise 7.1 *The* **Cube** *Class (continued)*

```
// -------- member function to compute the Cube's volume
int Cube::volume()
{
    return height * width * depth;
}
// ========== an application to use the cube
main()
{
    Cube thiscube(7, 8, 9);     // declare a Cube
    cout << thiscube.volume();  // compute & display volume
}
```

Exercise 7.1 displays the cube's volume, which is 504.

There are a lot of new C++ features packed into Exercise 7.1. The program begins by declaring the *Cube* class. The *Cube* has three private data members—the integers height, width, and depth—and three public functions: a constructor named *Cube*, a destructor named *~Cube*, and a member function named *volume*. You learn more about each of these kinds of functions as the chapter progresses.

Class Members

A class is a souped-up C structure. As such, a class has members, just as a structure does. A class's members are defined by the class declaration and consist of data members, the constructor and destructor functions, and member functions.

Class Member Visibility

The *private* and *public* access specifiers specify the visibility of the members that follow the access specifiers. The access mode set by an access specifier continues until another access specifier occurs or the class declaration ends. Private members can be accessed only by member functions of the same class. Public members can be accessed by member functions and by other functions that declare an instance of the class. There are exceptions to these general rules. The discussion later in this chapter of *friend* classes and functions addresses some of those exceptions.

The *Cube* class, therefore, specifies that its three integer data members are visible only to the constructor and destructor functions and to the *volume* member function, all three of which are visible to outside functions. You can use the *private* and *public* access specifiers as often as you want in a class declaration, but many programmers group the *private* and *public* members separately.

All class declarations begin with the *private* access specifier as the default mode, so you could omit it in Exercise 7.1. The exercise includes it for readability and to demonstrate its purpose. That point introduces what might come as a surprise. Chapter 5 discussed C++ structures briefly, deferring the more complicated subjects to this chapter. The surprise is that there are only a few small differences between the structure and the class. First, the structure begins with *public* access as the default, and the class begins with *private* access as the default. Second, if the structure is derived from a base class, the base class is public by default. If the class is derived from a base class, the base class is private by default. You have already learned about access specifiers. Chapter 9 discusses public and private base classes and class derivation—inheritance—in general. Many programmers adopt a style in which they define a structure when its form complies with the C definition of a structure. Otherwise, they define a class.

A third access specifier, the *protected* keyword, works the same as the *private* keyword except when you use class inheritance. For now, you will not use the *protected* access specifier.

Data Members

The data members of the class are the ones that are data types. A data member can be any valid C++ data type, including an instance of another another class or a reference. The *Cube* class has three data members: the integers *height, width,* and *depth.*

Initialization

The declaration of a class object can contain a list of initializers in parentheses. The declaration of *thiscube* in Exercise 7.1 contains three integer values. These values are passed to the class's constructor function, described soon. However, if the class has no private or protected members, has no virtual functions (discussed later), and is not derived from another class (Chapter 9), you can initialize an object of the class with a brace-delimited, comma-separated list of initializers, just as you initialize C structures, as shown here:

```
class Date  {
public:
    int mo, da, yr;
};
main()
{
    Date dt = {1,29,92};
    // ...
}
```

The same restrictions apply to structures, by the way. You cannot use a brace-delimited initializer list if a structure has any of the attributes just mentioned.

Member Functions

The member functions of the class are the functions that are declared within the class definition. You must provide the code for these functions just as you did for the functions in structures in Chapter 5.

There are several categories of member functions. The constructor and destructor, discussed soon, are two of them. The others are regular member functions, *friend* functions, and *virtual* functions. You learn about *friend* and *virtual* functions later. For now, note that the *Cube* class has one member function, named *volume*, which is neither *friend* nor *virtual*. Member functions are named with the class name followed by the :: operator followed by the function name. The name of the *Cube* class's *volume* member function is, therefore, *Cube::volume*.

The *Cube::volume* function returns the product of the *Cube* object's three dimensions. The program in Exercise 7.1 calls the *volume* function by using the same convention for calling a structure's function. Use structure member notation with the period operator, as illustrated in the following example:

```
int vol = thiscube.volume();
```

You can call the *volume* member function anywhere an object of type *Cube* is in scope. Member functions of a class can call one another as well by using the function name without the object name prefix. The compiler assumes that the call is being made for the same object that the calling member function was called for.

When a member function is private, only other member functions within the same class can call it.

Object-Oriented Class Design

Exercise 7.1 shows a convention that many C++ programmers follow because it is considered to be sound C++ object-oriented design. When designing a class, make all the data members private. Make public only those member functions that are necessary for a programmer to use the class in an application program.

A class design encapsulates the data members and algorithms into a user-defined *abstract data type*. The details of the type's *implementation* are hidden from the class user within the class's private members. The user's perception of the type is defined in its public *interface*, which is provided by public member functions. A class's hidden implementation can use private member functions, too, but these functions are not included in the public interface.

If you need to allow the class user to view or modify a private data value, do it with a public member function. This convention is not a hard and fast rule, and there will be rare times when you find it necessary to do otherwise. But if you use the convention as a guideline, your programs will be more object-oriented.

Is *Cube* in Exercise 7.1 an object? No, *Cube* is a *type*. Class declaration merely defines the class's format. It does not set aside any memory to hold an instance of the class. No instance of the class exists until a program declares one within the scope of the class declaration. A declared instance of a data type is an *object*. A class is a user-defined data type. Therefore, an instance of a class is an object. The *thiscube* variable in Exercise 7.1 is an object of type *Cube*. These are important distinctions in object-oriented programming.

The Scope of a Class Object

A class object is like any other data type with respect to scope. The object comes into scope when the program defines it, and it goes out of scope when the program exits the block in which the class object is defined.

An *extern* class comes into scope when the program begins and goes out of scope when the program ends.

If you give a local class object the *static* keyword, its scope appears to be the same as that of an automatic object, but its actual existence is the same as that of an *extern* object. This becomes a matter to consider because C++ classes involve those special functions called the constructor and destructor functions.

inline Functions

A class can have *inline* functions. You learned about regular *inline* functions in Chapter 2. The same guidelines apply when you decide whether a class member function should be *inline*. *Inline* functions should be small.

There is a special notation for defining *inline* functions for a class. You code the body of the function directly into the class declaration rather than coding a prototype. Both the *Cube* constructor function and the *Cube's volume* member function are small enough to be *inline* functions. By coding them as *inline* and removing the unnecessary destructor function, you can significantly reduce the size of the program's source code.

Exercise 7.2 illustrates a class member function coded to be an *inline* member function.

Exercise 7.2   *The **Cube** Class with **inline** Functions*

```
#include <iostream.h>
// ----------- a Cube class
class Cube    {
    int height, width, depth;      // private data members
public:
    // ------ inline constructor function
    Cube(int ht, int wd, int dp)
        { height = ht; width = wd; depth = dp; }
    // ----- inline member function
    int volume()
        { return height * width * depth; }
};
main()
{
    Cube thiscube(7, 8, 9);       // declare a Cube
    cout << thiscube.volume();    // compute & display volume
}
```

Exercise 7.2 displays the cube's volume, which is 504.

You often see *inline* class functions coded on a single line. This convention reinforces the idea that *inline* functions should be small. If you cannot get the function's body on a single line, then perhaps the function should not be an *inline* one.

CONSTRUCTORS

When an instance of a class comes into scope, a special function called the *constructor* executes. It does, that is, if you have defined one. You define the constructor when you define the class. The *Cube* class has a constructor function named *Cube*. Constructor functions always have the same name as the class, and they specify no return value, not even *void*.

The run-time system allocates enough memory to contain the data members of a class when an object of the class comes into scope. The system does not necessarily initialize the data members. The class's constructor function must do any initialization that the class requires. The data memory returns to the system when the class object goes out of scope.

The constructor function initializes the class object. The *Cube* constructor function in Exercise 7.2 accepts three integer parameters and uses these parameters to load the data members with values that describe the *Cube*.

Observe the declaration of *thiscube* in Exercise 7.2. It follows the C syntax for declaring a variable. First comes the data type—*Cube*, in this case—and then comes the name of the object, *thiscube*. That's the same way you would declare an *int*, for example. The declaration of a class object can contain an argument list in parentheses. This list represents class object initializers and contains the arguments that are passed to the constructor function. There must be a constructor function in the class declaration with a parameter list of data types that match those of the argument list in the class object declaration.

If the constructor function has an empty parameter list, the declaration of the object does not require the parentheses.

A constructor function returns nothing. You do not declare it as *void*, but it is *void* by default.

You may define multiple, overloaded constructor functions for a class. Each of these would have a distinct parameter list. More discussion of this feature follows later.

Constructors with Default Arguments

Perhaps you want to initialize a *Cube* with dimensions as you did in Exercise 7.1, but at other times you want a *Cube* with default dimensions.

Exercise 7.3 shows a *Cube* class that defaults to specified dimensions if you do not supply initializers.

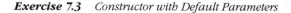

Exercise 7.3   *Constructor with Default Parameters*

```
#include <iostream.h>
// ----------- a Cube class
class Cube    {
    int height, width, depth;      // private data members
public:
    // ----- constructor function with default initializers
    Cube(int ht = 1, int wd = 2, int dp = 3)
        { height = ht; width = wd; depth = dp; }
    // ----- member function
    int volume() { return height * width * depth; }
};
main()
{
    Cube thiscube(7, 8, 9);        // declare a Cube
    Cube defaultcube;              // no initializers
    cout << thiscube.volume();     // volume of the Cube
    cout << '\n';
    cout << defaultcube.volume(); // volume of the default
}
```

Exercise 7.3 displays the initialized cube's volume, which is 504, followed by the default cube's volume, which is 6.

Overloaded Constructors

A class can have more than one constructor function. The several constructor functions for a class must have different parameter lists with respect to the number and types of parameters so that the compiler can tell them apart. You would code multiple constructors in cases where the declarations of a class can occur with different initialization parameters. Perhaps you want to initialize a *Cube* object with dimensions as you did in Exercise 7.1, but at other times you simply want an empty *Cube* with no initial dimensions—for example, to be on the receiving end of an assignment.

Exercise 7.4 shows the *Cube* with two constructor functions.

Exercise 7.4 *A Class with Two Constructors*

```
#include <iostream.h>
// ----------- a Cube class
class Cube    {
    int height, width, depth;    // private data members
public:
    // ------ constructor functions
    Cube() { /* does nothing */ }
    Cube(int ht, int wd, int dp)
        { height = ht; width = wd; depth = dp; }
    // ----- member function
    int volume() { return height * width * depth; }
};
main()
{
    Cube thiscube(7, 8, 9);    // declare a Cube
    Cube othercube;            // a Cube with no initializers
    othercube = thiscube;
    cout << othercube.volume();
}
```

Exercise 7.4 displays the cube's volume, which is 504, on the screen.

This exercise uses the simplest of differences between constructors: One constructor has initializers and the other one does not. The differences between constructors can be much greater depending on the types of the class's data members and the algorithms that associate with the constructor function. You will see more-complex constructor functions in later chapters.

CLASS CONVERSIONS

Use of C++ data types involves the implicit application of type conversion rules. If you use an *int* variable where the compiler expects a *long* variable, for example, the compiler invokes one of the type conversion rules to convert the original integer value to the new long format. Such conversions already exist for all pairs of data types that are compatible with respect to conversions. These implicit conversions come into play in assignments, function arguments, return values, initializers, and expressions.

Conversion Functions

You can build the same kind of implicit conversions into your classes by building conversion functions. When you write a function that converts any data type to a class, you tell the compiler to use the conversion function when the syntax of a statement implies that the conversion should take effect—that is, when the compiler expects an object of the class and sees the other data type instead.

There are two ways to write a conversion function. The first is to write a special constructor function; the second is to write a member conversion function.

Conversion Constructors

A constructor function with only one entry in its parameter list is a *conversion constructor* if the parameter is of a different type from the class of the constructor. A constructor conversion converts from an object of the type of the argument to an object of the class. The conversion constructor works like any other constructor when you declare an object of the class type with a matching initializer argument. It is an implicit conversion constructor when you use the argument type in a context where the class type is expected.

Exercise 7.5 demonstrates a constructor conversion function that converts the value returned by the standard time function to an object of the *Date* class.

Exercise 7.5   *Constructor Conversion Function*

```
#include <iostream.h>
#include <time.h>
class Date {
    int mo, da, yr;
public:
    Date() {}        // null constructor
    Date(time_t);    // constructor conversion function
    void display(void);
};
// ----- member function to display the date
void Date::display()
{
    cout << mo << '/' << da << '/' << yr;
}
// ------ constructor conversion function
Date::Date(time_t now)
{
    struct tm *tim = localtime(&now);
    da = tim->tm_mday;
    mo = tim->tm_mon + 1;
    yr = tim->tm_year;
}
main()
{
    time_t now = time(0); // today's date and time
    Date dt(now);    // invoke the conversion constructor
    dt.display();    // display today's date
}
```

Exercise 7.5 displays the current date in month/day/year format—for example, 5/3/94.

Member conversion functions

You use a *member conversion function* to convert from the class in which you define it to a different data type. A member conversion function uses the C++ *operator* keyword in its declaration. This usage is an early exposure to C++ operator overloading in classes, the subject of Chapter 8. To declare a member conversion function within a class, you code its prototype as illustrated by the following example:

```
operator long();
```

The *long* in this example is the type specifier of the converted data type. The type specifier can be any valid C++ type, including another class. You would define the member conversion function with the following notation:

```
Classname::operator long()
```

The *Classname* identifier is the type specifier of the class in which the function is declared and from which you convert to get the *long*. The function must return the data type to which it is converting, in this case a *long*.

There is not enough information in the *Date* class to convert it back to the *time_t* variable, but you can convert it to, for example, a long integer containing the number of days since the beginning of the century.

Exercise 7.6 shows how you would use a member function to make the conversion.

Exercise 7.6   *Member Conversion Function*

```
#include <iostream.h>
class Date {
    int mo, da, yr;
public:
    Date(int m, int d, int y) { mo = m; da = d; yr = y; }
    operator long();    // member conversion function
};
```

continued

Exercise 7.6   *Member Conversion Function (continued)*

```
// ---- the member conversion function
Date::operator long()
{
    static int dys[]={31,28,31,30,31,30,31,31,30,31,30,31};
    long days = yr;
    days *= 365;
    days += yr / 4;
    for (int i = 0; i < mo-1; i++)
        days += dys[i];
    days += da;
    return days;
}
main()
{
    Date xmas(12, 25, 89);
    long since = xmas;
    cout << '\n' << since;
}
```

Exercise 7.6 displays the number **32866**, which is the number of days from the turn of the century until Christmas of 1989.

Converting Classes

The conversion examples so far have converted a class to and from a fixed C++ data type. You can also define conversion functions that convert from one class to another.

Exercise 7.7 shows you how to convert class objects.

***Exercise* 7.7** *Converting Classes*

```
#include <iostream.h>
// -------- Julian date class
class Julian {
public:
    int da, yr;
    Julian() {}
    Julian(int d, int y) { da = d; yr = y;}
    void display(){ cout << '\n' << yr << '-' << da; }
};
// ------- date class
class Date {
    int mo, da, yr;
public:
    Date() {}
    Date(int m, int d, int y) { mo = m; da = d; yr = y; }
    Date(Julian);          // constructor conversion function
    operator Julian();     // member conversion function
    void display(){cout << '\n' << mo << '/' << da
                        << '/' << yr;}
};
static int dys[] = {31,28,31,30,31,30,31,31,30,31,30,31};
// -- constructor conversion function (Date <- Julian)
Date::Date(Julian jd)
{
    yr = jd.yr;
    da = jd.da;
    for (mo = 0; mo < 11; mo++)
        if (da > dys[mo])
            da -= dys[mo];
        else
            break;
    mo++;
}
```

continued

Exercise 7.7   *Converting Classes (continued)*

```
// ---- member conversion function (Julian <- Date)
Date::operator Julian()
{
    Julian jd(0, yr);
    for (int i = 0; i < mo-1; i++)
        jd.da += dys[i];
    jd.da += da;
    return jd;
}
main()
{
    Date dt(11,17,89);
    Julian jd;
    // ------- convert Date to Julian
    jd = dt;
    jd.display();
    // ------- convert Julian to Date
    dt = jd;
    dt.display();
}
```

Exercise 7.7 displays the two converted date formats as shown here:

```
89-321
11/17/89
```

This exercise has two classes: a *Julian* date and a *Date*. A *Julian* date is one that contains the year and the day of the year from 1 to 365. The conversion functions in Exercise 7.7 convert between the two date formats.

The date conversion algorithms in these exercises do not consider things such as the millennium or the leap year. These omissions are intentional to keep the exercises as simple as possible.

Both kinds of conversion functions are built into the *Date* class in Exercise 7.7. This approach works because you convert from the *Date* type to the *Julian* type with the member conversion function, and from the *Julian* type to the *Date* type with the constructor conversion function.

Note that it would not be legal to have a *Date* to *Julian* member conversion function in the *Date* class, and a *Date* to *Julian* conversion constructor function in the *Julian* class. This ambiguity would confuse the compiler about which function to call to perform the conversion.

Invoking Conversion Functions

There are three C++ forms that invoke a conversion function. The first is implicit conversion. For example, where the compiler expects to see a *Date* and the program supplies a *Julian*, the compiler calls the appropriate conversion function. The other two forms involve explicit conversions that you write into the code. The first of these conversions is implied by the C++ cast. The second is an explicit call to the conversion constructor or member conversion function.

Exercise 7.8 illustrates the three class conversion forms.

Exercise 7.8   *Invoking Conversions*

```
#include <iostream.h>
// -------- Julian date class
class Julian {
public:
    int da, yr;
    Julian() {}
    Julian(int d, int y) { da = d; yr = y;}
    void display(){cout << '\n' << yr << '-' << da;}
};
// ------- date class
class Date {
    int mo, da, yr;
public:
    Date(int m, int d, int y) { mo = m; da = d; yr = y; }
    operator Julian(); // conversion function
};
```

continued

Exercise 7.8 *Invoking Conversions (continued)*

```
static int dys[] = {31,28,31,30,31,30,31,31,30,31,30,31};
// ---- member conversion function (Julian <- Date)
Date::operator Julian()
{
    Julian jd(0, yr);
    for (int i = 0; i < mo-1; i++)
        jd.da += dys[i];
    jd.da += da;
    return jd;
}
main()
{
    Date dt(11,17,89);
    Julian jd;
    // ------- implicit conversion
    jd = dt;
    jd.display();
    // ------- convert Date to Julian via cast
    jd = (Julian) dt;
    jd.display();
    // ------- call the conversion function
    jd = Julian(dt);
    jd.display();
}
```

Exercise 7.8 displays the three Julian dates that were converted from conventional dates in three ways, as shown here.

```
89-321
89-321
89-321
```

N O T E

The cast in Exercise 7.8 uses traditional C++ notation. Contemporary C++ introduces new notations for casting. Chapter 13 discusses these new casting conventions.

The Contexts Where Conversions Occur

So far the exercises have invoked conversion functions through assignment. The following list identifies several other contexts in which a conversion function comes into play:

❖   As a function argument

❖   As an initializer

❖   As a return value

❖   In an expression

Exercise 7.9 illustrates some of the ways you can cause a conversion function to be called.

Exercise 7.9 *Contexts for Conversions*

```
#include <iostream.h>
// -------- Julian date class
class Julian {
public:
    int da, yr;
    Julian() {}
    Julian(int d, int y) { da = d; yr = y;}
    void display(){cout << '\n' << yr << '-' << da;}
};
```

continued

Exercise 7.9   *Contexts for Conversions (continued)*

```
// ------- date class
class Date {
    int mo, da, yr;
public:
    Date(int m, int d, int y) { mo = m; da = d; yr = y; }
    operator Julian(); // conversion function
};
// ----- a class that expects a Julian date as an initializer
class Tester {
    Julian jd;
public:
    Tester(Julian j) { jd = j; }
    void display() { jd.display(); }
};
static int dys[] = {31,28,31,30,31,30,31,31,30,31,30,31};
// ---- member conversion function (Julian <- Date)
Date::operator Julian()
{
    Julian jd(0, yr);
    for (int i = 0; i < mo-1; i++)
        jd.da += dys[i];
    jd.da += da;
    return jd;
}
// -------- a function that expects a Julian date
void dispdate(Julian jd)
{
    jd.display();
}
```

continued

Exercise 7.9 *Contexts for Conversions (continued)*

```
// --------- a function that returns a Julian Date
Julian rtndate()
{
    Date dt(10,11,88);
    return dt;        // this will be converted to Julian
}
main()
{
    Date dt(11,17,89);
    Julian jd;
    // ------- convert Date to Julian via assignment
    jd = dt;
    jd.display();
    // ---- convert Date to Julian via function argument
    dispdate(dt);
    // ------- convert Date to Julian via initializer
    Tester ts(dt);
    ts.display();
    // ------- convert Date to Julian via return value
    jd = rtndate();
    jd.display();
}
```

Exercise 7.9 displays the Julian dates converted from four different program contexts, as shown here:

```
89-321
89-321
89-321
88-284
```

Conversion within an expression occurs in those expressions where one type is expected and another type is found. This process is better illustrated when the conversion is to a numeric type instead of to another class.

Exercise 7.10 uses the earlier conversion of a date to a long integer to illustrate how the integral representation of a class can, through conversion, contribute directly to an expression.

Exercise 7.10   *Conversion in an Expression*

```
#include <iostream.h>
class Date {
    int mo, da, yr;
public:
    Date(int m, int d, int y) { mo = m; da = d; yr = y; }
    operator long();    // member conversion function
};
// ---- the member conversion function
Date::operator long()
{
    static int dys[]={31,28,31,30,31,30,31,31,30,31,30,31};
    long days = yr;
    days *= 365;
    days += yr / 4;
    for (int i = 0; i < mo-1; i++)
        days += dys[i];
    days += da;
    return days;
}
main()
{
    Date today(2, 12, 90);
    const long ott = 123;
    long sum = ott + today;    // today is converted to long
    cout << ott << " + " << (long) today << " = " << sum;
}
```

Exercise 7.10 displays this expression:

```
123 + 32915 = 33038
```

The implicit conversion from within an expression occurs for a class-to-class conversion if the converted class can appear in a conversion—that is, if the converted class can itself be converted to a numerical type, or if the expression invokes an overloaded operator that works with the class. Chapter 8 discusses overloading operators.

MANIPULATING PRIVATE DATA MEMBERS

All the data members in the *Julian* class in Exercises 7.7, 7.8, and 7.9 are public. This approach allows the conversion functions in the *Date* class to read and write the data members of the *Julian* object. Making the members public is one way to allow this access, but when you do, you make the members public to all other functions as well. You might not want to do that. Remember the convention for keeping the data members private and the interface member functions public. These exercises violated that convention to get their point across. Now you should consider alternative ways to get the same results within the bounds of the accepted conventions.

As a general rule, you make all the data members private and you provide member functions to read and write them.

Exercise 7.11 shows how the *Date* class can have member functions that provide controlled access to the data members.

Exercise 7.11   *Manipulating Data Members though Member Functions*

```
#include <iostream.h>
class Date {
    int mo, da, yr;
public:
    Date(int m, int d, int y) { mo = m; da = d; yr = y; }
    // ---- a member function to return the year
    int getyear() { return yr; }
    // ---- a member function to allow the year to be changed
    int& year() { return yr; }
};
```

continued

Exercise 7.11 *Manipulating Data Members though Member Functions (continued)*

```
main()
{
    // -------- set up a Date
    Date dt(4, 1, 89);
    // ------- use a member function to read the year value
    cout << "\nThe year is: " << dt.getyear();
    // ------ use a member function to change the year
    dt.year() = 90;
    cout << "\nThe new year is: " << dt.getyear();
}
```

Exercise 7.11 displays these messages:

```
The year is: 89
The new year is: 90
```

By consistently using this approach, you ensure that accesses and changes to the data of a class are managed by the member functions that are bound to the class. This binding strengthens a software design and makes it easier to maintain.

Exercise 7.12 uses the member function access technique to improve the code in the conversion function that converts a *Date* object to a *Julian* object.

Exercise 7.12 *Conversions with Proper Data Hiding*

```
#include <iostream.h>
// -------- Julian date class
class Julian {
    int da, yr;
public:
    Julian() {}
    Julian(int d, int y) { da = d; yr = y;}
    void display(){cout << '\n' << yr << '-' << da;}
    // ------ member function to read and write a day
    int& day() { return da; }
};
```

continued

Exercise 7.12   *Conversions with Proper Data Hiding (continued)*

```
// ------- date class
class Date {
    int mo, da, yr;
public:
    Date(int m, int d, int y) { mo = m; da = d; yr = y; }
    operator Julian(); // conversion function
};
static int dys[] = {31,28,31,30,31,30,31,31,30,31,30,31};
// ---- member conversion function (Julian <- Date)
Date::operator Julian()
{
    Julian jd(0, yr);
    for (int i = 0; i < mo-1; i++)
        jd.day() += dys[i];        // uses member function to
    jd.day() += da;            // change da in Julian class
    return jd;
}
main()
{
    Date dt(11,17,89);
    Julian jd;
    // ------- convert Date to Julian via assignment
    jd = dt;
    jd.display();
}
```

Exercise 7.12 displays this converted Julian Date:

    89-321

Restricting Access to Data Members

Observe that the *year* member function in Exercise 7.11 and the *day* member function in Exercise 7.12 return references. Because each function returns a reference, you can use the function call on the left side of an assignment the way the exercises show. This practice, however, compromises one of the principles of object-oriented design. It permits the using program to directly modify the value of a data member, thereby binding the user to the implementation of the class. A better way is to provide two member functions for the data member: one that returns its current value and one that accepts a new value with which to modify it, as shown below.

```
// ---- a member function to return the year
int getyear() { return yr; }
// ---- a member function to allow the year to be changed
void change_year(int y) { yr = y; }
```

This practice allows the class designer to change the implementation without affecting the code of the users.

There are valid uses of the reference return, and you will learn about some of them in Chapter 8.

const Member Functions

You can guarantee that a member function never modifies the object for which it is called by declaring it with the *const* qualifier as shown here:

```
// ---- a member function to return the year
int getyear() const;
```

No change to the *Date::getyear* function is permitted that modifies the data members in the object. This is a way to ensure that the member function's only purpose is to retrieve data values from the object.

FRIENDS

Having learned that hidden access to data members is best, you must now consider exceptions to that rule. There are times when a class declaration must allow specific outside functions to directly read and write the class's private data members.

The *friend* keyword in a class specifies that a particular function or all the member functions of another class can read and write the original class's private data members. This technique allows a class to maintain a private implementation in the view of its users while permitting access to that implementation to specified functions and classes.

Friend Classes

The first kind of friend is the class *friend*. A class can specify that all the member functions of another class can read and write the first class's private data members by identifying the other class as a friend.

Exercise 7.13 illustrates the use of the *friend* class.

Exercise 7.13   friend Classes

```
#include <iostream.h>
class Date;        // tells compiler a Date class is coming
// -------- Julian date class
class Julian {
    int da, yr;
public:
    Julian() {}
    Julian(int d, int y) { da = d; yr = y;}
    void display() {cout << '\n' << yr << '-' << da;}
    friend Date;    // allows Date member functions to see
                    // Julian private members
};
// ------- date class
class Date {
    int mo, da, yr;
public:
    Date(int m, int d, int y) { mo = m; da = d; yr = y; }
    operator Julian();
};
static int dys[] = {31,28,31,30,31,30,31,31,30,31,30,31};
```

continued

*Exercise 7.13 **friend** Classes (continued)*

```
// ---- member conversion function (Julian <- Date)
Date::operator Julian()
{
    Julian jd(0, yr);
    for (int i = 0; i < mo-1; i++)
        jd.da += dys[i];
    jd.da += da;
    return jd;
}
main()
{
    Date dt(11,17,89);
    Julian jd;
    jd = dt;
    jd.display();
}
```

Exercise 7.13 displays the converted Julian Date:

```
89-321
```

Observe this new construct in the *Julian* class of Exercise 7.13 in the following example:

```
friend Date;
```

This statement tells the compiler that member functions of the *Date* class have access to the private members of the *Julian* class. The conversion functions of the *Date* class need to see the individual data components of the *Julian* class, so the entire *Date* class is named as a friend of the *Julian* class.

Another new C++ construct is contained in Exercise 7.13. The beginning of the program has the following statement:

```
class Date;
```

This statement tells the compiler that a class named *Date* is defined later. The compiler needs to know about that because the *Julian* class refers to the *Date* class, and the *Date* class refers to the *Julian* class. One of them must be declared first, so the statement serves to resolve the forward reference to *Date* that occurs in the *Julian* class.

You can eliminate the need for the *class Date;* statement by including the *class* keyword in the *friend* declaration.

Exercise 7.14 modifies the Exercise 7.13 program by using the *class* keyword.

Exercise 7.14   friend Classes, Forward Reference

```
#include <iostream.h>
// -------- Julian date class
class Julian {
    int da, yr;
public:
    Julian() {}
    Julian(int d, int y) { da = d; yr = y;}
    void display() {cout << '\n' << yr << '-' << da;}
    friend class Date;    // <- forward reference to class
};
// ------- date class
class Date {
    int mo, da, yr;
public:
    Date(int m, int d, int y) { mo = m; da = d; yr = y; }
    operator Julian();
};
static int dys[] = {31,28,31,30,31,30,31,31,30,31,30,31};
```

continued

*Exercise 7.14 **friend** Classes, Forward Reference (continued)*

```
// ---- member conversion function (Julian <- Date)
Date::operator Julian()
{
    Julian jd(0, yr);
    for (int i = 0; i < mo-1; i++)
        jd.da += dys[i];
    jd.da += da;
    return jd;
}
main()
{
    Date dt(11,17,89);
    Julian jd;
    jd = dt;
    jd.display();
}
```

Exercise 7.14 displays this converted Julian Date:

```
89-321
```

Friend Functions

Sometimes you do not want an entire class to be a friend of another class. Unless it is necessary to access data in such a broad way, you should not do so. What you need is a way to specify that only selected member functions of another class may read and write the data members of the current class. In these cases, you may specify that a particular function rather than an entire class is a friend of a class.

Exercise 7.15 restricts the access to the data members of the *Julian* class to only the member function of the *Date* class that needs it.

Exercise 7.15 ***friend*** *Functions in a Class*

```cpp
#include <iostream.h>
class Julian;
// ------- date class
class Date {
    int mo, da, yr;
public:
    Date() {}
    Date(Julian);          // constructor conversion function
    void display()
        {cout << '\n' << mo << '/' << da << '/' << yr;}
};
// -------- Julian date class
class Julian {
    int da, yr;
public:
    Julian(int d, int y) { da = d; yr = y; }
    friend Date::Date(Julian); // friend conversion function
};
static int dys[] = {31,28,31,30,31,30,31,31,30,31,30,31};
// ---- constructor conversion function (Date <- Julian)
Date::Date(Julian jd)
{
    yr = jd.yr;
    da = jd.da;
    for (mo = 0; mo < 11; mo++)
        if (da > dys[mo])
            da -= dys[mo];
        else
            break;
    mo++;
}
main()
{
    Date dt;
    Julian jd(123, 89);
    dt = jd;          // convert Julian to Date
    dt.display();
}
```

Exercise 7.15 displays this date converted from a Julian Date:

```
5/3/89
```

Sometimes the function that is to be a friend is not a member of another class at all. You may specify that a regular function is a friend to a class. That function would then have the special privilege of reading and writing the class's private data members. This feature is particularly useful when you're overloading operators, the subject of Chapter 8.

A frequent use of nonmember *friend* functions is to bridge classes. A function that is friend to two classes can have access to the private members of both. Suppose you have a *Time* class and a *Date* class and you want a function that displays both.

Exercise 7.16 shows how a *friend* function that has access to the data members of both classes can bridge the two.

Exercise 7.16   *Bridging Classes with a friend Function*

```
#include <iostream.h>
class Time;
// ------- date class
class Date {
    int mo, da, yr;
public:
    Date(int m, int d, int y) { mo = m; da = d; yr = y;}
    friend void display(Date&, Time&); // bridge function
};
// ------- time class
class Time {
    int hr, min, sec;
public:
    Time(int h, int m, int s) { hr = h; min = m; sec = s;}
    friend void display(Date&, Time&); // bridge function
};
```

continued

Exercise 7.16 *Bridging Classes with a friend Function (continued)*

```
// -------- a bridge friend function
void display(Date& dt, Time& tm)
{
    cout << '\n' << dt.mo << '/' << dt.da << '/' << dt.yr;
    cout << ' ';
    cout << tm.hr << ':' << tm.min << ':' << tm.sec;
}
main()
{
    Date dt(2,16,90);
    Time tm(10,55,0);
    display(dt, tm);
}
```

Exercise 7.16 displays this date and time message:

```
2/16/90 10:55:0
```

DESTRUCTORS

When a class object goes out of scope, a special function called the *destructor* is called. You define the destructor when you define the class. The destructor function name is always that of the class with a tilde character (~) as a prefix.

There is only one destructor function for a class. A destructor function takes no parameters and returns nothing.

Until now, the exercises in this chapter have not included destructors because the classes in them have not required anything in the way of custom destruction. Destructors are a peculiar breed of function with their own set of problems to consider.

The destructor function for the *Cube* class used earlier in this chapter does nothing. Exercise 7.1 included it to show its format. You could omit it altogether and get the same result. However, on other occasions destructors are necessary. For example, some classes allocate memory from the free store in their constructors. These classes use destructors to return the memory to the free store.

To illustrate how destructors work, a new *Date* class includes a pointer to a string that contains the month spelled out. Exercise 7.17 shows the destructor function for the new *Date* class.

Exercise 7.17   *Destructors*

```
#include <iostream.h>
#include <string.h>
// ------- date class
class Date {
    int mo, da, yr;
    char *month;
public:
    Date();
    Date(int m, int d, int y);
    ~Date();
    void display();
};
// constructor that is called for an uninitialized Date
Date::Date()
{
    mo = 0; da = 0; yr = 0;
    month = 0;
}
```

continued

Exercise 7.17 *Destructors (continued)*

```
// constructor that is called for an initialized Date
Date::Date(int m, int d, int y)
{
    static char *mos[] = {
        "January", "February", "March", "April", "May",
        "June", "July", "August", "September", "October",
        "November", "December"
    };
    mo = m; da = d; yr = y;
    month = new char[strlen(mos[m-1])+1];
    strcpy(month, mos[m-1]);
}
// Destructor for a Date
Date::~Date()
{
    delete[] month;
}
// ----------- display member function
void Date::display()
{
    if (month != 0)
        cout << '\n' << month << ' ' << da << ", "
            << yr+1900;
}
main()
{
    Date birthday(6,24,40);
    birthday.display();
}
```

Exercise 7.17 displays this date:

```
June 24, 1940
```

Note that as the member functions get bigger, they are no longer *inline* functions.

The constructor function for the uninitialized *Date* object sets all the integer data members to zero and the month pointer to a null value.

The constructor function for the initialized *Date* object uses the *new* operator to allocate some free-store memory for the string name of the month. Then the constructor copies the name from its internal array into the *Date* object's *month* character pointer. Of course, in the context of this exercise you could have simply copied the pointer from the constructor's array into the class, but the point of the exercise is to discuss destructors. If you had copied the pointer, the object would have had nothing that needed destroying.

The destructor function deletes the *month* pointer, and this is where you can get into trouble. As programmed, the exercise has no problems, but as designed, the *Date* class can cause trouble when used in an assignment. Suppose you added the following code to the *main* function in Exercise 7.17:

```
Date newday;
newday = birthday;
```

You would construct an empty *Date* variable named *newday* and then assign the contents of *birthday* to it. That looks reasonable, but when you consider what the destructor function does, you see the problem.

C++ figures that if you do not tell it otherwise, a class assignment is a member-by-member copy. In this example, the *birthday* variable has *month*, a character pointer that was initialized by the constructor's use of the *new* operator. The destructor uses the *delete* operator to release the memory when *birthday* goes out of scope. But, when that happens, *newday* goes out of scope, too, and the destructor executes for it as well. The *month* pointer in *newday* is a copy of the *month* pointer in *birthday*. The constructor deletes the same pointer twice, giving unpredictable results, and that is a problem that you must deal with in your design of the class.

Furthermore, suppose that *newday* is an external object and *birthday* is automatic. When *birthday* goes out of scope, it deletes the *month* pointer in the *newday* object.

Now, suppose that you had two initialized *Date* variables and you assigned one to the other as in the following example:

```
Date birthday(6,24,40);
Date newday(7,29,41);
newday = birthday;
```

The problem compounds itself. When the two variables go out of scope, the *month* value originally assigned in *birthday* is in *newday* as a result of the assignment. The *month* value that the constructor's *new* operation put into *newday* has been overwritten by the assignment. Not only does the *month* value in *birthday* get deleted twice, but also the one that was originally in *newday* never gets deleted.

CLASS ASSIGNMENT

The solution to the problems just posed lies in recognizing when they occur and writing a special assignment operator function to deal with them. You can overload the assignment operator for assigning an object of a class to another object of the same class. It is with this technique that you solve the problem of assignment and destruction of free-store pointers in a class. (Chapter 8 discusses overloaded operators in detail.)

The technique you are about to learn is simple. Your class assignment function uses the *new* operator to get a different pointer from the free store. Then it copies the value pointed to in the assigning object, into the area pointed to in the assigned object.

Exercise 7.18 is an example of how the class-assignment technique works.

Exercise 7.18   *Class Assignment*

```
#include <iostream.h>
#include <string.h>
// ------- date class
class Date {
    int mo, da, yr;
    char *month;
public:
    Date();
    Date(int m, int d, int y);
    ~Date();
    void operator=(Date&); // overloaded assignment operator
    void display();
};
```

continued

Exercise 7.18   *Class Assignment (continued)*

```
// constructor that is called for an uninitialized Date
Date::Date()
{
    mo = 0; da = 0; yr = 0;
    month = 0;
}
// constructor that is called for an initialized Date
Date::Date(int m, int d, int y)
{
    static char *mos[] = {
        "January", "February", "March", "April", "May",
        "June", "July", "August", "September", "October",
        "November", "December"
    };
    mo = m; da = d; yr = y;
    month = new char[strlen(mos[m-1])+1];
    strcpy(month, mos[m-1]);
}
// Destructor for a Date
Date::~Date()
{
    delete[] month;
}
// ----------- display member function
void Date::display()
{
    if (month != 0)
        cout << '\n' << month << ' ' << da << ", "
            << yr+1900;
}
```

continued

Exercise 7.18 *Class Assignment (continued)*

```
// ---------- overloaded Date assignment
void Date::operator=(Date& dt)
{
    if (&dt == this) return;
    mo = dt.mo;
    da = dt.da;
    yr = dt.yr;
    delete[] month;
    if (dt.month != 0)    {
        month = new char [strlen(dt.month)+1];
        strcpy(month, dt.month);
    }
    else
        month = 0;
}
main()
{
    // ------ first date
    Date birthday(6,24,40);
    birthday.display();
    // ------ second date
    Date newday(7,29,41);
    newday.display();
    // ------ assign first to second
    newday = birthday;
    newday.display();
}
```

This exercise contains all the components of Exercise 7.17 except that the over-loaded assignment operator function is added to the *Date* class definition. The function makes the usual data-member assignments and then uses the *delete* operator to return the object's *month* string memory to the free store. Then, if the sending object's *month* pointer has been initialized (if not, the sender was never initialized), the function uses *new* to allocate memory for the receiving object and copies the sending object's *month* string to the receiver.

Exercise 7.18 displays the following messages:

```
June 24, 1940
July 29, 1941
June 24, 1940
```

You cannot always see the effects of the overloaded assignment function by observing a properly running program such as that in Exercise 7.18. The effects of leaving it out are different from compiler to compiler. In some cases, the code might even work for a time. The effects of deleting pointers that have already been deleted are undefined, and it is perfectly correct for the compiler to generate code that crashes if you do so. The effect of not deleting unneeded pointers is that you eventually exhaust the free store.

N O T E

The first statement in the overloaded *Date* assignment operator compares the address of the sending object to the *this* pointer (discussed next). This operation protects against the occasion when a program assigns an object to itself.

THE *this* POINTER

The *this* pointer is a special pointer that exists for a class while a nonstatic member function is executing. The *this* pointer is a pointer to an object of the type of the class, and it points to the object for which the member function is currently executing.

Note that *this* does not exist in a static member function (see the discussion on static members later in this chapter).

When you call a member function for an object, the compiler assigns the address of the object to the *this* pointer and then calls the function. Therefore, every reference to a data member from within a member function implicitly uses the *this* pointer. Both output statements in the following example are the same.

In this example, the second statement explicitly uses the pointer notation that the first statement uses implicitly:

```
void Date::month_display()
{
    cout << mo;       // these two statements
    cout << this->mo; // do the same thing
}
```

Returning *this*

One purpose of the *this* pointer is to allow member functions to return the invoking object to the caller. The overloaded assignment operator function in Exercise 7.18 returns nothing. With that function you would not be able to string assignments together in the C and C++ format as follows:

```
a = b = c;
```

Such an assignment works in C and C++ because every expression returns something unless it is a function returning *void*. The preceding example can be expressed the following way:

```
b = c;
a = b;
```

Because the first statement is an expression that returns the value assigned, the two expressions can be combined as follows:

```
a = (b = c);
```

Because the rightmost assignment operator has higher precedence than the leftmost one, the parentheses are not required, and the preceding example is thus expressed in the following way:

```
a = b = c;
```

To make your overloaded class assignments work the same way, you must make the assignment function return the result of the assignment, which happens to be the object being assigned to. This also happens to be what the *this* pointer points to while the assignment function is executing.

Exercise 7.19 modifies Exercise 7.18 by having the overloaded assignment function return a reference to a *Date*. The value returned is the object pointed to by the *this* pointer.

Exercise 7.19   *The**this** Pointer*

```
#include <iostream.h>
#include <string.h>
// ------- date class
class Date {
    int mo, da, yr;
    char *month;
public:
    Date();
    Date(int m, int d, int y);
    ~Date();
    Date& operator=(Date&); //overloaded assignment operator
    void display();
};
// constructor that is called for an uninitialized Date
Date::Date()
{
    mo = 0; da = 0; yr = 0;
    month = 0;
}
// constructor that is called for an initialized Date
Date::Date(int m, int d, int y)
{
    static char *mos[] = {
        "January", "February", "March", "April", "May",
        "June", "July", "August", "September", "October",
        "November", "December"
    };
    mo = m; da = d; yr = y;
    month = new char[strlen(mos[m-1])+1];
    strcpy(month, mos[m-1]);
}
```

continued

Exercise 7.19   *The* ***this*** *Pointer (continued)*

```
// Destructor for a Date
Date::~Date()
{
    delete[] month;
}
// ---------- display member function
void Date::display()
{
    if (month != 0)
        cout << '\n' << month << ' ' << da << ", "
            << yr+1900;
}
// ---------- overloaded Date assignment
Date& Date::operator=(Date& dt)
{
    if (&dt == this) return dt;
    mo = dt.mo;
    da = dt.da;
    yr = dt.yr;
    delete[] month;
    if (dt.month != 0)    {
        month = new char [strlen(dt.month)+1];
        strcpy(month, dt.month);
    }
    else
        month = 0;
    return *this;
}
```

continued

Exercise 7.19 *The **this** Pointer (continued)*

```
main()
{
    // ------ original date
    Date birthday(6,24,40);
    Date oldday, newday;
    // ------ assign first to second to third
    oldday = newday = birthday;
    birthday.display();
    oldday.display();
    newday.display();
}
```

Exercise 7.19 displays these three dates:

```
June 24, 1940
June 24, 1940
June 24, 1940
```

This use of the *this* pointer is sometimes difficult to grasp because it applies several C++ constructs that are unfamiliar to C programmers. Picture what is happening when you make the following assignment:

```
newday = birthday;
```

The assignment executes the overloaded assignment operator function for the *Date* class. That function has two parameters. The first parameter is implied. It is the address of the object for which the function is being called. In this case, the function is being called for the object on the left side of the assignment: the *newday* object. The second parameter is supplied as an argument and is the object on the right side of the assignment, in this case the *birthday* object. In the function, the *birthday* argument becomes the *dt* parameter. The first assignment statement in the function is as follows:

```
mo = dt.mo;
```

This statement can also be read the following way:

```
this->mo = dt.mo;
```

The statement assigns the value in the *mo* data member of the *birthday* object to the *mo* data member of the *newday* object. The other assignments work the same way. When the function is done, it returns what *this* points to: the *newday* object. Because the function really returns a reference, the compiler converts the return of what *this* points to into a reference to what *this* points to. The result is that the overloaded assignment operator function, in addition to performing the assignment, returns the object that received the assignment, making possible the following statement:

```
oldday = newday = birthday;
```

By understanding this mechanism and the subject of operator overloading (as discussed in Chapter 8), you can see how the chained *cout* statements used in previous exercises work. In many of the exercises, you have been using statements similar to the following example:

```
cout << a << b << c;
```

Using *this* to Link Lists

The *this* pointer is convenient in applications in which a data structure uses self-referential members. An example is the simple linked list.

Exercise 7.20 builds a linked list of a class named *ListEntry*.

Exercise 7.20 ***this*** *and the Linked List*

```
#include <iostream.h>
#include <string.h>
class ListEntry {
    char *listvalue;
    ListEntry *preventry;
public:
    ListEntry(char *);
    ~ListEntry() { delete[] listvalue; }
    ListEntry *PrevEntry() { return preventry; };
    void display() { cout << '\n' << listvalue; }
    // ---------- use the 'this' pointer to chain the list
    void AddEntry(ListEntry& le) { le.preventry = this; }
};
ListEntry::ListEntry(char *s)
{
    listvalue = new char[strlen(s)+1];
    strcpy(listvalue, s);
    preventry = 0;
}
main()
{
    ListEntry *prev = 0;
    // ---------- read in some names
    while (1)    {
        cout << "\nEnter a name ('end' when done): ";
        char name[25];
        cin >> name;
        if (strncmp(name, "end", 3) == 0)
            break;
```

continued

Exercise 7.20 ***this*** *and the Linked List (continued)*

```
        // -------- make a list entry of the name
        ListEntry *list = new ListEntry(name);
        if (prev != 0)
            // -------- add the entry to the linked list
            prev->AddEntry(*list);
        prev = list;
    }
    // ------- display the names in reverse order
    while (prev != 0)    {
        prev->display();
        ListEntry *hold = prev;
        prev = prev->PrevEntry();
        // -------- delete the ListEntry
        delete hold;
    }
}
```

Exercise 7.20 displays the prompting messages shown below. Enter names until you are finished and then enter **end**. The program displays the names in the reverse order in which you entered them.

```
Enter a name ('end' when done): Sonny
Enter a name ('end' when done): Jay
Enter a name ('end' when done): Alan
Enter a name ('end' when done): Wally
Enter a name ('end' when done): Julie
Enter a name ('end' when done): end

Julie
Wally
Alan
Jay
Sonny
```

The class in Exercise 7.20 has a string value and a pointer to the previous entry in the list. The constructor function gets memory for the string from the free store, copies the string value to the class, and sets the pointer to null. The destructor deletes the string memory.

Note that if you wanted to use this class in a broader scope to include assignments of objects of the class to one another, you would need to build an overloaded assignment operator like the one in Exercise 7.18.

A member function named *PrevEntry* returns the pointer to the previous entry in the list. Another member function displays the current entry.

The member function of concern here is the one named *AddEntry*. It builds the list by putting the address of the current entry into the pointer of the next entry. It does this by copying the *this* pointer into the *preventry* pointer of the argument entry.

The *main* function of the program prompts you to enter some names at the console. After the last name you should enter the word **end**. Then the function navigates the list and displays the entries. Because the list pointers point from the current to the previous entry, the names display in the opposite order in which you entered them.

Observe the use of the *new* operator to allocate memory for the *ListEntry* object to which the list pointer points. Chapter 3 addressed *new* and *delete* but did not discuss those operators with respect to classes because you had not learned about classes. A later section in this chapter discusses the free store as it pertains to objects of classes.

ARRAYS OF CLASS OBJECTS

Class objects are just like any other C++ data type in that you can declare pointers to them and arrays of them. The array notation is the same as that of an array of structures.

Exercise 7.21 shows an array of *Date* structures.

Exercise 7.21   *Arrays of Classes*

```cpp
#include <iostream.h>
// ------- date class
class Date {
    int mo, da, yr;
public:
    Date() { mo = 0; da = 0; yr = 0; }
    Date(int m, int d, int y) { mo = m; da = d; yr = y;}
    void display()
        { cout << '\n' << mo << '/' << da << '/' <<yr; }
};
main()
{
    Date dates[2];
    Date temp(6,24,40);
    dates[0] = temp;
    dates[0].display()
    dates[1].display();
}
```

The constructor function in Exercise 7.21 for declarations without initializers initializes the three data members to zero. The *main* function declares an array of two *Dates* and a single date with initialized values. It assigns the initialized *Date* to the first of the two *Dates* in the array and then displays both dates as follows:

```
6/24/40
0/0/0
```

Class Array Constructors

When you declare an array of objects of a class, the compiler calls the constructor function once for each element in the array. It is important that you understand this relationship when you design constructor functions.

Exercise 7.22 repeats Exercise 7.21, but it adds a display message to the constructor function to prove that the constructor gets called twice for one declaration.

Exercise 7.22   *Constructors for Arrays of Classes*

```
#include <iostream.h>
// ------- date class
class Date {
    int mo, da, yr;
public:
    Date();
    Date(int m, int d, int y) { mo = m; da = d; yr = y;}
    void display()
        { cout << '\n' << mo << '/' << da << '/' <<yr; }
};
// constructor that is called for each element in a Date array
Date::Date()
{
    cout << "\nDate constructor running";
    mo = 0; da = 0; yr = 0;
}
main()
{
    Date dates[2];
    Date temp(6,24,40);

    dates[0] = temp;
    dates[0].display();
    dates[1].display();
}
```

Exercise 7.22 displays the following messages:

```
Date constructor running
Date constructor running
6/24/40
0/0/0
```

As you can see, the constructor function executed twice—once for each of the elements in the array. There is no message displayed for the constructor of the *temp* object because it uses the constructor function that accepts initializers, which has no message.

CLASS ARRAY DESTRUCTORS

When an array of objects of a class goes out of scope, the compiler calls the destructor function once for each element of the array.

Exercise 7.23 illustrates calling destructors for class array elements.

Exercise 7.23   *Destructors for Arrays of Classes*

```
#include <iostream.h>
// ------- date class
class Date {
    int mo, da, yr;
public:
    Date() { mo = 0; da = 0; yr = 0; }
    Date(int m, int d, int y) { mo = m; da = d; yr = y;}
    ~Date();
    void display()
        { cout << '\n' << mo << '/' << da << '/' <<yr; }
};
// destructor that is called for each element in a Date array
Date::~Date()
{
    cout << "\nDate destructor running";
}
main()
{
    Date dates[2];
    Date temp(6,24,40);
    dates[0] = temp;
    dates[0].display();
    dates[1].display();
}
```

This exercise copies Exercise 7.22 except that there is a destructor function that does nothing except display its execution on the console to prove that it runs more than once for an array of objects. The following display shows that the destructor runs three times—twice for the two elements in the *dates* array and once for the *temp* object:

```
6/24/40
0/0/0
Date destructor running
Date destructor running
Date destructor running
```

STATIC MEMBERS

You can declare that a member of a class is *static*, in which case only one instance of it exists. It is accessible to all the member functions. No instance of the class needs to be declared for the static members to exist, although unless a static member is public, it cannot be seen by the rest of the program.

The declaration of a static member in a class does not, however, automatically define the variable. You must define it outside the class definition for it to exist.

Static Data Members

You would use a static data member to maintain a global value that applies to all instances of the class. Member functions can modify this value, and all other objects of the class then see the modified value. As an example, consider the simple linked list used in Exercise 7.20. The class merely defined the list entries. It was up to the using program to keep track of the end of the list.

Exercise 7.24 improves the linked-list example in Exercise 7.20 with a static data member that holds the address of the last entry in the list.

Exercise 7.24   *Static Members and the Linked List*

```
#include <iostream.h>
#include <string.h>
class ListEntry {
    static ListEntry *lastentry; // static list head pointer
    char *listvalue;
    ListEntry *nextentry;
public:
    ListEntry();
    ListEntry(char *);
    ~ListEntry() { delete[] listvalue;}
    ListEntry *NextEntry() { return nextentry; };
    void display() { cout << '\n' << listvalue; }
};
ListEntry *ListEntry::lastentry;
ListEntry::ListEntry()
{
    listvalue = 0;
    nextentry = 0;
    lastentry = this;
}
ListEntry::ListEntry(char *s)
{
    lastentry->nextentry = this;
    lastentry = this;
    listvalue = new char[strlen(s)+1];
    strcpy(listvalue, s);
    nextentry = 0;
}
```

continued

Exercise 7.24   Static Members and the Linked List (continued)

```
main ()
(
    ListEntry listhead;    // ---- this is the list head
    // ---------- read in some names
    while (1)    {
        cout << "\nEnter a name ('end' when done): ";
        char name[25];
        cin >> name;
        if (strncmp(name, "end", 3) == 0)
            break;
        // -------- make a list entry of the name
        new ListEntry(name);
    }
    ListEntry *next = listhead.NextEntry();
    // -------- display the names
    while (next != 0)    {
        next->display();
        ListEntry *hold = next;
        next = next->NextEntry();
        // -------- delete the ListEntry
        delete hold;
    }
}
```

Exercise 7.24 displays the prompting messages shown below. Enter names until you are finished and then enter **end**. The program displays the names in the order in which you entered them.

```
Enter a name ('end' when done): Fred
Enter a name ('end' when done): Joe
Enter a name ('end' when done): Al
Enter a name ('end' when done): Walter
Enter a name ('end' when done): Julian
Enter a name ('end' when done): end
```

```
Fred
Joe
Al
Walter
Julian
```

This exercise represents an improved linked-list class. By using a static data member to keep a record of the end of the list, the class assumes all the responsibility for list integrity. To use it, you must declare a class object with no initializers. The constructor for that form sets up a new list with a list entry as the list head. This constructor also initializes the static *lastentry* pointer to point to the list head entry. The *nextentry* pointer in that entry is initially null, but eventually it points to the first list entry that the program declares. That entry points to the one following it, and subsequent entries point to the ones following them. The last entry in the list always has a null value in its *nextentry* pointer.

The constructor function for a list entry adds the entry to the list, so there is no need for the *AddEntry* function of Exercise 7.20. Observe that Exercise 7.24 uses the *new* operator to declare a new entry, and that it does not assign to a pointer the address returned by the *new* operator. Because the constructor function records the address of the entry in the *nextentry* pointer of the previous entry, the program does not need to otherwise remember the address.

Finally, the linked-list class defined in Exercise 7.24 allows the program to retrieve the entries in the same order in which they were added. After you enter all the names and type the **end** input, the program displays those names in their original order, rather than in reverse order as did earlier versions of this program.

Static Member Functions

Member functions can be static. You can use static member functions to perform tasks in the name of the class or an object where the function does not need access to the members of any particular instance of the class. Usually you use a static member function when you need to access only the static data members of a class.

Static member functions have no *this* pointer. Inasmuch as they have no access to the nonstatic members, they cannot use the *this* pointer to point to anything.

Exercise 7.25 adds a static member function to the *ListEntry* class. In this exercise, the function displays the last entry in the list, which is always the entry you just keyed in.

Exercise 7.25 *Static Member Functions*

```
#include <iostream.h>
#include <string.h>
class ListEntry {
    static ListEntry *lastentry; // a static list head pointer
    char *listvalue;
    ListEntry *nextentry;
public:
    ListEntry();
    ListEntry(char *);
    ~ListEntry() { delete[] listvalue; }
    ListEntry *NextEntry() { return nextentry; };
    void display() { cout << '\n' << listvalue; }
    // ------- a static member function
    static void showlast();
};
ListEntry *ListEntry::lastentry;
ListEntry::ListEntry()
{
    listvalue = 0;
    nextentry = 0;
    lastentry = this;
}
ListEntry::ListEntry(char *s)
{
    lastentry->nextentry = this;
    lastentry = this;
    listvalue = new char[strlen(s)+1];
    strcpy(listvalue, s);
    nextentry = 0;
}
```

continued

Exercise 7.25   *Static Member Functions (continued)*

```
// ---------- a static member function
void ListEntry::showlast()
{
    lastentry->display();
    cout << " is the last entry in the list";
}
main()
{
    ListEntry listhead;     // ---- this is the list head
    // ---------- read in some names
    while (1)     {
        cout << "\nEnter a name ('end' when done): ";
        char name[25];
        cin >> name;
        if (strncmp(name, "end", 3) == 0)
            break;
        // -------- make a list entry of the name
        new ListEntry(name);
        // ----- call the static member function
        listhead.showlast();
    }
    // ------- delete the entries
    ListEntry *next = listhead.NextEntry();
    while (next != 0)     {
        ListEntry *hold = next;
        next = next->NextEntry();
        // -------- delete the ListEntry
        delete hold;
    }
}
```

Exercise 7.25 displays the prompting messages shown below. Enter names until you are done and then enter **end**. The program builds a linked list as you go and displays the last name in the list each time you enter a new one.

```
Enter a name ('end' when done): Alan
Alan is the last entry in the list
Enter a name ('end' when done): Sharon
Sharon is the last entry in the list
Enter a name ('end' when done): Wendy
Wendy is the last entry in the list
Enter a name ('end' when done): Tyler
Tyler is the last entry in the list
Enter a name ('end' when done): end
```

The *showlast* function is static. As such, it cannot read or write the member functions of the object for which it is called. But, because it needs to use the static *lastentry* pointer and nothing else, the function can be static, too.

Static Public Members

If a static member is public, it is accessible to the entire program and is not bound to a particular object. You can call a public static member function from anywhere without associating it with a particular instance of the class. The program in Exercise 7.25 called the *showlast* static member function in the name of the *listhead* object. In fact, the use of the object was for notational purposes only. Because the function is static, it could have been called in the name of any object. Further, because it is public, it can be called without an object reference at all. A public static member function is not quite global. It exists only within the scope of the class in which it is defined. You can, however, call it from anywhere within that scope by prefixing it with the class name and using the :: scope resolution operator.

Exercise 7.26 modifies Exercise 7.25 to demonstrate how to call a public static member function without associating it with a particular object of the class.

Exercise 7.26 *Public Static Member Functions*

```
#include <iostream.h>
#include <string.h>
class ListEntry {
    static ListEntry *lastentry; // a static list head pointer
    char *listvalue;
    ListEntry *nextentry;
public:
    ListEntry();
    ListEntry(char *);
    ~ListEntry() { delete[] listvalue; }
    ListEntry *NextEntry() { return nextentry; };
    void display() { cout << '\n' << listvalue; }
    // ------- a static member function
    static void showlast();
};
ListEntry *ListEntry::lastentry;
ListEntry::ListEntry()
{
    listvalue = 0;
    nextentry = 0;
    lastentry = this;
}
ListEntry::ListEntry(char *s)
{
    lastentry->nextentry = this;
    lastentry = this;
    listvalue = new char[strlen(s)+1];
    strcpy(listvalue, s);
    nextentry = 0;
}
```

continued

Exercise 7.26 *Public Static Member Functions (continued)*

```
// ---------- a static member function
void ListEntry::showlast()
{
    lastentry->display();
    cout << " is the last entry in the list";
}
main()
{
    ListEntry listhead;    // ---- this is the list head
    // ---------- read in some names
    while (1)    {
        cout << "\nEnter a name ('end' when done): ";
        char name[25];
        cin >> name;
        if (strncmp(name, "end", 3) == 0)
            break;
        // -------- make a list entry of the name
        new ListEntry(name);
        // ----- call the static member function
        // ----- with no object reference
        ListEntry::showlast();
    }
    // ------- delete the entries
    ListEntry *next = listhead.NextEntry();
    while (next != 0)    {
        ListEntry *hold = next;
        next = next->NextEntry();
        // -------- delete the ListEntry
        delete hold;
    }
}
```

Exercise 7.26 has the same displays and inputs as Exercise 7.25.

Public static members may be used when there is no instance of the class. Because they are both public and static and because you can call them in the name of the class alone, you can use one before you declare an object of the class.

Exercise 7.27 illustrates a class with a public static data member that the program initializes before declaring any objects of the class.

Exercise 7.27   *Using Public Static Members without Objects*

```
#include <iostream.h>
class. Date {
    int mo, da, yr;
public:
    static int format;     // 1 = mm/dd/yy, 2 = dd/mm/yy
    Date(int m , int d, int y) { mo = m; da = d; yr = y; }
    void display();
};
int Date::format;
void Date::display()
{
    if (format == 1)
        cout << mo << '/' << da;
    else
        cout << da << '/' << mo;
    cout << '/' << yr;
}
main()
{
    char ch = '0';
    while (ch != '3')    {
        cout << "\n  1 = mm/dd/yy";
        cout << "\n  2 = dd/mm/yy";
        cout << "\n  3 = quit\n  ";
        cin >> ch;
        if (ch == '1' || ch == '2')    {
            Date::format = ch - '0'; // no Date declared yet
```

continued

Exercise 7.27 *Using Public Static Members without Objects (continued)*

```
                // ---- declare and display a date
                Date dt(6, 24, 40);
                dt.display();
        }
    }
}
```

The *Date* class has a public static data member named *format* that controls whether the display member function displays the date in the mm/dd/yy or the dd/mm/yy format. The program displays the following menu:

```
1 = mm/dd/yy
2 = dd/mm/yy
3 = quit
```

When you enter a **1** or a **2**, the program initializes the format data member for the *Date* class even though no *Date* objects are in scope. Then the program declares and displays the *dt* variable. One of the following two displays occurs, depending on what you typed into the menu:

```
6/24/40
24/6/40
```

CLASSES AND THE FREE STORE

In Chapter 3, you learned about the C++ free store and the *new* and *delete* memory-management operators. This section discusses those operators and their special relationship to class definitions.

Using *new* and *delete* to Manage Object Scope

An automatic class object usually comes into scope when it is declared, and it goes out of scope when the program exits the block in which the object is declared. You can override this behavior by using the *new* operator to construct an object. The object exists until you use the *delete* operator to destroy it. To use this feature, you must remember the address returned by *new* so that you can send it to *delete*. You must also remember the type of object that the pointer points to, because *delete* must know what type of object you are deleting. The type of object to be deleted is a function of the type of the pointer that you send to the *delete* operator.

Constructors and *new,* Destructors and *delete*

You used *new* and *delete* in earlier exercises to get and release memory for classes. When you use *new* to get memory for a class, the *new* operator function calls the class's constructor function. When you use *delete* to return the memory, the *delete* operator function calls the class's destructor function.

Exercise 7.28 illustrates the relationships between *new* and the constructor functions and *delete* and the destructor function.

Exercise 7.28 new = Constructor, delete = Destructor

```
#include <iostream.h>
class Date    {
    int mo, da, yr;
public:
    Date();
    ~Date();
};
Date::Date()
{
    cout << "\nDate constructor";
}
Date::~Date()
{
    cout << "\nDate destructor";
}
```

continued

Exercise 7.28 **new** = *Constructor,* **delete** = *Destructor (continued)*

```
main()
{
    Date *dt = new Date;
    cout << "\nProcess the date";
    delete dt;
}
```

The exercise defines a *Date* class with a constructor and a destructor. These functions simply display messages that say they are running. When the *new* operator initializes the *dt* pointer, the constructor function executes. When the *delete* operator deletes the memory pointed to by the pointer, the operation calls the destructor function.

Exercise 7.28 displays the following messages:

```
Date constructor
Process the date
Date destructor
```

The Free Store and Class Arrays

You learned earlier that constructor and destructor functions are called once for every element in an array of class objects.

Exercise 7.29 illustrates an incorrect way to delete arrays of new classes.

Exercise 7.29   Deleting Arrays of **new** Classes

```
#include <iostream.h>
class Date    {
    int mo, da, yr;
public:
    Date()  { cout << "\nDate constructor"; }
    ~Date() { cout << "\nDate destructor";  }
};
main()
{
    Date *dt = new Date[5];
    cout << "\nProcess the dates";
    delete dt;                  // Not enough deletes!
}
```

The *dt* pointer points to an array of five dates. The *Date* constructor function executes five times from the *new* operator because that is what the array notation tells the compiler to do. But the compiler has no indication from the call to *delete* that the pointer points to more than one *Date* object, so it builds only one call to the destructor function.

Exercise 7.29 displays the following messages:

```
Date constructor
Date constructor
Date constructor
Date constructor
Date constructor
Process the dates
Date destructor
```

To solve this problem, C++ allows you to tell the *delete* operator that the pointer being deleted points to an array. You do so by adding the [] subscript operator to the *delete* operator like this:

```
delete[] pointername;
```

Exercise 7.30 illustrates the correct use of the *delete* operator where an array is involved.

Exercise 7.30 *Correctly Deleting Arrays of **new** Classes*

```
#include <iostream.h>
class Date    {
    int mo, da, yr;
public:
    Date()  { cout << "\nDate constructor"; }
    ~Date() { cout << "\nDate destructor";  }
};
main()
{
    Date *dt = new Date[5];
    cout << "\nProcess the dates";
    delete [] dt;                   // deleting 5 items
}
```

Exercise 7.30 displays the following messages:

```
Date constructor
Date constructor
Date constructor
Date constructor
Date constructor
Process the dates
Date destructor
Date destructor
Date destructor
Date destructor
Date destructor
```

If you use the [ ] notation in the *delete* of an object that has no destructors, the compiler ignores the notation. However, by convention you should include the [ ] notation whenever you're deleting memory that was allocated for an array even when the objects being deleted are not class objects or do not have destructors. The programs in this chapter have been doing just that.

Overloaded Class *new* and *delete*

Chapter 3 taught you how to manage memory by writing overloaded *new* and *delete* operator functions. Those overloaded operators were for global uses of *new* and *delete*. You can also overload *new* and *delete* from within the scope of a class declaration. This feature allows a class to have its own custom *new* and *delete* operators. You usually use this feature to gain a performance benefit from class-specific knowledge about the memory requirements of a class that can avoid the general-purpose overhead of the global *new* and *delete* operators.

Suppose that you know that there are never more than a certain small number of instances of a class at any one time. You can allocate the necessary memory for all instances of that class and use class-specific *new* and *delete* operators to manage the memory.

Exercise 7.31 illustrates a class with overloaded *new* and *delete* operators that are specific to the class.

Exercise 7.31   *Class-specific **new and delete** Operators*

```
#include <iostream.h>
#include <string.h>
#include <stddef.h>
const int MAXNAMES = 5;
class Names    {
    char name[25];
public:
    void setname(char *s) { strcpy(name, s); }
    void display() { cout << '\n' << name; }
    void *operator new(size_t);
    void operator delete(void *);
};
// -------- simple memory pool to handle fixed number of Names
char pool[MAXNAMES] [sizeof(Names)];
int inuse[MAXNAMES];
```

continued

Exercise 7.31   *Class-specific **new and delete** Operators (continued)*

```
// -------- overloaded new operator for the Names class
void *Names::operator new(size_t)
{
    for (int p = 0; p < MAXNAMES; p++)
        if (!inuse[p])    {
            inuse[p] = 1;
            return pool+p;
        }
    return 0;
}
// --------- overloaded delete operator for the Names class
void Names::operator delete(void *p)
{
    inuse[((char *)p - pool[0]) / sizeof(Names)] = 0;
}
main()
{
    Names *nm[MAXNAMES];
    for (int i = 0; i < MAXNAMES; i++)    {
        cout << "\nEnter name # " << i+1 << ": ";
        char name[25];
        cin >> name;
        nm[i] = new Names;
        nm[i]->setname(name);
    }
    for (i = 0; i < MAXNAMES; i++)    {
        nm[i]->display();
        delete nm[i];
    }
}
```

Exercise 7.31 prompts you for five names and then displays them as shown here:

```
Enter name # 1: Harpo
Enter name # 2: Chico
Enter name # 3: Groucho
Enter name # 4: Zeppo
Enter name # 5: Karl


Harpo
Chico
Groucho
Zeppo
Karl
```

A class of *Names* is defined in Exercise 7.31. The class has a member function that lets a user of the class set the name value of an object of the class. It also has a member function to display the name. Then it defines its own *new* and *delete* operators. Because the program is guaranteed never to exceed *MAXNAMES* names at one time, the programmer has decided to speed execution by overriding the default *new* and *delete* operators.

The simple memory pool that supports names is a *pool* character array with enough space to hold all the concurrent *Names* the program expects. The associated *inuse* integer array contains a true/false integer for each *Name* to indicate whether an entry in the pool is in use.

The overloaded *new* operator finds an unused entry in the pool and returns its address. The overloaded *delete* operator marks the specified entry as unused.

Even if a class design includes overloaded *new* and *delete* operators, the overloaded operator functions are not called for allocations of arrays of objects of the class. Suppose that the program in Exercise 7.31 included these statements:

```
Names *nms = new Names[10];
// ...
delete [] nms;
```

These statements would call the global *new* and *delete* operators rather than the overloaded ones.

Overloaded *new* and *delete* functions within a class definition are always static and have no *this* pointer associated with the object being created or deleted. This is because the compiler calls the *new* function before it calls the class's constructor function, and it calls the *delete* function after it calls the destructor.

Exercise 7.32 demonstrates the sequence in which the constructor, destructor, and overloaded *new* and *delete* operator functions execute.

Exercise 7.32 *Class-specific **new** and **delete** Operators with Constructor, Destructor*

```
#include <iostream.h>
#include <stddef.h>
class Name    {
    char name[25];
public:
    Name()  { cout << "\nName constructor running"; }
    ~Name() { cout << "\nName destructor running";    }
    void *operator new(size_t);
    void operator delete(void *);
};
// -------- simple memory pool to handle one Name
char pool [sizeof(Name)];
// -------- overloaded new operator for the Name class
void *Name::operator new(size_t)
{
    cout << "\nName's new running";
    return pool;
}
// --------- overloaded delete operator for the Name class
void Name::operator delete(void *)
{
    cout << "\nName's delete running";
}
```

continued

```
main()
{
    cout << "\nBuilding a new name";
    Name *nm = new Name;
    cout << "\nDeleting a name";
    delete nm;
}
```

Exercise 7.32 does nothing with the class except display the following messages as the various functions execute:

```
Building a new name
Name's new running
Name constructor running
Deleting a name
Name destructor running
Name's delete running
```

As you can see, the *new* function executes before the constructor function. The *new* function may not access any of the class's members because no memory exists for them until *new* allocates it, and because the constructor function has not yet performed any other class-specific initializations. Likewise, because the *delete* operator executes after the destructor function, the *delete* operator may not have access to the class members.

COPY CONSTRUCTORS

A copy constructor is a constructor that executes when you initialize a new object of the class with an existing object of the same class, when you pass a copy of an object of the class by value as an argument to a function, and when you return an object of the class by value. The copy constructor is similar to the conversion constructor function that you learned about earlier in this chapter. Conversion constructors convert the values in one class object to the format of an object of a different class. Copy constructors initialize the values from an existing object of a class to a new instantiated object of that same class.

Earlier in this chapter you learned how to overload the assignment operator (=) to manage the assignment of an object of a class to another object of the same class when the default assignment provided by the compiler would cause problems. Similar problems occur when you initialize an object with the contents of another object, so you must have copy constructor functions.

The difference between initialization of an object with another object, and assignment of one object to another is this: Assignment assigns the value of an existing object to another existing object; initialization creates a new object and initializes it with the contents of the existing object. The compiler can distinguish between the two by using your overloaded assignment operator for assignments and your copy constructor for initializers. If you omit either one, the compiler builds a default member-by-member copy operation for the one you omit.

Initializing an object with the contents of another object of the same class requires the use of a copy constructor function, which is a constructor that can be called with a single argument of the same class as the object being constructed.

Exercise 7.33 demonstrates the copy constructor.

Exercise 7.33   *Copy Constructor*

```
#include <iostream.h>
#include <string.h>
// ------- date class
class Date {
    int mo, da, yr;
    char *month;
public:
    Date(int m, int d, int y);
    Date(Date&);  // copy constructor
    ~Date();
    void display();
};
```

continued

Exercise 7.33 *Copy Constructor (continued)*

```cpp
// constructor that is called for an initialized Date
Date::Date(int m, int d, int y)
{
    static char *mos[] = {
        "January", "February", "March", "April", "May",
        "June", "July", "August", "September", "October",
        "November", "December"
    };
    mo = m; da = d; yr = y;
    month = new char[strlen(mos[m-1])+1];
    strcpy(month, mos[m-1]);
}
// ---------- Date copy constructor
Date::Date(Date& dt)
{
    mo = dt.mo;
    da = dt.da;
    yr = dt.yr;
    month = new char [strlen(dt.month)+1];
    strcpy(month, dt.month);
}
// Destructor for a Date
Date::~Date()
{
    delete[] month;
}
// ---------- display member function
void Date::display()
{
    if (month != 0)
        cout << '\n' << month << ' ' << da << ", "
            << yr+1900;
}
```

continued

Exercise 7.33   *Copy Constructor (continued)*

```
main()
{
    // ------ first date
    Date birthday(6,24,40);
    birthday.display();
    // ------ second date
    Date newday = birthday;
    newday.display();
    // ------ third date
    Date lastday(birthday);
    lastday.display();
}
```

The copy constructor in this exercise resembles the overloaded assignment operator in Exercise 7.18. The difference is that the copy constructor function executes when you declare a new *Date* object that is to be initialized with the contents of an existing *Date* object. The exercise shows that there are two ways to do this. One way uses the usual C++ variable initializer syntax as shown here.

```
Date newday = birthday;
```

The second way uses the constructor calling convention, in which the initializing object is an argument to the function's parameter as shown here:

```
Date lastday(birthday);
```

REFERENCES IN CLASSES

Chapter 6 taught you about references. Everything that you learned about using references with the standard C++ data types and structures applies equally to objects of classes. Using references to class objects as function parameters and return values adds a measure of efficiency that would not exist if you had to pass every object by value.

You can also declare references as class data members, but there are some things to consider. First, remember that a reference must be initialized. You do not usually initialize a class object with a brace-surrounded initialization list as you do a structure; you initialize it with a constructor. Therefore, class member references must be initialized by the class constructor. Remember, too, that references are aliases. References in classes behave just as if they were data members of the class with the same notational syntax, but operations on member references actually operate on the objects that are used to initialize them. Exercise 7.34 shows the use of a class that has reference data members.

Exercise 7.3   *A Class with a Reference*

```
#include <iostream.h>
class Date  {
    int da, mo, yr;
public:
    Date(int d,int m,int y)
        { da = d; mo = m; yr = y; }
    void Display()
        { cout << da << '/' << mo << '/' << yr; }
};
class Time  {
    int hr, min, sec;
public:
    Time(int h, int m, int s)
        { hr = h; min = m; sec = s; }
    void Display()
        { cout << hr << ':' << min << ':' << sec; }
};
```

continued

Exercise 7.3   *A Class with a Reference (continued)*

```
class DateTime {
    Date& dt;        // reference to Date
    Time& tm;        // reference to Time
public:
    // --- constructor with reference initializers
    DateTime(Date& d, Time& t) : dt(d), tm(t)
        { /* empty */ }
    void Display()
        { dt.Display(); cout << ' '; tm.Display(); }
};
main()
{
    Date today(25,3,93);
    Time now(4,15,0);
    DateTime dtm(today, now);
    dtm.Display();
}
```

Observe the *DateTime* constructor specification. The colon operator specifies that a list of initializers follows. You must initialize references in this manner. You cannot wait and do it in the body of the constructor. If the constructor is not *inline*, as this one is, you put the colon and list in the constructor's definition rather than in its prototype in the class declaration.

Exercise 7.34 displays the following:

```
3/25/93 4:15:0
```

THE MANAGEMENT OF CLASS SOURCE AND OBJECT FILES

In all the previous exercises, each program has been a single, stand-alone source module. The entire program was contained in one source module that represented the exercise. In practice, you do not organize a C++ source program that way. You use the traditional C convention of having common definitions in header files, common executable code in separately compiled object libraries, and separately compiled source code files for the code that supports your application.

Class Definitions in a Header

The convention for C++ header files resembles that of C. Put things in header files that do not reserve memory but that declare structures, classes, and externally declared items to the source modules that include header files. When a class uses the definitions of other classes, its include file includes those of the other classes. This opens the possibility for multiple or circular inclusions. You should use a code convention that prevents the errors that can occur if a source file is included twice or if source file A includes source file B, which includes source file C, which includes source file A.

If you have a class named *Date*, for example, you might put its definition in a header file named **date.h**. If you use the *#ifndef* preprocessor directive shown in the following listing, you can prevent those cases in which a header file might be included more than once or where header file inclusion wraps around:

```
#ifndef DATE_H
#define DATE_H
// --- the contents of date.h
#endif
```

Class Member Functions in a Library

As a rule, you should separately compile the member functions of your classes and maintain them as separate object files, perhaps in object library files. The source files for the member functions include the header files that define the classes to which the functions belong, as well as those for any classes that they may use and that might not be included from within the class header.

SUMMARY

This chapter taught you about C++ classes. Chapter 8 is about overloaded operators, a feature touched on here and in Chapter 3. In Chapter 3, you learned to overload the *new* and *delete* operators to insert your own memory-management functions into the program. In this chapter you learned the same technique, but at the individual class level. You also learned to overload the assignment operator to build conversion functions and to manage class copying when member-by-member copy would not work.

The potential for overloaded operators extends beyond the uses you've learned so far. With them you can perform arithmetic, comparisons, and many other operations on your classes as if they were standard C++ data types. Chapter 8 describes these features.

CHAPTER 8

Overloaded Operators

This chapter is about extending the C++ language by adding operators to classes. A C++ class adds a new data type to the language. You learned how to add dates and other such types by binding data structures and functions. Now you will add to those classes the behavior of C++ operators. You will learn how to overload:

- ❖ Arithmetic operators
- ❖ Relational operators
- ❖ Assignment operators
- ❖ Auto increment and decrement operators
- ❖ Unary operators
- ❖ The subscript operator
- ❖ The function call operator
- ❖ The pointer to member operator

Consider a class to implement a numerical type. The using program must compute the sum of a column of objects of the type. It must also be able to increment, decrement, and add and subtract other numerical types to and from objects of the class. The program needs to compare two of the objects to see whether they are equal or which is greater. You could build special class member functions to perform these operations and call them the way you call, for example, the standard C function *strcmp*. There is, however, a better way.

C++ lets you build operators that implement unary and binary operations on objects of classes. This feature is called *operator overloading*, and with it you add member functions to the class to implement the overloaded operators.

In Chapters 3 and 7 you overloaded the *new* and *delete* operators to build custom memory management. In Chapter 7 you overloaded the assignment operator for your classes. You have already used overloaded operators extensively in most of the exercises. Every time you display a value on the *cout* object, you use the << bit-wise shift left operator, which is overloaded by the *ostream* class.

Overloading an operator means that you write a function to make the operator do your bidding. For example, you can do these operations with a *Date* class:

```
Date dt1(1,2,83);
Date dt2(2,4,93);
dt1 += 100;              // add 100 days
int dif = dt2-dt1;       // compute the delta
if (dt2 < dt1)           // compare two dates
    dt1 = dt2;           // assign dates
cout << dt1 << ' ' << dt2; // display the dates
```

Look at the last of the examples just shown. You will learn how to overload the << and >> operators in Chapter 10.

Overloaded operators must obey some rules:

1. The overloaded operator must comply with the syntax of the language. For example, you cannot do the following in C++:

```
int a;
/ a;      // error: / is not a unary operator
```

Therefore, you also cannot overload the / operator to do the following:

```
Date dt(1,2,83);
/ dt;    // error: / is not a unary operator
```

2. If you can put an operator between two identifiers, then you can overload it for custom use with your classes, even if the operator would not otherwise be acceptable to the compiler. Consider the following statement:

```
cout << "Hello";
```

Without an overloaded << operator, that expression seems to shift *cout* a number of bits equal to the value of the pointer to the string, none of which would have passed the compiler's error check. But the statement is correct syntax, so you can write an overloaded operator function that executes when this construct appears. The compiler sees the overloaded operator in the context of the two data types and associates this statement with it.

3. You cannot overload the way an operator works with the intrinsic C++ data types. For example, you cannot overload the binary integer addition operator.

4. You cannot invent new operators that do not exist in the C++ language. For example, the dollar sign ($) is not a C++ operator, so it cannot be an overloaded operator.

5. You cannot overload these operators:

Operator	Definition
.	*Class member operator*
.*	*Pointer-to-member operator*
::	*Scope resolution operator*
?:	*Conditional expression operator*

6. You cannot change the precedence of operator evaluation.

BINARY ARITHMETIC OPERATORS

Consider a *Date* class such as the ones in Chapter 7. You want to compute a new *Date* object by adding an integer number of days to an existing one. You could write a member function and call it as shown here:

```
newdate.AddToDate(100);
```

Rather than calling a function to make the addition, you prefer to use this more intuitive syntax:

```
newdate = newdate + 100;
```

Assuming that *newdate* is an object of type *Date* with a value already in it and that you have correctly overloaded the binary addition operator (+) in this context, the result would be the *newdate* object of type *Date* with the effective month, day, and year incremented by 100 days.

Class Member Operator Functions

To perform the kind of addition on objects of a class just shown, you write a class member function that overloads the binary addition (+) operator when it appears between a *Date* object and an integer.

Exercise 8.1 overloads an operator to compute the sum of an integer and an object of the *Date* class, returning an object of the *Date* class.

Exercise 8.1   *Overloading the + Operator*

```cpp
#include <iostream.h>
class Date {
    int mo, da, yr;
public:
    Date(int m=0, int d=0, int y=0)
        { mo = m; da = d; yr = y; }
    void display(
        { cout << mo << '/' << da << '/' << yr; }
    Date operator+(int);        // overloaded + operator
};
static int dys[]={31,28,31,30,31,30,31,31,30,31,30,31};
// -------- overloaded + operator
Date Date::operator+(int n)
{
    Date dt = *this;
    n += dt.da;
    while (n > dys[dt.mo-1])    {
        n -= dys[dt.mo-1];
        if (++dt.mo == 13)    {
            dt.mo = 1;
            dt.yr++;
        }
    }
    dt.da = n;
    return dt;
}
main()
{
    Date olddate(2,20,90);
    Date newdate;
    newdate = olddate + 21;    // three weeks hence
    newdate.display();
}
```

Exercise 8.1 displays the following date:

```
3/13/90
```

Here is how the overloaded operator function works. When the compiler sees the expression *olddate + 21*, it recognizes that *olddate* is an object of type *Date* and that the *Date* class includes an overloaded binary addition operator function. The compiler substitutes a call to the overloaded operator function with the integer value as the argument. You could code the substituted call yourself this way:

```
newdate = olddate.operator+(21);
```

The *operator+* part of the statement is the name of the member function. The 21 is the integer argument. Although you can call an overloaded operator function this way, these functions are meant to be used in the context of an expression that uses the operator, as in:

```
newdate = olddate + 21;
```

Remember the discussion on the overloaded assignment operator in Chapter 7. If the *Date* class has an overloaded assignment operator function, the statement just shown will call it after calling the overloaded binary addition operator function to assign the result to *newdate*. Exercise 8.1 has no overloaded assignment operator, so the compiler creates a default one to make a copy of the original.

Observe that the overloaded binary addition operator function in Exercise 8.1 does not modify the *Date* object in the expression. The *olddate* object declared in the *main* function retains its value. This behavior mimics that of similar expressions with intrinsic numerical types. This is a valuable lesson. Strive to overload operators in intuitive ways.

Nonmember Operator Functions

Exercise 8.1 overloads the + operator by using a member function. Like other member functions, overloaded operator member functions are associated with objects for which the operator function executes. In this case, the object is the *olddate* object taken from the left side of the binary expression. But suppose you also wanted to support the following expression:

```
Date newdate = 100 + olddate;
```

There is no way to design a class member overloaded operator function to support an expression like that. You can, however, write a nonmember function to overload the operator and get what you want.

Exercise 8.2 adds a *friend* function to the program in Exercise 8.1 to overload the binary addition (+) operator.

Exercise 8.2   *Overloading the + Operator*

```
#include <iostream.h>
class Date {
    int mo, da, yr;
public:
    Date(int m=0, int d=0, int y=0)
        { mo = m; da = d; yr = y; }
    void display()
        { cout << mo << '/' << da << '/' << yr; }
    // ----- overloaded + operators
    Date operator+(int);
};
```

continued

Exercise 8.2 *Overloading the + Operator (continued)*

```
static int dys[]={31,28,31,30,31,30,31,31,30,31,30,31};
// -------- overloaded + operator: Date + int
Date Date::operator+(int n)
{
    Date dt = *this;
    n += dt.da;
    while (n > dys[dt.mo-1])     {
        n -= dys[dt.mo-1];
        if (++dt.mo == 13)     {
            dt.mo = 1;
            dt.yr++;
        }
    }
    dt.da = n;
    return dt;
}
// ----- overloaded operator: int + Date
Date operator+(int n, Date& dt)
{
    return dt + n;
}
main()
{
    Date olddate(2,20,90);
    Date newdate;
    newdate = 11 + olddate + 10;   // three weeks hence
    newdate.display();
}
```

Exercise 8.2 displays the same output as Exercise 8.1.

The overloaded function uses the class's overloaded *operator+* function to perform the addition. If the class did not have such a function, the class could have declared the overloaded *operator+* function to be a friend as shown here:

```
class Date {
    friend Date operator+(int n, Date& );
    // ...
};
```

Overloaded operator functions such as the one in Exercise 8.2 have both parameters declared. The function is not a member of a class. Because it does not execute as a class member function, there is no implied object.

NOTE

You could have written the first overloaded binary addition function as a friend function as well. Some programmers overload all their class operators as friend functions for consistency.

Observe that the expression in the using program now uses two integer constants to compute the result. The effective expression is *(11+olddate)+10*. The first part uses the overloaded nonmember function, and the second part uses the overloaded member function. With these two overloaded functions you can write an expression that consists of a *Date* object and any number of integer expressions and compute the effective new *Date* object. You would probably not add two dates; the result would not be meaningful. You could, however, use overloaded subtraction to compute the number of days between two dates.

NOTE

Nothing says that an overloaded binary addition operator function must perform addition. For example, string classes overload the plus operator to concatenate strings the way that Basic does. An overloaded operator function does whatever you design it to do. It causes the compiler to call the function when the operator is applied in a context that matches the parameter types. Then the function does whatever you code it to do. You might have guessed by now that you could overload the addition operator to perform subtraction. Yes, you could, but it is not a wise thing to do.

The examples just given deal with addition. You can use the same approaches to develop overloaded subtraction, multiplication, division, relational, modulus, Boolean, and shifting operator functions. Once again, nothing requires you to make those functions perform intuitively, and a lot of C++ programs have wildly overloaded operators that only their creators can understand. If you must overload operators, always try to overload them so that they perform operations that resemble their use with intrinsic data types in the C++ language.

RELATIONAL OPERATORS

Suppose you want to compare dates. Perhaps you need to use an expression such as the following one:

```
if (newdate < olddate)
// ....
```

You can overload relational operators in the same way that you overloaded the addition operator.

Exercise 8.3 shows the *Date* class with overloaded operators that compare dates.

Exercise 8.3 *Overloading Relational Operators*

```
#include <iostream.h>
class Date {
    int mo, da, yr;
public:
    Date(int m=0, int d=0, int y=0)
        { mo = m; da = d; yr = y; }
    void display()
        { cout << mo << '/' << da << '/' << yr; }
    // ----- overloaded operators
    int operator==(Date& dt);
    int operator<(Date&);
};
// ----- overloaded equality operator
int Date::operator==(Date& dt)
{
    return (this->mo == dt.mo &&
            this->da == dt.da &&
            this->yr == dt.yr);
}
```

continued

Exercise 8.3   *Overloading Relational Operators (continued)*

```
// ----- overloaded less than operator
int Date::operator<(Date& dt)
{
    if (this->yr == dt.yr)    {
        if (this->mo == dt.mo)
            return this->da < dt.da;
        return this->mo < dt.mo;
    }
    return this->yr < dt.yr;
}
main()
{
    Date date1(12,7,41),
        date2(2,22,90),
        date3(12,7,41);

    if (date1 < date2)    {
        date1.display();
        cout << " is less than ";
        date2.display();
    }
    cout << '\n';
    if (date1 == date3)    {
        date1.display();
        cout << " is equal to ";
        date3.display();
    }
}
```

The *Date* class in Exercise 8.3 has two overloaded relational operators: the equal to (==) and the less than (<) operators. The *main* function declares three dates, compares them, and displays the following messages:

```
12/7/41 is less than 2/22/90
12/7/41 is equal to 12/7/41
```

You could easily build the other relational operators as variations on the two in the exercise. For example, the != (not equal) operator could be coded the following way:

```
int operator!=(Date& dt) { return !(*this == dt); }
```

MORE ASSIGNMENT OPERATORS

You learned how to overload the assignment operator (=) in the discussion on class assignment in Chapter 7. C++ has other assignment operators (+=, -=, <<=, >>=, |=, &=, ^=) in which the assignment includes an arithmetic, Boolean, or shift operation applied to the receiving field. You can overload these operators to work with your classes.

Exercise 8.4 adds the overloaded += operator to the *Date* class by using the overloaded + operator that the class already has.

Exercise 8.4   *Overloading the += Operator*

```
#include <iostream.h>
class Date {
    int mo, da, yr;
public:
    Date(int m=0, int d=0, int y=0)
        { mo = m; da = d; yr = y; }
    void display()
        { cout << mo << '/' << da << '/' << yr; }
    // --------- overloaded + operator
    Date operator+(int);
    // --------- overloaded += operator
    Date operator+=(int n)
        { *this = *this + n; return *this; }
};
```

continued

Exercise 8.4   *Overloading the += Operator (continued)*

```
static int dys[]={31,28,31,30,31,30,31,31,30,31,30,31};
// -------- overloaded + operator
Date Date::operator+(int n)
{
    Date dt = *this;
    n += dt.da;
    while (n > dys[dt.mo-1])    {
        n -= dys[dt.mo-1];
        if (++dt.mo == 13)    {
            dt.mo = 1;
            dt.yr++;
        }
    }
    dt.da = n;
    return dt;
}
main()
{
    Date olddate(2,20,90);
    olddate += 21;           // three weeks hence
    olddate.display();
}
```

Exercise 8.4 displays the same output as Exercises 8.1 and 8.2.

AUTO-INCREMENT AND AUTO-DECREMENT

You can overload the auto-increment (++) and the auto-decrement (--) operators and specify whether these operators are prefix or postfix.

```
Date dt;
++dt;   // calls the overloaded prefix ++ operator
dt++;   // calls the overloaded postfix ++ operator
```

Exercise 8.5 adds the overloaded auto-increment (++) prefix and postfix operators to the *Date* class by using the overloaded binary addition operator that the
class already has.

Exercise 8.5 *Overloading the ++ Operator*

```
#include <iostream.h>
class Date {
    int mo, da, yr;
public:
    Date(int m=0, int d=0, int y=0)
        { mo = m; da = d; yr = y; }
    void display()
        { cout << '\n' << mo << '/' << da << '/' << yr;}
    Date operator+(int);        // overloaded +
    // --------- overloaded prefix ++ operator
    Date operator++()
        { *this = *this + 1; return *this; }
    // --------- overloaded postfix ++ operator
    Date operator++(int)
        { Date dt=*this; *this=*this+1; return dt; }
};
static int dys[]={31,28,31,30,31,30,31,31,30,31,30,31};
// -------- overloaded + operator
Date Date::operator+(int n)
{
    Date dt = *this;
    n += dt.da;
    while (n > dys[dt.mo-1])    {
        n -= dys[dt.mo-1];
        if (++dt.mo == 13)    {
            dt.mo = 1;
            dt.yr++;
        }
    }
    dt.da = n;
    return dt;
}
```

continued

Exercise 8.5 *Overloading the ++ Operator (continued)*

```
main()
{
    Date olddate(2,20,90);
    olddate++;
    olddate.display();
    ++olddate;
    olddate.display();
}
```

Exercise 8.5 displays these dates:

```
2/21/90
2/22/90
```

As shown in the exercise, you can specify that the auto-increment and auto-decrement operators are prefix or postfix, as shown here:

```
Date operator++();      // prefix ++ operator
Date operator++(int);   // postfix ++ operator
```

The compiler will call the overloaded prefix operator function when it sees the prefix notation. The unnamed *int* parameter in the overloaded postfix operator function declaration tells the compiler to call this function for the postfix operator. Note that the compiler makes no further distinction except to call the correct function. The code in the functions is responsible for supporting prefix or postfix operations. In Exercise 8.5, the overloaded *operator++()* function increments the object and returns it. The overloaded *operator++(int)* function saves the value of the object before incrementing it and then returns the saved object.

ADDRESS-OF AND REFERENCE-TO OPERATOR

You can overload the unary address-of (&) operator to change its behavior. One possible use for the overloaded & operator is to take the address of one of the data members, usually the most significant one, to pass to a library function that expects an address. Exercise 8.6 overloads the & operator to return the address of a data member.

Exercise 8.6   *Overloaded & Operator*

```
#include <iostream.h>
#include <string.h>
class Name {
    char name[25];
public:
    void display()
        { cout << '\n' << name; }
    // ---- add a name
    void AddName(char *nm)
        { strncpy(name, nm, 24); name[24] = '\0'; }
    // ---- overloaded & address-of operator
    const char * operator&() const
        { return name; }
};
main()
{
    char nm[25];
    Name names[5];
    for (int i = 0; i < 5; i++)    {
        cout << "\nEnter a name: ";
        cin >> nm;
        names[i].AddName(nm);
    }
    for (i = 0; i < 5; i++)
        cout << '\n' << &names[i];
}
```

In Exercise 8.6, you enter five names in response to the prompt. The program then displays the names in the order in which you entered them:

```
Enter a name: John
Enter a name: Bill
Enter a name: Terry
Enter a name: Warren
Enter a name: Jay


John
Bill
Terry
Warren
Jay
```

The exercise overloads the & operator to return the address of the *name* array from within the class. The operator returns a *const* character pointer, which means that users of the function may not use the address to modify the data values in the object. The address may be used only in contexts where a *const* character pointer is expected. The input from *cin* may not, therefore, go to that address. The class uses the *AddName* member function to change an object's data value.

Conversely, the output to *cout* may go to the address that the overloaded operator function returns because that context expects a *const* pointer and does not intend to modify the data.

Note that if you overload the & operator with a class for any purpose, you can no longer use the operator to take the address of an object of the class. Rather than overloading &, you should use a member function to return the address of the data member of an object and let the & operator perform its normal function.

UNARY PLUS AND MINUS OPERATORS

You can overload the unary plus and minus operators to work with a class. Suppose you have a class that describes an inventory quantity and you need to express that quantity with the plus and minus unary operators. Exercise 8.7 is an example of how overloading the unary minus operator might work.

Exercise 8.7   Overloaded Unary Minus

```
#include <iostream.h>
#include <string.h>
class ItemQty {
    int onhand;
    char desc[25];
public:
    ItemQty(int oh, char *d)
        { onhand = oh; strcpy(desc, d); }
    void display()
        { cout << '\n' << desc << ": " << onhand; }
    // ---- overloaded unary - operator
    int operator-() { return -onhand; }
};
main()
{
    ItemQty item1(100, "crankshaft");
    ItemQty item2(-50, "driveshaft");
    item1.display();
    cout << '\n' << -item1;  // invoke the overloaded -
    item2.display();
    cout << '\n' << -item2;  // invoke the overloaded -
}
```

The exercise declares two *ItemQty* objects: one with a positive *onhand* value and one with a negative. It calls the *display* function to display the record contents and then uses the overloaded unary minus operator to display the quantity with the unary minus operator applied, as shown in the following display:

```
crankshaft: 100
-100
driveshaft: -50
50
```

SUBSCRIPT OPERATOR

Overloading the subscript ([]) operator is sometimes useful. For example, a *String* class that stores a string value can overload the subscript operator to provide subscripted access to the character positions of the string value.

Exercise 8.8 overloads the [] operator in a small string class.

Exercise 8.8 *Overloaded [ ] Operator*

```
#include <iostream.h>
#include <string.h>
class String    {
    char *sptr;
public:
    String(char *s = 0);
    ~String() { delete sptr; }
    void display()
        { cout << '\n' << sptr; }
    // --- overloaded [] operator
    char& operator[] (int n)
        { return *(sptr + n); }
};
String::String(char *s)
{
    if (s)  {
        sptr = new char[strlen(s)+1];
        strcpy(sptr, s);
    }
    else
        sptr = 0;
}
```

continued

```
main()
{
    String mystring("The Ides of March");
    mystring.display();
    cout << '\n' << mystring[4];
    mystring[4] = '1';
    mystring[5] = '5';
    mystring[6] = 't';
    mystring[7] = 'h';
    mystring.display();
    strncpy(&mystring[4], "21st", 4);
    mystring.display();
}
```

The exercise declares a string with a value. The overloaded [] operator function allows the program to retrieve a single character from the string and display it. Because the [] operator function returns a reference to the character being subscripted, the program can use the expression on the left side of an assignment. With that notation, the program inserts the value '15th' one character at a time into the string and displays it. Then, by using the address of the value returned, the program uses *strncpy* to insert the value '21st' into the string and displays it.

Exercise 8.8 displays the following messages when you run it:

```
The Ides of March
I
The 15th of March
The 21st of March
```

Note that the overloaded [] subscript operator must be a nonstatic member function. Furthermore, you cannot implement it as a *friend* function as you can other operators.

Suppose you wanted to continue the similarity between your string classes and the character arrays of C++, where the following expressions are equivalent:

```
mystring[5]
*(mystring+5)
```

The following expressions are also equivalent:

```
&mystring[5]
mystring+5;
```

Exercise 8.9 shows how the overloaded + operator can simulate dereferenced pointer notation in a string class.

Exercise 8.9   *Overloaded + Operator*

```
#include <iostream.h>
#include <string.h>
class String    {
    char *sptr;
public:
    String(char *);
    ~String() { delete sptr; }
    void display()
        { cout << '\n' << sptr; }
    // --- overloaded [] operator
    char& operator[] (int n)
        { return *(sptr + n); }
    // --- overloaded () operator
    char *operator+ (int n)
        { return sptr + n; }
};
String::String(char *s)
{
    if (s)  {
        sptr = new char[strlen(s)+1];
        strcpy(sptr, s);
    }
    else
        sptr = 0;
}
```

continued

Exercise 8.9   *Overloaded + Operator (continued)*

```
main()
{
    String mystring("The Ides of March");
    mystring.display();
    cout << '\n' << *(mystring+4);
    *(mystring+4) = '1';
    *(mystring+5) = '5';
    *(mystring+6) = 't';
    *(mystring+7) = 'h';
    mystring.display();
    strncpy(mystring+4, "21st", 4);
    mystring.display();
}
```

The exercise adds the overloaded + operator and changes its notation from subscripted array accesses of the string to dereferenced pointer accesses. Except for those differences, Exercise 8.9 is the same as Exercise 8.8.

This particular usage would not prevent you from using the + operator as a Basic-like string concatenation operator as well. As shown here, you can overload an overloaded operator function by using different parameter types in the same way that you can for other functions:

```
class String  {
    // ...
public:
    // ...
    char *operator+(int n);
    String& operator+(String& s);
};
```

N O T E   The String class in these examples is not complete. Its purpose is to illustrate operator overloading and is not intended to be used as a rugged string class. Contemporary C++ implements a standard *string* class, which Chapter 15 describes. Future C++ defines a *string* class template that adjusts to wide international character sets.

FUNCTION CALL OPERATOR

Overloading the ( ) function call operator makes your object's name look like a function that accepts whatever arguments you specify. How you use the overloaded ( ) function call operator depends on your class and your imagination. Whether you want to do it depends on how far from traditional C++ styles you want to wander. As with all operator overloading, you should be reluctant to overload ( ) where its purpose is not apparent.

Exercise 8.10 illustrates one possibility for using the overloaded ( ) operator.

Exercise 8.10   *Overloaded ( ) Operator*

```
#include <iostream.h>
#include <string.h>
class Name {
    char name[25];
public:
    Name(char *s)
        { strcpy(name, s); }
    void operator() (char *s, int n)
        { strncpy(s, name, n); *(s+n) = '\0'; }
};
main()
{
    Name nm("Charlie");
    char newname[25];
    // --- use overloaded () to get name value
    nm(newname, sizeof newname -1);
    cout << newname;
}
```

Exercise 8.10 displays the name **Charlie** on the screen.

The exercise uses the overloaded ( ) operator with a *char* pointer as an argument to deliver the contents of the *Name* class to the caller. You can use several different versions of the overloaded ( ) operator as long as each one has a distinct parameter list.

Note that the overloaded ( ) function call operator must be a nonstatic member function. You cannot implement it as a *friend* function in the manner of other operators.

POINTER-TO-MEMBER OPERATOR

The -> operator, when overloaded, is always a postfix unary operator with the class object (or reference to same) on its left. The overloaded operator function returns the address of an object of some class.

Although the overloaded -> operator is postfix unary, its use requires the name of a member on the right side of the expression. That member must be a member of the class for which the overloaded operator returns an address.

You can overload the -> operator to ensure that a pointer to a class object always has a value—in other words, a smart pointer to an object. The pointer always guarantees that it points to something meaningful, and you avoid problems associated with dereferencing null and garbage pointers.

To illustrate the need for a smart pointer, Exercise 8.11 uses the usual *Date* class and, at the beginning of the program, a pointer to an object of the *Date* class.

Exercise 8.11   *Pointer to Class Object*

```
#include <iostream.h>
class Date {
    int mo, da, yr;
public:
    Date(int m=0, int d=0, int y=0)
        { mo = m; da = d; yr = y; }
    void display()
        { cout << '\n' << mo << '/' << da << '/' << yr; }
};
```

continued

Exercise 8.11 *Pointer to Class Object (continued)*

```
main()
{
    Date *dp;           // date pointer with garbage in it
    Date dt(3,17,90);   // Date
    dp = &dt;           // put address of date in pointer
    dp->display();      // display date through the pointer
}
```

Exercise 8.11 displays the date **3/17/90** on the screen.

The program declares a *Date* object, puts its address in the pointer, and calls the *display* member function through the pointer. Nothing is wrong with that. However, if the programmer neglects to assign a valid address of a *Date* object to the pointer, the program crashes because the pointer points nowhere meaningful. Whatever gets executed by that function call is not likely to be a valid function.

Exercise 8.12 overloads the -> operator to add a so-called smart pointer to the program.

Exercise 8.12 *Overloaded -> Operator*

```
#include <iostream.h>
class Date {
    int mo, da, yr;
public:
    Date(int m=0, int d=0, int y=0)
            { mo = m; da = d; yr = y; }
    void display()
        { cout << '\n' << mo << '/' << da << '/' << yr; }
};
```

continued

Exercise 8.12   *Overloaded -> Operator (continued)*

```
// ----------- "smart" Date pointer
class DatePtr {
    Date *dp;
public:
    DatePtr(Date *d = 0) { dp = d; }
    Date *operator->();
};
Date *DatePtr::operator->()
{
    static Date nulldate(0,0,0);
    if (dp == 0)            // if the pointer is null
        return &nulldate;   // return the dummy address
    return dp;              // otherwise return the pointer
}
main()
{
    DatePtr dp;        // date pointer with nothing in it
    dp->display();     // use it to call display function
    Date dt(3,17,90);  // Date
    dp = &dt;          // put address of date in pointer
    dp->display();     // display date through the pointer
}
```

Exercise 8.12 displays an empty date and a real one, as shown here:

```
0/0/0
3/17/90
```

An object of the *DatePtr* class is a pointer that knows whether a value has ever been assigned to it. If the program tries to use the pointer without first assigning the address of a *Date* object to it, the pointer contains the address of a null *Date* instead of garbage. The *DatePtr* object always returns the address of a *Date* object or the address of the null *Date* because the *DatePtr* conversion constructor function accepts no value that is not the address of a *Date* and substitutes zero if a *DatePtr* is constructed without a parameter. When the overloaded ->

operator function sees that the *dp* pointer is 0, it returns the address of the null *Date* object rather than the value in the pointer.

Note that the overloaded -> pointer operator must be a nonstatic member function. You cannot implement it as a friend function in the manner of other operators.

SUMMARY

This chapter showed you how to overload C++ operators to work with your classes. As you apply these techniques, try to keep a rein on your enthusiasm. You can get carried away with overloaded operators, and your code can become difficult to understand. Always overload operators in intuitive ways, and always use liberal comments in class definition header files to document the behavior of the operators you overload. One industry sage observed that C++ programmers first learn to overload operators. Then they learn not to.

CHAPTER 9

Class Inheritance

Class inheritance is the technique that is used to build new classes from existing ones and to build object-oriented class hierarchies. You can build layers of classes derived from other classes. You can build hierarchies of classes by using single and multiple inheritance. This chapter describes these processes by using small classes to demonstrate the features of inheritance. You will learn about:

- ❖ Base and derived classes
- ❖ Protected class members
- ❖ Public and private base classes
- ❖ Overriding base class functions
- ❖ Pointers and references to base and derived classes
- ❖ Virtual and pure virtual functions
- ❖ Polymorphism
- ❖ Virtual destructors
- ❖ Constructors and destructors in a hierarchy
- ❖ Multiple inheritance
- ❖ Virtual base classes

187

BASE AND DERIVED CLASSES

In *inheritance*, you derive a new class from an existing class. The class from which you derive is called the *base class*, and the new class is called the *derived class*. A base class has derived classes, each of which can be the base of other derived classes, all of which forms a class hierarchy. With *multiple inheritance*, a derived class can have more than one base class, each of which can have one or more base classes of its own.

A derived class inherits the characteristics of its bases. The derived class automatically possesses the data members and member functions, of the base. The derived class can add its own data members and member functions and it can override the member functions of the base. Adding and overriding members is how you modify the behavior of a base class to form a derived class.

There are two reasons to derive a class. One is that you want to modify the behavior of an existing class. The other is that you are building a well-organized, object-oriented class hierarchy in which the user-defined data types descend from one root class. These two reasons are design approaches, but the class inheritance behavior of C++ that supports them is the same, with the same rules and boundaries.

Why use inheritance to modify the behavior of an existing class? Why not just change the base class, making it do what you want it to do? There are several reasons.

First, the base class might be used by other parts of your program and by other programs, and you want its original behavior to remain intact for those objects that already use it. By deriving a class from the base, you define a new data type that inherits all the characteristics of the base class without changing the base class's operation in the rest of the program and in other programs.

Second, the source code for the base class might not be available to you. To use a class, all you need are its definition and the object code for its member functions. If you are using class libraries from other sources, you might not have the source code for the member functions and you could not change it.

Third, the base class might be an *abstract base class*, which is one that is designed to be a base class only. A class hierarchy can contain general-purpose classes that do nothing on their own. Their purpose is to define the behavior of a generic data structure to which derived classes add implementation details.

Fourth, you might be building a class hierarchy to derive the benefits of the object-oriented approach. One of these benefits is the availability of general-purpose class methods that modify their own behavior based on the characteristics of the subclasses that use them. The class hierarchy approach supports this ability through the virtual function mechanism. You will learn about this technique later in the chapter.

SINGLE INHERITANCE

You have been dealing with potential base classes since Chapter 5. All C++ structures and classes can have derived classes. The base class does not define inheritance; the derived class does. The base class has nothing in it that tells it which classes, if any, are derived from it. A derived class specifes its base.

The exercises in this book have, until now, been independent, stand-alone programs. To learn about inheritance, you will define classes in header files, put member functions in separate class-specific source files, and link the object code compiled from those multiple source files to make running programs.

Immediately following are a header file named **timeday.h** and a source file named **timeday.cpp**. They contain the definition and implementation of a *Time* class and are similar to the class definitions that you learned in Chapter 7.

```
// Header file to define the Time class
// ---------- timeday.h
#ifndef TIMEDAY_H
#define TIMEDAY_H
#include <iostream.h>
//
// A Time Class
//
class Time    {
    int hours, minutes, seconds;
public:
    Time(int hr, int min, int sec);
    void display();
};
#endif


// ----- timeday.cpp
#include "timeday.h"
Time::Time(int hr, int min, int sec)
{
    hours = hr;
    minutes = min;
    seconds = sec;
}
void Time::display()
{
    cout << hours << ':' << minutes << ':' << seconds;
}
```

The next two files are **date.h** and **date.cpp**, which define the *Date* class used in subsequent exercises.

```
// --------- date.h
// ------ base Date class
class Date {
protected:
    int month, day, year;
public:
    Date(int m=0, int d=0, int y=0);
    virtual void display();
};
```

```
// --------- date.cpp
#include <iostream.h>
#include "date.h"
Date::Date(int m, int d, int y)
{
    month = m;
    day = d;
    year = y;
}
void Date::display()
{
    cout << month << '/' << day << '/' << year;
}
```

When you compile the exercises that use these classes, remember to link the source files from these classes into your executable progams.

DESIGNING A DERIVED CLASS

You haven't used the *Time* class for anything yet. Perhaps other programs use it regularly. You determine that although you need its basic properties for storing the time of day, your programs must record and report the time zone in addition to hours, minutes, and seconds. You can't modify the *Time* class because that might affect other programs that use it. You can, however, derive a class from it and add the new requirements.

Following are **timezone.h** and **timezone.cpp**, header and source files that define and implement the *TimeZone class*, which maintains and displays the time along with its time zone. To use your new class in an application program, you would include **timezone.h** in your source and link the compiled **timezone.cpp** with your program.

```cpp
// Header to define derived TimeZone class
// ---------- timezone.h
#ifndef TIMEZONE_H
#define TIMEZONE_H
#include "timeday.h"
//
// A TimeZone Class
//
enum timezone { gmt, est, cst, mst, pst };
class TimeZone : public Time {
    timezone zone;
protected:
    const char *Zone();
public:
    TimeZone(int hr, int min, int sec, timezone zn);
    void display();
};
#endif
```

```
// ---------- timezone.cpp
#include "timezone.h"
static const char *TZ[] = { "GMT","EST","CST","MST","PST" };
TimeZone::TimeZone(int hr, int min, int sec, timezone zn)
            : Time(hr, min, sec)
{
    zone = zn;
}
void TimeZone::display()
{
    Time::display();
    cout << ' ' << Zone();
}
const char *TimeZone::Zone()
{
    return TZ[zone];
}
```

The *TimeZone* class is derived from the base class *Time*. You specify a base class with the colon (:) operator following the derived class name, as illustrated in the following statement:

```
class TimeZone : public Time { /* ... */ };
```

Protected Members

Observe the protected access specifier that appears ahead of the data member in **timezone.h**. You learned about public and private members in Chapter 7. Protected members behave just like private members until a new class is derived from a base class that has protected members.

If a base class has private members, those members are not accessible to the derived class. Protected members are public to derived classes but private to the rest of the program. Use of the *protected* keyword is the only acknowledgment by the *TimeZone* class in **timezone.h** that it might ever be a base class.

When you design a class, you should proceed as if the class would someday be derived even if you have no such intentions. Specify the *protected* keyword for members that could be accessible to derived classes.

The *TimeZone* class has one protected data member, the *zone* variable. It also has, indirectly, three other data members. These are the three private data members of the *Time* class: *hours*, *minutes*, and *seconds*. But because these members are private to the *Time* class, the member functions of the *TimeZone* class cannot have access to them except through the public member functions of the *Time* class.

Public and Private Base Classes

A derived class can specify that a base class is public or private by using the following notation in the definition of the derived class:

```
class TimeZone : private Time { /* ... */ };
class DispTime : public Time  { /* ... */ };
```

The *private* access specifier means that the protected and public members of the base class are private members of the derived class. The *public* access specifier means that the protected members of the base class are protected members of the derived class and that the public members of the base class are public members of the derived class.

If you do not provide an access specifier, the compiler assumes that the access is private unless the base class is a structure, in which case the compiler assumes that the access is public.

Constructors in the Base and Derived Classes

When you declare an object of a derived class, the compiler executes the constructor function of the base class followed by the constructor function of the derived class.

The parameter list for the derived class's constructor function could be different from that of the base class's constructor function. Therefore, the constructor function for the derived class must tell the compiler what values to use as arguments to the constructor function for the base class.

The derived class's constructor function specifies the arguments to the base class's constructor function in **timezone.cpp** as follows:

```
TimeZone::TimeZone(int hr, int min, int sec, timezone zn)
        : Time(hr, min, sec)
```

The colon (:) operator after the derived constructor's parameter list specifies in this case that an argument list for a base class's constructor follows. The argument list is in parentheses and follows the name of the base class.

The arguments to the constructor function of the base class are expressions that may use constants and the parameter list of the derived class's constructor function. They can be any valid C++ expressions that match the types of the base constructor's parameter list. In this case, the *TimeZone* constructor passes its arguments to the *Time* constructor.

When a base class has more than one constructor function, the compiler decides which one to call based on the types of the arguments in the base constructor argument list as specified by the derived class constructor function.

Overriding Base Class Functions in the Derived Class

When a base and a derived class have public member functions with the same name and parameter list types, the function in the derived class overrides that in the base class when the function is called as a member of the derived class object.

Both the base *Time* class and the derived *TimeZone* class have functions named *display*. A program that declares an object of type *TimeZone* can call the *display* function for that type, and the function in the derived class object executes. Exercise 9.1 is a program that uses the derived TimeZone class.

Exercise 9.1   *Using a Derived Class*

```
#include "timezone.h"
main()
{
    TimeZone tz(10, 26, 0, est);
    tz.display();
}
```

You must compile **timezone.cpp** and the exercise independently. Then you link them to build the executable program.

Exercise 9.1 displays the following message:

```
10:26:0 EST
```

A program can declare objects of both the base and the derived classes. The two objects are independent of each other.

Exercise 9.2 shows a program that uses *Time* and *TimeZone* objects.

Exercise 9.2   *Using a Base and a Derived Class*

```
#include <iostream.h>
#include "timezone.h"
main()
{
    Time tm(23, 15, 45);
    tm.display();
    cout << '\n';
    TimeZone tz(10, 26, 0, est);
    tz.display();
}
```

Exercise 9.2 displays the following messages, showing that each object uses the display function of its own class:

```
23:15:45
10:26:0 EST
```

CLASSES DERIVED FROM DERIVED BASE CLASSES

You can derive a class from a base class that was itself derived from another base class. Suppose that neither the *Time* class nor the *TimeZone* class fully satisfies a new requirement.

The *Time* class maintains the 24-hour military clock. (Actually, it records and displays whatever value you care to write into the hour with your initializers. A more comprehensive class would validate its initializers.) But suppose there is a new requirement to display the time in a 12-hour format with the time zone indicator and with a.m. or p.m. notation. You can derive a class from the *TimeZone* base that incorporates the new requirements.

Following are **disptime.h** and **disptime.cpp**, header and source files that define and implement the *DispTime* class, which is derived from the *TimeZone* class.

```cpp
// Header to define derived DispTime class
// ---------- disptime.h
#ifndef DISPTIME_H
#define DISPTIME_H
#include <stdio.h>
#include "timezone.h"
//
// A DispTime Class
//
class DispTime : public TimeZone {
protected:
    char ampm;
public:
    DispTime(int hr, int min, int sec, timezone zn);
    void display();
};
#endif
```

```
// ---------- disptime.cpp
#include "disptime.h"
inline int adjust(int hour)
{
    return hour > 12 ? hour - 12 : (hour == 0 ? 12 : hour);
}
inline char makeampm(int hour)
{
    return hour < 12 ? 'a' : 'p';
}
DispTime::DispTime(int hr, int min, int sec, timezone zn)
            : TimeZone(adjust(hr), min, sec, zn)
{
    ampm = makeampm(hr);
}
void DispTime::display()
{
    Time::display();
    cout << ' ' << ampm << 'm';
    cout << ' ' << Zone();
}
```

The **disptime.cpp** source file begins with two *inline* functions. The first, *adjust*, adjusts the 0 to 24 hour value to one that is correct for a 12-hour clock. Zero becomes 12, and 13 to 23 become 1 to 11. The second *inline* function, *makeampm*, returns the letter *a* if the hour is less than 12; otherwise it returns *p*.

This use of *inline* functions shows how the *inline* keyword can replace the preprocessor's *#define* statement for macros with parameters. The *inline* format is better because it enjoys all the notational convenience and type-checking of a function declaration.

Note that the argument list for the base *TimeZone* constructor uses the *adjust* function to initialize the *hours* data member all the way up in the base *Time* class. When you use the *DispTime* class, hours are always 1 to 12.

The *DispTime* constructor initializes the *ampm* data member by calling the *makeampm* function with the *hr* parameter as an argument.

The class definitions for *TimeZone* and *DispTime* have protected data members. The class definition for *Time* did not. This circumstance reflects what you are likely to run into when you deal with classes from other sources. A designer of a derived class is sensitive to how a base class definition can help the process. If you needed the data members from the *Time* class to be protected, you could always change the header file that defines *Time*. This is not a good practice. It is not wise to change code that might be in use elsewhere even if the change appears to be harmless.

Exercise 9.3 is a program that uses the *DispTime* class.

Exercise 9.3   *Using a Derived Class from a Derived Class*

```
#include "disptime.h"
main()
{
    DispTime dt(21, 42, 12, pst);
    dt.display();
}
```

Exercise 9.3 initializes the object with a 24-hour clock value and uses the class's *display* function to display the following message:

```
9:42:12 pm PST
```

POINTERS TO BASE AND DERIVED CLASSES

The three classes *Time*, *TimeZone*, and *DispTime* represent three generations in a straight line of inheritance. Each class has a function named *display* that performs differently. You can use these characteristics to observe how C++ behaves with class inheritance.

A pointer to a base class can be assigned the address of one of the base's derived class objects. If the derived class overrides members of the base, the compiler associates pointer deferenced accesses with the base class components of the object. This means that if a derived class member overrides a base class member, the pointer ignores the override.

Exercise 9.4 is a program that has a single object of type *DispTime* and three pointers to classes—one to each of the three types.

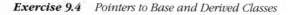

Exercise 9.4   *Pointers to Base and Derived Classes*

```
#include <iostream.h>
#include "disptime.h"
main()
{
    DispTime dt(21, 42, 12, pst);
    Time     *tp = &dt;
    TimeZone *zp = &dt;
    DispTime *dp = &dt;
    tp->display();
    cout << '\n';
    zp->display();
    cout << '\n';
    dp->display();
}
```

Exercise 9.4 displays the following messages showing that the compiler selects the member function based on the type of the pointer rather than on the type of the object:

```
9:42:12
9:42:12 PST
9:42:12 pm PST
```

SCOPE RESOLUTION OPERATOR WITH BASE AND DERIVED CLASSES

A program can use the scope resolution operator (::) to bypass the override of a member that a derived class has overridden.

Exercise 9.5 declares an object of type *DispTime* and a pointer to same.

Exercise 9.5   *Scope Resolution in Base and Derived Classes*

```
#include <iostream.h>
#include "disptime.h"
main()
{
    DispTime dt(21, 42, 12, pst);
    DispTime *dp = &dt;
    // -------- use the DispTime display function
    dp->display();
    cout << '\n';
    dt.display();
    cout << '\n';
    // -------- use the TimeZone display function
    dp->TimeZone::display();
    cout << '\n';
    dt.TimeZone::display();
    cout << '\n';
    // -------- use the Time display function
    dp->Time::display();
    cout << '\n';
    dt.Time::display();
    cout << '\n';
}
```

Exercise 9.5 calls the *display* function of the *DispTime* class twice—once directly via the object and once through the pointer. Then it uses the scope resolution operator to specify that it intends to use the *display* function for *TimeZone*, the base class of *DispTime*. Finally, it uses the same override to call the *display* function for *Time* (the base class of *TimeZone*), which is two generations removed from the object's *DispTime* class. The program displays the following messages:

```
9:42:12 pm PST
9:42:12 pm PST
9:42:12 PST
9:42:12 PST
```

```
9:42:12
9:42:12
```

Using the scope resolution operator without specifying a type on its left compiles a call to a global, nonmember function with the same name and parameter list. If no such function exists, the compiler issues an error message.

References to Base and Derived Classes

A reference to a base class can be initialized with one of the base's derived class objects. If the derived class overrides members of the base, the compiler associates operations made through that reference with the base class components of the object. If a derived class member overrides a base class member, the reference ignores the override.

Exercise 9.6 is a program that has a single object of type *DispTime* and three references to classes—one to each of the three types.

Exercise 9.6   *References to Base and Derived Classes*

```
#include <iostream.h>
#include "disptime.h"
main()
{
    DispTime dt(21, 42, 12, pst);
    Time&     tp = dt;  ·
    TimeZone& zp = dt;
    DispTime& dp = dt;
    tp.display();
    cout << '\n';
    zp.display();
    cout << '\n';
    dp.display();
}
```

Exercise 9.6 displays the same messages as Exercise 9.4 :

```
9:42:12
9:42:12 PST
9:42:12 pm PST
```

This display demonstrates that the compiler selects the member function based on the type of the reference rather than on the type of the object.

VIRTUAL FUNCTIONS

A *virtual* function is one that is defined in a base class and that expects to be overridden by a function in a derived class with the same name and parameter types. You saw earlier that when a pointer to a base class points to a derived class object, a call to an overridden function through the pointer calls the function that is a member of the base class rather than the one belonging to the object. A virtual function, on the other hand, passes the calls to the matching function in a derived class when the call is made from an object of the derived class. This is true regardless of the type of the pointer or reference that calls the function.

Time Classes with Virtual Functions

For the next exercise, modify the header files **timeday.h**, **timezone.h**, and **disptime.h** so that the member functions named *display* in all the classes are now virtual functions:

```
virtual void display();
```

This exercise reflects one of those times when you modify a class rather than derive from it. In this case, the original class is still under development, and you are improving on it.

Recompile **timeday.cpp**, **timezone.cpp**, and **disptime.cpp**. Link these compiled modules with the compiled output from Exercises 9.4 and 9.6. When you run the new programs, you see this output:

```
9:42:12 pm PST
9:42:12 pm PST
9:42:12 pm PST
```

When you compare these messages with those displayed by Exercises 9.4 and 9.6, you can see that the compiler now elects to use the *display* function in the *DispTime* class even when the reference is to the type *Time* or *TimeZone*.

Overriding the Virtual Function Override

If you want a virtual function to execute even when the calling object has an overriding function, you can use the scope resolution operator (::) to specify that the virtual function is to execute.

Exercise 9.7 modifies the program from Exercise 9.6 so that the virtual *TimeZone.display* function executes even though the *DispTime* object has an overriding display function.

Exercise 9.7 *Overriding the Virtual Function Override*

```
#include <iostream.h>
#include "disptime.h"
main()
{
    DispTime dt(21, 42, 12, pst);
    Time&     tp = dt;
    TimeZone& zp = dt;
    DispTime& dp = dt;
    tp.Time::display();
    cout << '\n';
    zp.TimeZone::display();
    cout << '\n';
    dp.display();
}
```

The modified program in Exercise 9 displays the same messages that Exercise 9.4 displayed and that Exercise 9.6 displayed before you made the display functions in the classes virtual:

```
9:42:12
9:42:12 PST
9:42:12 pm PST
```

Virtual Functions without Derived Overrides

If the derived class has no function to override the base class's virtual function, then the base class's function executes regardless of the pointer or reference type.

Exercise 9.8 derives a class from *Time* to demonstrate that a virtual function in a base class executes if the derived class of the invoking object has no overriding function.

Exercise 9.8 *Virtual Function with No Derived Override*

```
#include <iostream.h>
#include "timeday.h"
class NewTime : public Time    {
public:
    NewTime(int hr,int min,int sec) : Time(hr,min,sec)
        { /* empty */ }
};
class MoreTime : public NewTime    {
public:
    MoreTime(int hr,int min,int sec) : NewTime(hr,min,sec)
        { /* empty */ }
};
main()
{
    MoreTime dt(21, 42, 12);
    NewTime *nt = &dt;
    Time& tp = dt;

    dt.display();
    cout << '\n';
    tp.display();
    cout << '\n';
    nt->display();
    cout << '\n';
}
```

Neither the *NewTime* class nor the *MoreTime* class in Exercise 9.8 has a *display* function to override the virtual *display* function of the *Time* class. Therefore, all three calls to the *display* function execute the virtual function in the *Time* class, and the program displays the following messages:

```
21:42:12
21:42:12
21:42:12
```

Pure Virtual Functions

A base class can specify a *pure virtual* function, which means that the base class is an *abstract base class*. The base class provides no function body for the pure virtual function. In this case, the program may not declare any objects of the base class, and a derived class must declare the function. A class derived directly from the base declaration does not have to declare the function as long as somewhere down the class hierarchy a lower derived class declares it.

The following code shows you how to specify a pure virtual function:

```
class Time {
  // ...
public:
    virtual void display() = 0;
}
```

The zero initializer identifies the function as a pure virtual function. The class may not supply a function body, and a program may not declare an object of the base class.

Exercise 9.9 modifies the program in Exercise 9.8 by specifying a pure virtual *display* function for the *Time* class and by replacing the display function in the *TimeZone* class.

Exercise 9.9 *Pure Virtual Function*

```
#include <iostream.h>
#include "timeday.h"
class NewTime : public Time    {
public:
    NewTime(int hr,int min,int sec) : Time(hr,min,sec)
        { /* empty */ }
    virtual void Showit() = 0;
};
class MoreTime : public NewTime    {
public:
    MoreTime(int hr,int min,int sec) : NewTime(hr,min,sec)
        { /* empty */ }
    void Showit() { display(); }
};
main()
{
    MoreTime dt(21, 42, 12);
    NewTime *nt = &dt;

    dt.Showit();
    cout << '\n';
    nt->Showit();
    cout << '\n';
}
```

The program in Exercise 9.9 derives a *NewTime* class from the base *Time* class. The *NewTime* class has a pure virtual function named *Showit*. The *main* function declares an object of type *MoreTime* and a pointer to type *NewTime*, which contains the address of the *MoreTime* object. The program calls the *Showit* function directly for the object and then through the pointer. In both cases, the *MoreTime::Showit* function is called. It calls *display*, which is a public member function of the base *Time* class. Exercise 9.9 displays the following messages:

```
. 21:42:12
  21:42:12
```

Virtual Functions and Multiple Derived Classes

If a base class has more than one derived class and more than one of them overrides a virtual function, the compiler selects the function from the class for which the calling object is declared.

Exercise 9.10 defines an abstract *Date* class and two derived classes: *NumDate* and *AlphaDate*. The *Date* class has a pure virtual function named *display* that is overridden by *display* functions in the derived classes.

> **Exercise 9.10** *Virtual Functions and Multiple Derived Classes*

```cpp
#include <iostream.h>
// --------- abstract date class
class Date {
protected:
    int mo, da, yr;
public:
    Date(int m, int d, int y)
        {mo = m; da = d; yr = y;}
    virtual void display() = 0;
};
// --------- derived numeric date class
class NumDate : public Date {
public:
    NumDate(int m, int d, int y) : Date(m, d, y)
        { /* ... */ }
    void display()
    { cout << mo << '/' << da << '/' << yr; }
};
```

continued

Exercise 9.10 *Virtual Functions and Multiple Derived Classes (continued)*

```
// -------- derived alphabetic date class
class AlphaDate : public Date {
public:
    AlphaDate(int m, int d, int y) : Date(m, d, y)
        { /* ... */ }
    void display();
};
// ------ Display function for AlphaDate
void AlphaDate::display()
{
    static char *mos[] = {
        "January","February","March","April",
        "May","June","July",August",
        "September","October","November","December"
    };
    cout << mos[mo-1] << ' ' << da << ", " << yr+1900;
}
main()
{
    NumDate nd(7,29,41);
    AlphaDate ad(11,17,41);

    Date& dt1 = nd;
    Date& dt2 = ad;
    dt1.display();
    cout << '\n';
    dt2.display();
}
```

The program in Exercise 9.10 declares objects of types *NumDate* and *AlphaDate*. The two dates have different initialized values so that you can tell them apart. Then the program declares two references to *Date* objects, initializing one to refer to the *NumDate* object and the other to refer to the *AlphaDate* object. The important point is that both references, as defined, refer to the base class, but as initialized they refer to the derived class objects.

The program calls the *display* function by using the *Date* references and displays the following messages:

```
7/29/41
November 17, 1941
```

When the program calls the *display* function through a reference to the *Date* class, the compiler must select a function to execute. Because the *display* function in the *Date* class is virtual, the compiler selects the *display* function for the object to which the *Date* reference refers.

Polymorphism

Polymorbism is the ability of different objects in a class hierarchy to exhibit unique behavior in response to the same message. *Employee* and *Contractor* classes derived from a base *Worker* class, for example, can have different behavior even when a message is sent to their objects through a reference to their base *Worker* class.

In the next exercise you have a string of base and derived classes such as the following:

```
OrgEntity - Company - Division - Department
```

OrgEntity is the root base, and *Department* is the lowest derived class. The *OrgEntity* class is an abstract class, which means that its sole purpose is to be a base class. It has a function named *number_employees*, and every class in the hierarchy has a virtual function named *office_party*. The functions return the variable number of employees assigned to each organizational entity and a constant amount per employee budgeted for the annual office party.

Following are **org.h** and **org.cpp**, the header and source files that define and implement these four base and derived classes. The files contain code to support several subsequent exercises.

```
// ------------ org.h
#ifndef COMPANY_H
#define COMPANY_H
#include <iostream.h>
#include <string.h>
class OrgEntity {
    char name[25];
    int employee_count;
public:
    OrgEntity(char *s, int ec);
    int number_employees()
        { return employee_count; }
    char *org_name()
        { return name; }
    virtual int office_party() = 0;
};
class Company : public OrgEntity    {
public:
    Company(char *s, int ec);
    virtual int office_party();
};
class Division : public Company    {
public:
    Division(char *s, int ec);
    virtual int office_party();
};
class Department : public Division    {
public:
    Department(char *s, int ec);
    int office_party();
};
#endif
```

```
// ------- org.cpp
#include "org.h"
OrgEntity::OrgEntity(char *s, int ec)
{
    strcpy(name, s);
    employee_count = ec;
}
Company::Company(char *s, int ec) : OrgEntity(s, ec)
{
    // empty constructor
}
int Company::office_party()
{
    return 100;
}
Division::Division(char *s, int ec) : Company(s, ec)
{
    // empty constructor
}
int Division::office_party()
{
    return 75;
}
Department::Department(char *s, int ec) : Division(s, ec)
{
    // empty constructor
}
int Department::office_party()
{
    return 50;
}
```

It might appear that each of the three lower classes in **org.h** could simply derive from the *OrgEntity* base class. So they could, but, although not shown in the exercise, in practice such classes would contain other specialized and inherited members related to the organizational entities they represent. Tiered layers of inheritance would, therefore, be appropriate.

Somewhere in the organization's accounting system is a budget management process that generates annual budget reports. It does not necessarily know what kind of organizational entity it is working with at the time, so it must rely on the design of the class hierarchy to cause each class to behave in its own unique way.

Exercise 9.11 is a program that emulates this relationship. The *main* function stubs the exercise by declaring objects of the classes and calling the budget function for each one.

Exercise 9.11   *A Company's Budget Program*

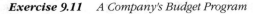

```
#include <iostream.h>
#include "org.h"
void budget(OrgEntity& oe);
main()
{
    Company company("Bilbo Software, Inc.", 35);
    Division div("Vertical Applications", 12);
    Department dept("Medical Practice", 4);
    budget(company);
    budget(div);
    budget(dept);
}
void budget(OrgEntity& oe)
{
    cout << "\n---- Budget Report ----\n";
    cout << oe.org_name();
    cout << " $" << oe.number_employees() * oe.office_party();
    cout << '\n';
}
```

The *budget* function represents a part of a software system that does not necessarily know which of the classes derived from *OrgEntity* it is dealing with. The virtual *office_party* function represents a way that each derived class can provide its own specialized behavior for a given process. The program displays the following messages:

```
---- Budget Report ----
Bilbo Software, Inc. $3500
---- Budget Report ----
Vertical Applications $900
---- Budget Report ----
Medical Practice $200
```

This ability for each derived class to provide its own custom version of a general function and for the compiler to select the correct one based on the object being processed is called *polymorphism* in the object-oriented lexicon.

VIRTUAL DESTRUCTORS

When an object of a derived class goes out of scope, the destructor for the derived class executes and then the destructor for the base class executes. There are potential problems in this process. If the destructor executes as the result of the *delete* operator and if the pointer type is the base class, the base destructor executes instead of the derived destructor.

Exercise 9.12 illustrates this destructor-execution behavior in base and derived classes.

Exercise 9.12   *Base and Derived Destructors*

```
#include <iostream.h>
#include <string.h>
// ------------- OrgEntity Class
class OrgEntity  {
    char *name;
public:
    OrgEntity(char *s);
    ~OrgEntity();
    void org_name();
};
OrgEntity::OrgEntity(char *s)
{
    name = new char[strlen(s)+1];
    strcpy(name, s);
}
OrgEntity::~OrgEntity()
{
    cout << "\nOrgEntity destructor";
    delete[] name;
}
void OrgEntity::org_name()
{
    cout << name;
}
```

continued

Exercise 9.12   *Base and Derived Destructors (continued)*

```
    // ------------ Division Class
class Division : public OrgEntity  {
    char *manager;
public:
    Division(char *s, char *mgr);
    ~Division();
};
Division::Division(char *s, char *mgr) : OrgEntity(s)
{
    manager=new char[strlen(mgr)+1];
    strcpy(manager, mgr);
}
Division::~Division()
{
    cout << "\nDivision destructor";
    delete[] manager;
}
main()
{
    OrgEntity *orgs[3];
    orgs[0] = new OrgEntity("Bilbo Software, Inc.");
    orgs[1] = new Division("Vert Apps", "Ron Herold");
    orgs[2] = new Division("Horiz Apps", "Bob Young");
    for (int i = 0; i < 3; i++)     {
        // ....... process the organization objects
        delete orgs[i]; // not always right destructor
    }
}
```

When you design a class hierarchy, you must consider each method with respect to whether it should be a virtual function. If you are defining a member function whose method is specific to the class, you must ask whether any derived class might have a similar function with the same name. The *display* function you have seen in many exercises in this book is a good example of a general-purpose function whose operation could be overridden by a derived class. Next, you must ask whether calls to the function are always in the name of the actual object or whether they might be through a pointer or reference to a base class. Answering that, you must determine whether such calls need the services of the function that is a member of the pointer/reference class or whether they need a virtual function that finds its way to the member function of the actual class of which the object is a type. These are the kinds of decisions that face the designer of an object-oriented class hierarchy.

Exercise 9.12 has a base *OrgEntity* class and a derived *Division* class. Both classes have destructors because they both contain pointer data members that are initialized with free store memory by their constructors. Both classes should also have copy constructors and overloaded assignment operators for the same reason, which you learned about in Chapter 7.

The destructor functions of both classes display messages to show that they are executing, and they both delete the free store memory to which their member pointers point.

The *main* function declares an array of pointers to the *OrgEntity* class, initializes one of them with a pointer to a new *OrgEntity* object, and initializes the other two with pointers to new *Division* objects. Because these objects were built by the *new* operator, they must be destroyed by the *delete* operator.

The *main* function uses a *for* loop to process and delete the objects. However, the pointers in the array are *OrgEntity* types, so the *delete* operator calls the destructor function for the *OrgEntity* class only—even when the pointer points to a *Division* object. The result is that the free store memory allocated to the two *Division* class objects for their manager members never gets deleted. Exercise 9.12 displays the following messages to prove that only the *OrgEntity* destructor ever gets called:

```
OrgEntity destructor
OrgEntity destructor
OrgEntity destructor
```

The solution to the problem revealed by Exercise 9.12 is to declare the destructor function for the base class to be virtual. When a base class destructor is virtual, all the destructors below it in the hierarchy are automatically virtual, and the compiler can call the correct destructor function.

N O T E

Even though destructor functions can be virtual, constructor functions cannot.

Change the *OrgEntity* destructor prototype in the class definition in Exercise 9.12 to a virtual destructor this way:

```
virtual ~OrgEntity();
```

Following that change, recompile and run the program to see that it now displays the following messages:

```
OrgEntity destructor
Division destructor
OrgEntity destructor
Division destructor
OrgEntity destructor
```

The first *OrgEntity* destructor message comes when the program deletes the *OrgEntity* object. The next two pairs of messages—for the *Division* destructor and *OrgEntity* destructor—come when the program deletes the two *Division* objects.

MULTIPLE INHERITANCE

In multiple inheritance, a derived class has more than one base class. This technique allows you to define a new class that inherits the characteristics of several unrelated base classes.

You specify more than one base class when you define a derived class with multiple inheritance. The following notation defines a *FileStamp* class derived from the *Time* and *Date* classes:

```
class FileStamp : public Time, public Date {
    // ...
};
```

The constructor function declaration in a class derived from multiple bases specifies the arguments for the constructors of all the base classes, as shown here:

```
FileStamp::Filestamp(int dd,int mm,int yy,
                         int hr,int mn,int sc)
    : Time(hr, mn, sc), Date(mm, dd, yy)
```

Exercise 9.13 is a program that derives the *FileStamp* class from two bases: the *Time* class and the *Date* class. In this exercise, the *FileStamp* class records the date and time when something happens to a file. It has its own data member to store the name of the file, and it uses the properties it inherits from the *Date* and *Time* classes to manage the date and time.

Exercise 9.13   *Multiple Inheritance*

```
#include <iostream.h>
#include <string.h>
#include "timeday.h"
#include "date.h"
// ------ derived FileStamp class
class FileStamp : public Time, public Date    {
protected:
    char filename[15];
public:
    FileStamp(char *fn, int mm, int dd, int yy,
                      int hr, int mn, int sc);
    void display();
};
FileStamp::FileStamp(char *fn, int mm, int dd, int yy,
                             int hr, int mn, int sc)
        : Time(hr, mn, sc), Date(mm, dd, yy)
{
    strcpy(filename, fn);
}
```

continued

Exercise 9.13 *Multiple Inheritance (continued)*

```
void FileStamp::display()
{
    cout << filename << ' ';
    Date::display();
    cout << ' ';
    Time::display();
}
main()
{
    FileStamp fs("DATAFILE", 4, 6, 90, 13, 32, 27);
    fs.display();
}
```

The *Date* and *Time* classes have *display* functions to display their contents. The *FileStamp* function overrides those functions with its own *display* function. The *FileStamp::display* function uses the virtual *display* functions of the two base classes by using the global scope resolution operator to call them.

Exercise 9.13 displays the following message:

```
DATAFILE 4/6/90 13:32:27
```

Ambiguities with Multiple Inheritance

Suppose that the *FileStamp* class in Exercise 9.13 had no *display* function to override the virtual *display* functions of the two base classes. This would not be a problem as long as the program did not attempt to call the *display* function through an object of type *FileStamp* or a pointer or reference to one. If it did, however, the program would not compile because the compiler would not know which of the two *display* functions to execute. The program can resolve this ambiguity by using the scope resolution operator to specify which class's *display* function to use, as shown in the following example:

```
fs.Date::display();
```

The same ambiguities can exist with data members. If both base classes have data members with the same name and if the derived class has no such data member, the member functions of the derived class must use the scope resolution operator to resolve which base class's data member to use.

If the data members are public, the program cannot access such an ambiguous data member directly through the object. The program must use the scope resolution operator and the base class name in the same manner that is shown above for member functions.

Constructor Execution with Multiple Inheritance

When the program declares an object of a class that is derived from multiple bases, the constructors for the base classes are called first. The order of execution is the order in which the base classes are declared as bases to the derived class. Consider the following example:

```
class FileStamp : public Time, public Date {
    // ...
};
```

The constructor for the *Time* class executes first, followed by the constructor for the *Date* class. The constructor for the *FileStamp* class executes last.

If the class definition includes another class as a member, that class's constructor executes after the constructors for the base classes and before the constructor for the class being defined. Consider the following example:

```
class Name { /* ... */ };
class FileStamp : public Time, public Date {
    Name filename;
    // ...
};
```

The order of constructor execution is *Time*, *Date*, *Name*, and *FileStamp*.

Destructor Execution with Multiple Inheritance

When an object of a class goes out of scope, the destructors execute in the reverse order of the constructors.

VIRTUAL BASE CLASSES

Multiple inheritance has the potential for a derived class to have too many instances of one of the bases. Consider the following class:

```
class BillingItem {
protected:
    char name[25];
    int cost;
public:
    virtual void display() = 0;
};
```

The *BillingItem* class is an abstract base class that is the base class for two derived classes in a system that supports the sale of products and services. The following are the derived classes:

```
class Product : public BillingItem {
protected:
    int qty_sold;
public:
    Product(char *nm, int qty, int cst)
        { qty_sold = qty; }
    void display() { cout << qty_sold; }
};
class Service : public BillingItem {
protected:
    int manhours;
public:
    Service(char *nm, int mh, int cst)
        { manhours = mh; }
    void display() { cout << manhours; }
};
```

A program that declares an object of either of these classes has access to the *name* and *cost* data members of the base *BillingItem* class. That, combined with the *display* functions of the derived classes, gives the program the ability to report the details of individual product and service sales.

Suppose that the system also needs to support the sale of installed products; the sale involves a number of products and the labor hours to perform the installation. It is reasonable to want to build a new class that inherits the characteristics of the two existing classes. Such a new class is shown as follows:

```
class Installation : public Product, public Service    {
public:
    Installation(char *nm, int qty, int hrs, int cst)
        : Product(nm, qty, cst), Service(nm, hrs, cst)  { }
    void display();
};
```

A problem arises because the *Product* and *Service* classes are both derived from the *BillingItem* class; therefore, the *Installation* class inherits two copies of it. You do not want that to happen. An installation is one billing item with one name and one cost. It does not need two representations of these data members. Furthermore, any attempt to address *name* or *cost* for an *Installation* object would result in a compile-time ambiguity that the program could resolve only by applying the scope resolution operator to associate the member with one of the intermediate base classes.

C++ allows you to specify in the definition of a derived class that a base class is virtual. As a result, all virtual occurrences of the class throughout the class hierarchy share one actual occurrence of it. To specify a virtual base class, use the following notation:

```
class Product : public virtual BillingItem {
    // ...
};
```

There are rules, however, about how a virtual base class can itself be specified. A class that uses a constructor that accepts parameters cannot be a virtual base class. If this restriction did not exist, the compiler would not know which constructor argument list from which derived class to use. Note that a pointer to a virtual base class cannot be cast to a class that is derived from it, either directly or further down the class hierarchy.

Exercise 9.14 shows the use of a virtual base class such as the one just discussed.

Exercise 9.14   *Virtual Base Classes*

```
#include <iostream.h>
#include <string.h>
class BillingItem    {
protected:
    char name[25];
    int cost;
public:
    virtual void display() = 0;
};
    void display();
};
Product::Product(char *nm, int qty, int cst)
{
        qty_sold = qty;
        strcpy(name, nm);
        cost = cst;
}
void Product::display()
{
        cout << qty_sold;
}
class Service : public virtual BillingItem    {
    int manhours;
public:
    Service(char *nm, int mh, int cst);
    void display();
};
```

continued

Exercise 9.14   *Virtual Base Classes (continued)*

```
Service::Service(char *nm, int mh, int cst)
{
      manhours = mh;
      strcpy(name, nm);
      cost = cst;
}
void Service::display()
{
      cout << manhours;
}


        : Product(nm, qty, cst), Service(nm, hrs, cst) { }
    void display();
};
void Installation::display()
{
    cout << "\nInstalled ";
    Product::display();
     cout << ' ' << name << 's';
    cout << "\nLabor: ";
    Service::display();
    cout << " hours";
    cout << "\nCost: $" << cost;
}
main()
{
    Installation inst("refrigerator", 2, 3, 75);
    inst.display();
}
```

Both the *Product* and the *Service* class definitions specify that the *BillingItem* base class is virtual. Observe that the constructors for these two classes take care of initializing the data members for the *BillingItem* class because it cannot have a constructor with a parameter list. The *Installation* class is derived from the *Product* and *Service* classes.

The *main* function declares an *Installation* object, initializes it with some values, and uses its *display* function to display the following messages:

```
Installed 2 refrigerators
Labor: 3 hours
Cost: $75
```

SUMMARY

There is more than just language to know about the C++ language development environment. Along with implementations of the language comes a library of standard stream input/output classes and functions. You have already used that library extensively by including **iostream.h** in the exercises and using the *cin* and *cout* objects to read and write the console. Chapter 10 is about C++ input/output streams and how you can use their advanced features for file input/output as well as for the console.

CHAPTER 10

C++ Input/Output Streams

The exercises in this book have used the C++ *iostream* class library to read input from the keyboard and display results on the screen. The *iostream* class library has capabilities beyond those that read and write the console, however. The library is the C++ equivalent to the Standard C stream input/output functions, and you can use it to manage console and file input/output.

The *iostream* classes have more features than this chapter describes. After mastering the usages in the exercises given here, you should refer to the *iostream* documentation that comes with your compiler to see how to use its more advanced features. This chapter provides sufficient knowledge to use the streams in the ways that support most programming problems. You will learn:

- ❖ Input and output stream classes
- ❖ Buffered and formatted output
- ❖ *put* and *write* member functions
- ❖ *get, getline,* and *read* member functions
- ❖ Overloading << and >>
- ❖ File input/output

227

C++ has no input/output operators as intrinsic or integral parts of the language. Just as C relies on function libraries to extend the language with input/output functions, C++ depends on class libraries for its input and output.

C++ manages file and console input and output as streams of characters. C++ programs manage data values as data types such as integers, structures, classes, and so on. The *iostream* library provides the interface between the data types that a program views and the character streams of the input/output system.

Most of the exercises in this book include the **iostream.h** header file. You can learn a lot about the design of class hierarchies by reading this file. You can also answer some of your own questions about the use of the streams by looking at how they are implemented in the header file.

When the first edition of this book was written, the *iostream* class library was relatively new. Different compiler vendors implemented it according to their own interpretations of the AT&T specification. The implementations today tend to follow the emerging ANSI/ISO standard but with a few minor differences reflecting the compiler writers' interpretations of the standard. Not all compilers deliver the same output, so you might see different results from these exercises depending on which compiler you use. Do not worry about that. Learn the basics and then learn how your compiler behaves.

STREAMS

Chapter 1 introduced the C++ *iostream* class library and showed some of the ways to use it. That introduction allowed you to proceed with the exercises in this book, most of which use console input/output. Without knowing about C++ classes, you were not prepared to understand how the classes and their objects are implemented. Now that you have classes, overloaded operators, and inheritance under your belt, you are ready to learn to use the features of the *iostream* libraries.

The *ios* Class

C++ streams are implemented as classes. The *cout* and *cin* objects are global instances of those classes, which derive from a base class named *ios* and which are declared by the system. There is not much to know about *ios*, although later you will use the *enum* values that *ios* defines. A program deals mostly with objects of types derived from the *ios* class.

The *ostream* Class

Stream output is managed by a class named *ostream*, which is derived from *ios*. You learned to display a message on the screen with a statement such as the following one:

```
cout << "Hello, Dolly";
```

The *cout* object is an external object of the *ostream* class. The *cout* object is declared in the library, and an *extern* declaration of it appears in **iostream.h** so that it is available to be used by any program that includes **iostream.h**.

In addition to *cout*, **iostream.h** declares other objects as instances of the *ostream* class. The *cerr* object writes to the standard error device and uses unbuffered output. The *clog* object also writes to the standard error device, but it uses buffered output. A later part of this chapter describes buffered output.

A program writes to an *ostream* object by using the overloaded << insertion operator. The exercises in this book have used this feature extensively. The *ostream* class provides sufficient overloaded << insertion operators to support writing most standard C++ data types to the output stream. Later you will learn how to overload the << insertion operator to write your own classes to an *ostream* object.

The *istream* Class

The *istream* class manages stream input in the same way that the *ostream* class manages output. The *istream* class is externally declared in **iostream.h**. The *cin* object reads data values from the standard input device.

The *istream* class uses the overloaded >> extraction operator to read input. There are sufficient overloaded extraction >> operators to support reading the standard C++ data types, and a user-defined class can overload the >> extraction operator to read data from an *istream* object. You will learn how to do this later.

The *iostream* Class

The *iostream* class is derived from the *istream* and *ostream* classes. A program uses it for the declaration of objects that do both input and output. You do not often need to deal with the *iostream* class in basic input/output operations. The *fstream* class, which manages file input/output, derives from the *iostream* class, and that is as close as most programmers need to come to *iostream*.

BUFFERED OUTPUT

The data characters written to an *ostream* object are usually buffered. For example, the *ostream* class collects output bytes into a buffer and does not write them to the actual device associated with the object until the one of the following events occurs: the buffer fills, the program tells the object to flush its buffer, the program terminates, or, if the output object is *cout*, the program reads data from the *cin* object. The *cout* and *clog* objects use buffered output. The *cerr* object does not.

Exercise 10.1 displays a "please wait" message, which does extensive processing—in this case, just a five-second wait loop—and then proceeds.

Exercise 10.1   *A Buffered Stream Object*

```
#include <iostream.h>
#include <time.h>
main()
{
    time_t tm = time((time_t *)NULL) + 5;
    cout << "Please wait...";
    while (time((time_t *)NULL) < tm)
        ;
    cout << "\nAll done";
}
```

The "please wait" message does not always display when it should, because *cout* is a buffered object.

N O T E

Not all compilers exhibit the same behavior. The Borland C++ compiler displays the "please wait" message immediately. Microsoft C++ waits until the timer loop expires and the "\nAll done" message flushes the buffer.

The solution is to tell *cout* to flush itself as soon as you want the message to display. A program tells an *ostream* object to flush itself by sending it the *flush* manipulator.

Exercise 10.2 uses the *flush* manipulator to cause the program in Exercise 10.1 to work the way it is intended.

Exercise 10.2   *Flushing a Buffered Stream*

```
#include <iostream.h>
#include <time.h>
main()
{
    time_t tm = time((time_t *)NULL) + 5;
    cout << "Please wait..." << flush;
    while (time(NULL) < tm)
        ;
    cout << "\nAll done";
}
```

FORMATTED OUTPUT

Chapter 1 included discussions on the *dec, oct,* and *hex* manipulators. These manipulators set the default format for input and output. If you insert the *hex* manipulator into the output stream, for example, the object translates the internal data representation of the object into the correct display. Exercise 1.6 in Chapter 1 demonstrated this behavior.

Output Width

By default, objects of type *ostream* write data without padding . The exercises in this book insert the space character between data values in the output stream to separate them. You might want some displays to be lined up in columns, which means that displays need to be written with a fixed width.

A program can specify a default width for every item displayed by inserting the *setw* manipulator into the stream or by calling the *width* member function. The *setw* manipulator and the *width* member function both take a width parameter.

Exercise 10.3 is a program that displays a column of numbers.

Exercise 10.3   *Displaying Columns of Numbers*

```
#include <iostream.h>
main()
{
    cout.unsetf(ios::scientific);
    cout.setf(ios::fixed);
    static double values[] =
        { 1.23, 35.36, 653.7, 4358.224 };
    for (int i = 0; i < 4; i++)
        cout << values[i] << '\n';
}
```

Exercise 10.3 displays the following output:

```
1.23
35.36
653.7
4358.224
```

Some compilers pad the decimal places with zeros as shown here:

```
1.230000
35.360000
653.700000
4358.224000
```

Observe the calls to the *unsetf* and *setf* member functions for the *cout* object. These calls clear and set flags that are related to the object and that control output format. The *scientific* flag, which this exercise clears, formats a *double* or *float* output with exponential notation. The *fixed* flag formats the output with decimal positions. The default flag is *scientific*.

Exercise 10.4 demonstrates how the *width* member function manages output width. By calling the *width* function with an argument of 10, the program specifies that the displays are to appear in a column at least 10 characters wide.

Exersise 10.4 *The width Member Function*

```
#include <iostream.h>
main()
{
    cout.setf(ios::fixed, ios::scientific);
    static double values[] = { 1.23, 35.36, 653.7, 4358.224 };
    for (int i = 0; i < 4; i++)    {
        cout.width(10);
        cout << values[i] << '\n';
    }
}
```

Exercise 10.4 displays the following output:

```
      1.23
     35.36
     653.7
  4358.224
```

The *setf* call in Exercise 10.4 differs from the one in Exercise 10.3. This variation on the call has two parameters: the flag to set and a mask that defines the flags to clear.

Sometimes a report needs to use different widths for different data elements, and it is convenient to insert width commands into the stream. The *setw* manipulator provides this capability.

Exercise 10.5 demonstrates the use of the *setw* manipulator to display columns that have data elements with different width requirements.

Exercise 10.5 *The **setw** Manipulator*

```
#include <iostream.h>
#include <iomanip.h>
main()
{
    cout.setf(ios::fixed, ios::scientific);
    static double values[] =
        { 1.23, 35.36, 653.7, 4358.224 };
    static char *names[] =
        {"Zoot", "Jimmy", "Al", "Stan"};
    for (int i = 0; i < 4; i++)
        cout << setw(6)  << names[i]
             << setw(10) << values[i] << '\n';
}
```

You must include **iomanip.h** to use the *setw* manipulator.

Exercise 10.5 displays the following output:

```
Zoot      1.23
Jimmy     35.36
Al        653.7
Stan   4358.224
```

Note that using *setw* or *width* does not cause any truncation. If the data value being displayed is wider than the current width value, the entire data value still displays. You should be aware of this behavior when you design well-formatted displays that use the *setw* manipulator or the *width* member function.

Note also that the default width you specify applies only to the object for which you specified it and not for other objects of the class.

To return the object to the default width, use the *width* member function or the *setw* manipulator with a zero argument.

You can use the *fill* member function to set the value of the padding character for output that has a width other than the default width.

Exercise 10.6 demonstrates this usage by padding a column of numbers with asterisks.

Exercise 10.6 *The **fill** Member Function*

```
#include <iostream.h>
main()
{
    cout.setf(ios::fixed, ios::scientific);
    static double values[] =
        { 1.23, 35.36, 653.7, 4358.224 };
    for (int i = 0; i < 4; i++)     {
        cout.width(10);
        cout.fill('*');
        cout << values[i] << '\n';
    }
}
```

Exercise 10.6 displays the following output:

```
******1.23
*****35.36
*****653.7
**4358.224
```

Output Justification

Suppose that you want the names in Exercise 10.5 to be left-justified and the number to remain right-justified. You can use the *setiosflags* manipulator to specify that the output is to be left- or right-justified.

Exercise 10.7 demonstrates *setiosflags* by modifying the display from Exercise 10.5 so that the names are left-justified.

Exercise 10.7 *The **setiosflags** and **resetiosflags** Manipulators*

```
#include <iostream.h>
#include <iomanip.h>
main()
{
    cout.setf(ios::fixed, ios::scientific);
    static double values[] =
        { 1.23, 35.36, 653.7, 4358.224 };
    static char *names[] =
        {"Zoot", "Jimmy", "Al", "Stan"};
    for (int i = 0; i < 4; i++)
        cout << setiosflags(ios::left)
            << setw(6)  << names[i]
            << resetiosflags(ios::left)
            << setiosflags(ios::right)
            << setw(10) << values[i] << '\n';
}
```

Exercise 10.7 displays the following output:

```
Zoot       1.23
Jimmy     35.36
Al        653.7
Stan   4358.224
```

The exercise sets the left-justification flag by using the *setiosflags* manipulator with an argument of *ios::left*. This argument is an *enum* value that is defined in the *ios* class, so its reference must include the *ios::* prefix. The *resetiosflags* manipulator turns off the left-justification flag to return to the default right justification mode.

Precision

Suppose you wanted the floating-point numbers in Exercise 10.7 to display with only one decimal place. The *setprecision* manipulator tells the object to use a specified number of digits of precision.

Exercise 10.8 adds the *setprecision* manipulator to the program.

Exercise 10.8 *The setprecision Manipulator*

```cpp
#include <iostream.h>
#include <iomanip.h>
main()
{
    static double values[] = { 1.23, 35.36, 653.7, 4358.224 };
    static char *names[] = {"Zoot", "Jimmy", "Al", "Stan"};
    for (int i = 0; i < 4; i++)
        cout << setiosflags(ios::left)
             << setw(6)
             << names[i]
             << resetiosflags(ios::left)
             << setiosflags(ios::right)
             << setw(10)
             << setprecision(1)
             << values[i]
             << '\n';
}
```

Exercise 10.8 displays the following output:

```
Zoot        1.2
Jimmy      35.4
Al       6.5e+02
Stan     4.4e+03
```

The scientific notation displayed by Exercise 10.8 might not be what the program needs to display. There are two flags—*ios::fixed* and *ios::scientific*—that control how a floating-point number displays. A program can set and clear these flags with the *setiosflags* and *resetiosflags* manipulators.

Some compilers display the values as shown here:

```
Zoot          1
Jimmy     4e+001
```

```
Al        7e+002
Stan      4e+003
```

Exercise 10.9 uses the *setiosflags* manipulator to set the *ios::fixed* flag so that the program does not display in scientific notation.

Exercise 10.9   *Setting the **ios::fixed** Flag*

```
#include <iostream.h>
#include <iomanip.h>
main()
{
    static double values[] = { 1.23, 35.36, 653.7, 4358.224 };
    static char *names[] = {"Zoot", "Jimmy", "Al", "Stan"};
    for (int i = 0; i < 4; i++)
        cout << setiosflags(ios::left)
            << setw(6)
            << names[i]
            << resetiosflags(ios::left)
            << setiosflags(ios::fixed)
            << setiosflags(ios::right)
            << setw(10)
            << setprecision(1)
            << values[i]
            << '\n';
}
```

Exercise 10.9 displays the following output:

```
Zoot        1.2
Jimmy      35.4
Al        653.7
Stan     4358.2
```

Manipulators, Flags, and Member Functions

The exercises in this discussion have used manipulators and member functions to change the various modes of display, which are controlled by flags. The *ios* class keeps the current settings of the flags in member data items. The class defines the mnemonic values for the settings in an *enum* data type. Many of the modes can be changed with either a manipulator or a member function. Which one you use depends on how convenient it might be for the display at hand. Some of the mode changes remain in place until you change them again. Others reset themselves to their default values after every output message.

INPUT/OUTPUT MEMBER FUNCTIONS

There are several member functions associated with the *ostream* and *istream* classes that perform input and output. These member functions are alternatives to the extraction and insertion operators providing better ways to manage certain kinds of input and output.

Output Member Functions

The *ostream* class includes two member functions that write characters and memory blocks to output stream objects.

put

The *put* member function writes a single character to the output stream. The following two statements are the same:

```
cout.put('A');
cout << 'A';
```

write

The *write* member function writes any block of memory to the stream in binary format. Because *write* does not terminate when it sees a null, it is useful for writing the binary representations of data structures to stream files, which are discussed later. Exercise 10.10 illustrates the *write* function with the *cout* object.

Exercise 10.10 *The **ostream write** Function*

```
#include <iostream.h>
main()
{
    static struct    {
        char msg[23];
        int alarm;
        int eol;
    } data = { "It's Howdy Doody time!", '\a', '\n' };

    cout.write( (char *) &data, sizeof data);
}
```

In Exercise 10.10, the message is displayed. The program writes the message, sounds the alarm, and advances to the next line.

Note the cast to *char** before the address of the structure object. The *write* function accepts *char* pointers and unsigned *char* pointers only. The address of the structure must be cast to one of these. See Chapter 13 for a discussion on the ANSI/ISO new-style casts.

Input Member Functions

The >> extraction operator has a limitation that programs sometimes need to overcome: The extraction operator bypasses white space. If you type characters on a line that is being read by the extraction operator, only the nonspace characters come into the receiving character variable. The spaces are skipped. Likewise, if the program uses the extraction operator to read a string of words, the input stops when it finds a space character. The next word is read into the next (if any) use of the extraction operation on the *istream* object, and all spaces between the words are lost.

The *istream* class includes the *get* and *getline* member functions to handle reading input characters that must include white space.

get

The *get* member function works just like the >> extraction operator except that white space characters are included in the input.

Exercise 10.11 demonstrates the difference between the two operations.

Exercise 10.11   *The **istream get** Member Function*

```
#include <iostream.h>
main()
{
    char line[25], ch = 0, *cp;

    cout << " Type a line terminated by 'x'\n>";
    cp = line;
    while (ch != 'x')    {
        cin >> ch;
        *cp++ = ch;
    }
    *cp = '\0';
    cout << ' ' << line;

    cout << "\n Type another one\n>";
    cp = line;
    ch = 0;
    while (ch != 'x')    {
        cin.get(ch);
        *cp++ = ch;
    }
    *cp = '\0';
    cout << ' ' << line;
}
```

In Exercise 10.11, two strings are read from the keyboard one character at a time. The first input uses the extraction operator, and the second one uses the *get* member function. If you typed **now is the timex** for both entries, the screen would look like the following display:

```
Type a line terminated by 'x'
now is the timex                (entered by you)
```

```
nowisthetimex                (echoed by the program)
Type another one
now is the timex             (entered by you)
now is the timex             (echoed by the program)
```

You can see that the extraction operator skips over the white space and the *get* function does not. The program needs the **x** terminator because it needs to know when to stop reading. Because *cin* is a buffered object, the program does not begin to start seeing characters until you type the carriage return, and that character is not seen by the program.

A variation of the *get* function allows a program to specify a buffer address and the maximum number of characters to read.

Exercise 10.12 shows how the *get* function can specify a buffer address and length instead of a character variable to receive the input.

Exercise 10.12 *Using **get** with a Buffer and Length*

```
#include <iostream.h>
main()
{
    char line[25];
    cout << " Type a line terminated by carriage return\n>";
    cin.get(line, 25);
    cout << ' ' << line;
}
```

Exercise 10.12 reads whatever you type into the structure and echoes it to the screen.

The length value minus one is the maximum number of characters that are read into the buffer. You can type more than that number, but the excess characters are discarded.

getline

The *getline* function works the same as the variation of the *get* function demonstrated in Exercise 10.12. Both functions allow a third argument that specifies the terminating character for input. If you do not include that argument, its default value is the *newline* character.

Exercise 10.13 uses the *getline* function with a third argument to specify a terminating character for the input stream.

Exercise 10.13 *The **istream getline** Member Function*

```
#include <iostream.h>
main()
{
    char line[25];
    cout << " Type a line terminated by 'q'\n>";
    cin.getline(line, 25, 'q');
    cout << ' ' << line;
}
```

If you type after this I quit, the program screen looks like the following:

```
Type a line terminated by 'q'
after this I quit          (entered by you)
after this I               (echoed by the program)
```

Observe that some compilers include the terminating character in the final string, as shown here:

```
after this I q             (echoed by the program)
```

read

The *istream* class's *read* member function is the input equivalent of the *write* function. It reads the binary representation of the input data into the buffer without bypassing white space. It is usually used with file input/output, described later.

Exercise 10.14 is an example of using the *read* function to read a string of characters from the keyboard into a structure.

Exercise 10.14 *The* ***istream read*** *Function*

```
#include <iostream.h>
main()
{
    struct    {
        char msg[23];
    } data;

    cin.read( (char *) &data, sizeof data);
    cout << data.msg;
}
```

Exercise 10.14 reads whatever you type into the structure and echoes it to the screen.

OVERLOADING THE << INSERTION AND >> EXTRACTION OPERATORS

The overloaded insertion and extraction operators work with the standard C++ data types. A user-defined class can overload them to work with the data formats of the class itself, making a program more readable. It is clearer when a program can use the second of the following two statements:

```
dt.display(); // call a member function to display
cout << dt;   // send the dt object to the cout object
```

The second statement is also more flexible, as you will soon see. The overloaded insertion operator can work with *ostream* objects other than just *cout*. Similarly, the overloaded extraction operator can work with *istream* objects other than *cin*. You might, for example, display a class on the *cerr* stream or write it to a file.

Overloading <<

Consider the *Date* class that the exercises in this book have used extensively. Usually the *Date* class in an exercise also has a *display* member function that sends the data members to the *cout* object in a date format. The following is a more intuitive way to display a class object:

```
Date dt(1,2,88);
cout << dt;
```

To get the *cout* object to accept a *Date* object along with the insertion operator, the program must overload the insertion operator to recognize an *ostream* object on the left and a *Date* on the right. The overloaded << operator function must then be a friend to the *Date* class definition so that it can access the private data members of the *Date*.

Exercise 10.15 overloads the << insertion operator with an *iostream* object on the left and a *Date* object on the right.

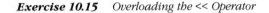

Exercise 10.15   *Overloading the << Operator*

```
#include <iostream.h>
class Date {
    int mo, da, yr;
public:
    Date(int m, int d, int y) { mo = m; da = d; yr = y; }
    friend ostream& operator<< (ostream& os, Date& dt);
};
ostream& operator<< (ostream& os, Date& dt)
{
    os << dt.mo << '/' << dt.da << '/' << dt.yr;
    return os;
}
main()
{
    Date dt(5, 6, 77);
    cout << dt;
}
```

Exercise 10.15 displays the date **5/6/77** on the screen.

Overloading >>

Overloading the >> extraction operator allows a class to have an intelligent class input function that knows about the input requirements of the class's data members. Exercise 10.16 is an example of overloading the extraction operator to read a date into the *Date* class.

Exercise 10.16 *Overloading the >> Operator*

```
#include <iostream.h>
class Date {
    int mo, da, yr;
public:
    Date() {}
    friend ostream& operator<< (ostream& os, Date& dt);
    friend istream& operator>> (istream& is, Date& dt);
};
ostream& operator<< (ostream& os, Date& dt)
{
    os << dt.mo << '/' << dt.da << '/' << dt.yr;
    return os;
}
istream& operator>> (istream& is, Date& dt)
{
    is >> dt.mo >> dt.da >> dt.yr;
    return is;
}
main()
{
    Date dt;
    cout << "Enter a date (mm dd yy): ";
    cin >> dt;
    cout << dt;
}
```

Exercise 10.16 displays a date that you enter, as shown here:

```
Enter a date (mm dd yy): 6 29 90
6/29/90
```

With the overloaded >> operator in the exercise, the user enters the three components of a date with intervening spaces. The overloaded >> operator in *istream* skips white space, so the *Date* overloaded >> operator function uses that feature to collect three integers from *cin*. You might prefer to read the date into a string with intervening slashes or dashes and then use the Standard C *atoi* function to parse the values into the *Date* class data members. A complete date input function would validate the values for the month, day, and year.

FILE INPUT/OUTPUT

A file stream is an extension of a console stream. File stream classes are derived from the console stream classes and inherit all the characteristics of the console. But files have some requirements of their own that character devices such as the console do not have. Files have distinct names. A program can append data to an existing file. A program can seek to a specified position in a file. The class inheritance facility of C++ is a natural way to build file classes from console classes, and that is how the file stream classes work.

A program that uses the file stream classes must include the **fstream.h** header file where the classes are defined. The program might also include **iostream.h**, but it is not necessary because **fstream.h** itself includes **iostream.h**.

The *ofstream* Class

The *ofstream* class objects are files that a program can write to. In the most elementary use of *ofstream*, the program declares an object of type *ofstream*, gives it a name, and writes to it. When the object goes out of scope, the file closes.

Exercise 10.17 uses an *ofstream* object in its simplest form.

Exercise 10.17 *File Output*

```
#include <fstream.h>
main()
{
    ofstream tfile("test.dat");
    tfile << "This is test data";
}
```

The program creates a file and writes a string to it.

You can use the *ofstream* class to append to an existing file. Exercise 10.18 appends a string to the file that Exercise 10.17 created.

Exercise 10.18 *Appending to an Output File*

```
#include <fstream.h>
main()
{
    ofstream tfile("test.dat", ios::app);
    tfile << ", and this is more";
}
```

The *write* member function works well with *ofstream* classes. Exercise 10.19 shows how the *write* function can record the binary representation of a class object into a data file.

Exercise 10.19 *The **write** Member Function*

```
#include <fstream.h>
class Date    {
    int mo, da, yr;
public:
    Date(int m, int d, int y)
        { mo = m; da = d; yr = y; }
};
```

continued

Exercise 10.19 *The **write** Member Function (continued)*

```
main()
{
    Date dt(6, 24, 40);
    ofstream tfile("date.dat");
    tfile.write((char *) &dt, sizeof dt);
}
```

The program creates the file and writes the binary value of the *Date* object into it. The *write* function does not stop writing when it reaches a null character, so the complete class structure is written regardless of its content.

The *ifstream* Class

The *ifstream* class objects are input files. A program can declare an input file stream object and read it. A program can use the >> extraction operator, the *get* function, or the *getline* function just as if the stream were the console device rather than a file. A program can also use the *read* member function to read binary blocks into memory.

Exercise 10.20 is a program that reads the *Date* object from xthe file written by Exercise 10.19.

Exercise 10.20 *The **read** Member Function*

```
#include <fstream.h>
class Date    {
    int mo, da, yr;
public:
    Date() { }
    friend ostream& operator<< (ostream& os, Date& dt);
};
ostream& operator<< (ostream& os, Date& dt)
{
    os << dt.mo << '/' << dt.da << '/' << dt.yr;
    return os;
}
```

continued

Exercise 10.20 *The **read** Member Function (continued)*

```
main()
{
    Date dt;
    ifstream tfile("date.dat");
    tfile.read((char *) &dt, sizeof dt);
    cout << dt;
}
```

Exercise 10.20 displays the date **6/24/40** on the screen.

Streams have a number of status bits that reflect the current state of the stream. The values of the bits are defined in an *enum* in the *ios* class, and there are member functions that can test and change the bits. The *eof* member function returns a true value if the stream has reached the end of its character stream.

Exercise 10.21 reads a text file a one character at a time, sending each character to *cout* and stopping at end-of-file.

Exercise 10.21 *Testing End-of-File*

```
#include <fstream.h>
main()
{
    ifstream tfile("test.dat");
    while (!tfile.eof())    {
        char ch;
        tfile.get(ch);
        cout << ch;
    }
}
```

Exercise 10.21 displays this message:

```
This is test data, and this is more
```

Seeking

Disk drives are random access devices. A program can modify the current position of a file stream by using one of the member functions *seekg* and *seekp*. The *seekg* function changes the position of the next input operation. The *seekp* functions changes the position of the next output operation.

Exercise 10.22 opens a file, changes the input position, and then reads to end-of-file.

Exercise 10.22   *The **seekg** Member Function*

```
#include <fstream.h>
main()
{
    ifstream tfile("test.dat");
    tfile.seekg(5);          // seek five characters in
    while (!tfile.eof())    {
        char ch;
        tfile.get(ch);
        cout << ch;
    }
}
```

Exercise 10.22 displays this message:

```
is test data, and this is more
```

By adding an argument to the function call, a program can specify that a *seekg* or *seekp* operation occurs relative to the beginning of the file, the end of the file, or the current position. The argument is defined in an *enum* in the *ios* class. The following are examples of the function calls:

```
tfile.seekg(5, ios::beg);
tfile.seekg(10, ios::cur);
tfile.seekg(-15, ios::end);
```

If you do not provide the second argument, the seek occurs from the beginning of the file.

You can determine the current position for input with the *tellg* member function and the current position for output with the *tellp* member function.

Exercise 10.23 illustrates the *tellg* function.

Exercise 10.23   *The* ***tellg*** *Function*

```
#include <fstream.h>
main()
{
    ifstream tfile("test.dat");
    while (!tfile.eof())    {
        char ch;
        streampos here = tfile.tellg();
        tfile.get(ch);
        if (ch == ' ')
            cout << "\nPosition " << here << " is a space";
    }
}
```

Exercise 10.23 displays these messages:

```
Position 4 is a space
Position 7 is a space
Position 12 is a space
Position 18 is a space
Position 22 is a space
Position 27 is a space
Position 30 is a space
```

The program reads the file built by earlier exercises and displays messages showing the character positions where it finds spaces. The *tellg* function returns an integral value of type *streampos*, a *typedef* defined in **iostream.h**.

The *fstream* Class

The *fstream* class supports file stream objects that a program opens for both input and output. Typical examples are database files in which a program reads records, updates them, and writes them back to the file.

An object of type *fstream* is a single stream with two logical substreams: one for input and one for output. Each of the two substreams has its own position pointer. The pointers follow each other. There are two pointers because they are defined in the *ifstream* and *ofstream* classes and are also available to objects of those classes.

Files opened in append mode always write to the end of the file. They also change the input position pointer to just past the last character after every write.

Exercise 10.24 is a program that reads the text file from the earlier exercises into a character array and writes an uppercase-only copy of the bytes at the end of the file.

Exercise 10.24   An fstream File

```
#include <fstream.h>
#include <ctype.h>
main()
{
    fstream tfile("test.dat", ios::in | ios::app);
    char tdata[100];
    int i = 0;
    while (!tfile.eof())
        tfile.get(tdata[i++]);
    tfile.clear();
    for (int j = 0; j < i; j++)
        tfile.put((char)toupper(tdata[j]));
}
```

The program must include the call to the *clear* member function before starting the writes because the stream is at end-of-file. The *clear* member function clears the end-of-file and all other indicators, and that allows the program to proceed with the output.

Opening and Closing a Stream File

A program can declare an *ifstream*, *ofstream*, or *fstream* object without a name. When it does, the object exists but no file is associated with it. You must then use the *open* member function to associate a file with the *fstream* object. You can disassociate the file from the object by calling the *close* member function. This technique allows a single object to represent different files at different times.

Exercise 10.25 demonstrates the use of the *open* function to associate the stream object with a file and the *close* function to disassociate the object from a file.

*Exercise 10.25   **open** and **close** Member Functions*

```
#include <fstream.h>
main()
{
    ofstream tfile;    // an ofstream object without a file
    tfile.open("test1.dat");
    tfile << "This is TEST1";
    tfile.close();
    tfile.open("test2.dat");
    tfile << "This is TEST2";
    tfile.close();
}
```

The *iostream* classes include conversion functions that return true or false values if you use the object name in a true/false conditional expression. Suppose you declare a file stream object without an initializing name and do not associate a name with that object. The following code shows how you might test for that condition:

```
fstream tfile;    // no file name given
if (tfile)        // this test returns false
    // ...
```

How to Open a File

The C and C++ stream facilities for opening files are less than instantly intuitive. Veteran programmers still have to stop and think when they are about to open a file. Does the file already exist? May the file already exist? If the file exists, should the program truncate it? Append to it? If the file does not exist, should the program create it? The variations on this theme go on and on.

The *open* member function and the implied open operation performed by the constructor take an *open_mode* integer value as a parameter. The argument values for the *open_mode* parameter are defined in the *ios* class. You optionally provide one or more of these parameters in a logical OR expression depending on how you want the file to be opened.

Following is a list of the *open_mode* bits defined in the *ios* class.

ios::app	Append to an output file. Every output operation is performed at the physical end-of-file, and the input and output file pointers are repositioned immediately past the last character written.
ios::ate	The open operation includes a seek to the end of the file. This mode can be used with input and output files.
ios::in	This is an input file and is an implied mode for ifstream objects. If you use *ios::in* as an *open_mode* for an *ofstream* file, it prevents the truncation of an existing file.
ios::out	This is an output file and is an implied mode for *ofstream* objects. When you use *ios::out* for an *ofstream* object without *ios::app* or *ios::ate*, *ios::trunc* is implied.
ios::nocreate	The file must exist; otherwise, the open fails.
ios::noreplace	The file must not exist; otherwise, the open fails.
ios::trunc	Delete the file if it already exists and re-create it.

There are seven of these bits. There are three types of objects: *ofstream*, *ifstream*, and *fstream*. Therefore, there are 381 possible open statements for you to code. Not all of them would be logical, but you could code them all. For each of them, the file might exist or it might not. Therefore, there are 762 possible circumstances. Covering them all is beyond the scope of this book. However, here are some of the most common circumstances:

1. You want to create a file. If it exists, delete the old one.

   ```
   ofstream ofile("FILENAME");  // no open_mode
   ```

2. You want to read an existing file. If it does not exist, an error has occurred.

   ```
   ifstream ifile("FILENAME");  // no open_mode
   if (ifile.fail())
       // the file does not exist ...
   ```

3. You want to read and write an existing file. This is an update mode. You might read records, seek to records, rewrite existing records, and add records to the end of the file.

   ```
   fstream ffile("FILENAME", ios::in | ios::out | ios::nocreate);
   if (ffile.fail())
   // the file does not exist ...
   ```

4. You want to write to an existing file without deleting it first.

   ```
   ofstream ofile("FILENAME", ios::in);
   ```

5. You want to append records to an existing file, creating it if it does not exist.
   ```
   ofstream ofile("FILENAME", ios::out | ios::app);
   ```

Testing Errors

A program can and should test errors when it uses input/output file streams. Each stream object has its own set of condition flags that change according to the current state of the object. You used one of these flags when you tested for end-of-file with the *eof* member function. Other member functions that test for flag settings are *bad*, *fail*, and *good*. The *bad* function returns a true value if your program attempts to do something illegal such as seek beyond the end of the file. The *fail* function returns a true value for all conditions that include the *bad* positive return plus any valid operations that fail such as trying to open an unavailable file or trying to write to a disk device that is full. The *good* function returns true whenever *fail* would return false.

Exercise 10.26 attempts and fails to open a nonexisting file for input.

Exercise 10.26 *File Error Checking*

```
#include <fstream.h>
main()
{
    ifstream ifile;
    ifile.open("noname.fil", ios::in | ios::nocreate);
    if (ifile.fail())
        cout << "Cannot open";
    else    {
        // ...
        ifile.close();
    }
}
```

Exercise 10.26 displays the **Cannot open** message on the screen.

Observe the use of the *ios::nocreate* mode value as an argument to the *open* member function. This argument tells the *open* function to fail if the file does not exist. Therefore, the call to the *fail* member function returns true because the file does not exist. This function works the same way whether you open the file with the *open* member function or specify the file name as an initializer in the declaration of the stream object.

SUMMARY

The C++ stream library has many other features and facilities. For example, there is a set of classes that supports in-memory formatting much like the *sprintf* and *sscanf* functions of C but with all the insertion and extraction operations and member functions of the *iostream* classes.

With the introduction in this chapter, you have learned how to use C++ stream classes as they apply to most input/output applications. After you have used them for a while you might want to read the description of their advanced features in the documentation that accompanies your compiler.

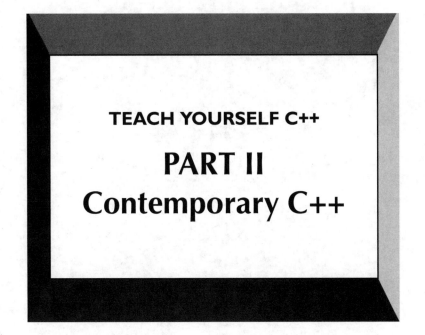

TEACH YOURSELF C++

PART II
Contemporary C++

CHAPTER 11

Templates

Contemporary C++ adds templates, exception handling, runtime type information, and a new casting mechanism to the language. This chapter shows you how and when to use templates. Future C++, addressed in Part III of this book, significantly modifies how templates work. This chapter discusses the implementation as it exists in contemporary compilers. You will learn about:

❖   Class templates
❖   Function templates

CLASS TEMPLATES

Class templates, sometimes called *parameterized data types*, allow you to describe a generic data type to manage other data types. Class templates are typically used to build general-purpose container classes, such as stacks, lists, and queues, in which the maintenance of the container is generic but the item in the container is specific.

Consider the *ListEntry* linked list class that you used in Exercises 7.20 and 7.24. These particular linked list classes manage lists of character pointers. A program might need several linked lists, with each one managing a different data type.

By using a class template, you can define a generic linked list class with an unspecified data type to be in the list. You can then associate specific classes with the template.

The format of a class template specification is shown in this example:

```
template<class T>
class LinkedList {
    T& p;
    // ...
public:
    // ...
    void AddEntry(T &entry);
};
```

The template specifies objects of type *LinkedList* with an unspecified data type as a parameter. Users of the template specify the data type to be managed by the list.

The first part of a class template definition and its member function definitions is the template specifier as shown here:

```
template<class T>
```

The *T* identifier represents the parameterized data type throughout the definition. The identifier can be any C++ data type, including intrinsic types and classes. The use of *T* for the primary template parameter is a convention, although you can use any valid C++ identifier instead.

As with normal classes, you must provide the member functions for a class template. The *LinkedList* example has an *AddEntry* member function. You define the function as shown here:

```
template<class T>
void LinkedList<T>::AddEntry(T &entry)
{
    // ...
}
```

In contemporary C++, these function definitions are in the header file that contains the class definition. They must be visible to the program that declares objects of the class template. They do not generate any code until they are used.

Future C++ proposes to provide for template member functions that can be defined outside the file scope of the using program. The compiler would resolve references to member functions and compile and instantiate relevant functions to match the parameterized types.

N O T E

You declare an object of a class template by specifying the name of the class and its parameterized data type:

```
LinkedList<int> IntList;
```

This statement declares an object from the *LinkedList* template with the *int* data type as the parameter.

Think of contemporary C++ templates as macros. The compiler uses the object declaration to build the class definition and functions. The compiler substitutes the template argument, which is *int* in the example just shown, for the template parameter, which is *T* in the *LinkedList* template example.

You can declare more than one object of a class template in the same program. For example, given the *LinkedList* template just shown, a program can declare two different linked lists, as shown here:

```
LinkedList<char *> StrList;
LinkedList<Date> DateList;
```

These statements declare two *LinkedList* objects. The first one is a list of character pointers. The second one is a list of *Date* objects. These two statements cause the compiler to generate two copies of the member functions in the template. Each copy is customized to work with the type specified in the declaration. In this example, there is a copy of the code for character pointers and one for the *Date* class. Wherever the template definition uses *T*, the compiler substitutes *char** for the first object and *Date* for the second. That means that the code in the template's member functions must work in the context of those types.

If you use the same data types for two different objects of the same template, as shown next, the compiler generates only one set of code for the two.

```
LinkedList<int> monthList;
LinkedList<int> yearList;
```

The using program calls a class template's member functions just as it calls member functions of other classes. For example, you can add entries to the *LinkedList* objects with these calls:

```
Date dt(6,24,93);        // a date
DateList.AddEntry(dt);   // add the date to DateList

char *name = "Dolly";    // a string
StrList.AddEntry(name);  // add the string to StrList

int n = 123;             // an int
IntList.AddEntry(n);     // add the int to IntList
```

A template can contain more than one data type parameter, making it possible to build parameterized data types of considerable complexity. The parameters can be classes, which are identified by the *class* keyword. Other parameters can be specific data types, as shown here:

```
template <class T, class S, int b>
```

At least one parameter should be a class. When you declare an object of the class template, you must use actual types where they are called for. In the example just shown, you can use any type for the first two parameters, but the third type must be an *int*.

Exercise 11.1 illustrates how a class template works.

Exercise 11.1 *A Simple Class Template*

```
#include <iostream.h>
template<class T1, class T2>
class MyTemp {
    T1 t1;
    T2 t2;
public:
    MyTemp(T1 tt1, T2 tt2)
        { t1 = tt1; t2 = tt2; }
    void display()
        { cout << t1 << ' ' << t2 << '\n'; }
};
main()
{
    int a = 123;
    double b = 456.789;
    MyTemp<int, double> mt(a, b);
    mt.display();
}
```

The template in Exercise 11.1 builds a parameterized type from two parameters. The class template stores values and displays them. The main function declares an object of the type with an *int* and a *double* as the parameters. Then it tells the object to display itself. Exercise 11.1 displays this output:

```
123 456.789
```

The template in Exercise 11.1 points out something to consider when you use a template. The template sends its parameterized types to the *cout* object by using the << insertion operator. Therefore, any type that you use with the template must be compatible with that operation. Exercise 11.1 works because *iostreams* can accept *ints* and *doubles* with the << operator. If a class template uses relational operators to compare objects of the parameterized type, then the type must be able to use those operators, too. C++ intrinsic types would work with such a template, but your user-defined types would not work if you have not overloaded the relational operators.

A Bounded Array Class Template

C and C++ programmers often build bugs into their programs because the language does not test whether an array subscript is within the bounds of the array. The following code passes the compiler's error tests and executes with no run-time bounds-checking.

```
main()
{
    int array[10];
    for (int i = 0; i <= 10; i++)
        array[i] = 123;
}
```

The problem with the code is that the subscript is allowed to go beyond the end of the array. The array has 10 elements. The subscript is allowed to go as high as 10, which references the 11th element, which does not exist. However, the program writes an integer into the next integer position in memory beyond the array. The result depends on the program and the compiler. If you are lucky, the program aborts early in testing and you find the problem. If you are not so lucky, the 11th array element is in a harmless position, and you do not encounter the bug until much later when it is more difficult to isolate.

Other languages have bounded arrays. The run-time system does not allow you to address an array with a subscript that is beyond its limits. The cost is in run-time efficiency.

You can use the template to add bounded arrays to your programs without adding a lot of overhead. The technique depends on your understanding not only of templates but also of the Standard C *assert* macro. Immediately following is **barray.h**, the class template for the bounded array.

Barray.h

```
// ------ barray.h
#include <assert.h>
// --- a bounded array template
template <class T, int b>
class Array    {
    T elem [b];
public:
    T& operator[] (int sub)
    {
        assert(sub >= 0 && sub < b);
        return elem[sub];
    }
};
```

This simple template has one purpose: to check all subscripted references to array elements and abort the program if a subscript is out of bounds. Observe that the template specifier has two parameter types:

```
template <class T, int b>
```

NOTE

If the template included non-inline member functions, the statement just shown would be immediately ahead of the function definitions as well.

The overloaded subscript operator ([]) function in the *Array* class template grants read-write subscripted access to elements of the array. The *assert* macro validates the subscript's value. If the value is less than zero or greater than the array's dimension minus one, the *assert* macro displays an error message on the *stderr* device and aborts the program.

Exercise 11.2 is a program that uses the bounded array template.

Exercise 11.2   *Using a Bounded Array Template*

```
#include <iostream.h>
#include <iomanip.h>
#include "barray.h"
#include "date.h"
main()
{
    // ---- a bounded array of dates
    Array<Date, 5> dateArray;
    // ----- some dates
    Date dt1(12,17,37);
    Date dt2(11,30,38);
    Date dt3(6,24,40);
    Date dt4(10,31,42);
    Date dt5(8,5,44);
    // ----- put the dates in the array
    dateArray[0] = dt1;
    dateArray[1] = dt2;
    dateArray[2] = dt3;
    dateArray[3] = dt4;
    dateArray[4] = dt5;
    // ------ display the dates
    for (int i = 0; i < 5; i++)    {
        dateArray[i].display();
        cout << '\n';
    }
    cout << flush;
    // ---- try to put a date in the array
    //      outside the range of the subscript
    Date dt6(1,29,92);
    dateArray[5] = dt6;  // template's assertion aborts
}
```

Make sure that you link this program with the **date.cpp** program from Chapter 9. The program declares an *Array* object of *Date* objects with a subscript limit of five. Then it declares five *Date* objects, which it puts into the array. After displaying all five objects, the program flushes *cout* and then tries to put another *Date* object into the array's sixth position, which does not exist. The *assert* macro's test is false, and the program aborts. Exercise 11.2 displays this output:

```
12/17/37
11/30/38
6/24/40
10/31/42
8/5/44
Assertion failed: sub >= 0 && sub < b,
file barray.h, line 11
Abnormal program termination
```

The format of the error message depends on the compiler, but the information displayed is the same.

After your program is fully tested, you can remove the assertion code by inserting this line before the *include* of **assert.h**:

```
#define NDEBUG
```

When to Use Class Templates

Templates surround other types with generic management. The types that you provide as parameters have their own behavior. The class templates provide a way to contain objects of those classes in general-purpose containers. The details of their containment are unrelated to their purposes. A *Date* class has its own behavior. So does a *string* class. So does a class that encapsulates a person's name, address, and phone number. Their participation in a queue, list, bag, linked list, balanced tree, or any other kind of container is unrelated to their purpose. It is natural and proper to use the features of a programming language to separate these two unrelated behaviors.

Before C++ supported templates, programmers used inheritance to associate data types with container classes. In other cases they built cumbersome classes that used *void* pointers and casts to manage the containment of unrelated types in various containers. These approaches worked well enough, but they are not always the best ones. As a rule you should use inheritance when the derived class modifies the functional behavior of the base. When the relationship manages objects of the class without changing the class's behavior, you should use templates.

There are other considerations, however. If the management algorithm entails a lot of code in the class definition and its member functions and if you plan to instantiate many different parameterized versions of the template, think twice before you build the entire algorithm as a template. Remember that each distinct use of the template generates a new copy of the code. If the template manages a significant number of different types, the executable program can be big. Programmers often separate the common code that is not influenced by the parameterized type into a base class from which they derive the class template. The base class code is instantiated only once irrespective of the number of discrete type instantiations of the derived class template.

A Linked List Template

You used the *LinkedList* class at the beginning of this chapter to see how templates work. Now you implement a complete *LinkedList* class template. Immediately following is **linklist.h**, the header file that defines the *LinkedList* template.

Linklist.h

```
// ------------ linklist.h
// a template for a linked list
template <class T>
// --- the linked list entry
class ListEntry     {
    T thisentry;
    ListEntry<T> *nextentry;
    ListEntry<T> *preventry;
    ListEntry(T& entry);
    friend class LinkedList<T>;
};
```

continued

Linklist.b *(continued)*

```
template <class T>
// ---- construct a linked list entry
ListEntry<T>::ListEntry(T &entry)
{
    thisentry = entry;
    nextentry = 0;
    preventry = 0;
}
template <class T>
// ---- the linked list
class LinkedList    {
    // --- the listhead
    ListEntry<T> *firstentry;
    ListEntry<T> *lastentry;
    ListEntry<T> *iterator;
    void RemoveEntry(ListEntry<T> *lentry);
    void InsertEntry(T& entry, ListEntry<T> *lentry);
public:
    LinkedList();
    ~LinkedList();
    void AppendEntry(T& entry);
    void RemoveEntry(int pos = -1);
    void InsertEntry(T&entry, int pos = -1);
    T *FindEntry(int pos);
    T *CurrentEntry();
    T *FirstEntry();
    T *LastEntry();
    T *NextEntry();
    T *PrevEntry();
};
```

continued

Linklist.b (continued)

```
template <class T>
// ---- construct a linked list
LinkedList<T>::LinkedList()
{
    iterator = 0;
    firstentry = 0;
    lastentry = 0;
}
template <class T>
// ---- destroy a linked list
LinkedList<T>::~LinkedList()
{
    while (firstentry)
        RemoveEntry(firstentry);
}
template <class T>
// ---- append an entry to the linked list
void LinkedList<T>::AppendEntry(T& entry)
{
    ListEntry<T> *newentry = new ListEntry<T>(entry);
    newentry->preventry = lastentry;
    if (lastentry)
        lastentry->nextentry = newentry;
    if (firstentry == 0)
        firstentry = newentry;
    lastentry = newentry;
}
```

continued

Linklist.b *(continued)*

```
template <class T>
// ---- remove an entry from the linked list
void LinkedList<T>::RemoveEntry(ListEntry<T> *lentry)
{
    if (lentry == 0)
        return;
    if (lentry == iterator)
        iterator = lentry->preventry;
    // ---- repair any break made by this removal
    if (lentry->nextentry)
        lentry->nextentry->preventry = lentry->preventry;
    if (lentry->preventry)
        lentry->preventry->nextentry = lentry->nextentry;
    // --- maintain listhead if this is last and/or first
    if (lentry == lastentry)
        lastentry = lentry->preventry;
    if (lentry == firstentry)
        firstentry = lentry->nextentry;
    delete lentry;
}
template <class T>
// ---- insert an entry into the linked list
void LinkedList<T>::InsertEntry(T& entry, ListEntry<T> *lentry)
{
    ListEntry<T> *newentry = new ListEntry<T>(entry);
    newentry->nextentry = lentry;
    if (lentry)    {
        newentry->preventry = lentry->preventry;
        lentry->preventry = newentry;
    }
    if (newentry->preventry)
        newentry->preventry->nextentry = newentry;
    if (lentry == firstentry)
        firstentry = newentry;
}
```

continued

```
template <class T>
// ---- remove an entry from the linked list
void LinkedList<T>::RemoveEntry(int pos)
{
    FindEntry(pos);
    RemoveEntry(iterator);
}
template <class T>
// ---- insert an entry into the linked list
void LinkedList<T>::InsertEntry(T& entry, int pos)
{
    FindEntry(pos);
    InsertEntry(entry, iterator);
}
template <class T>
// ---- return the current linked list entry
T *LinkedList<T>::CurrentEntry()
{
    return iterator ? &(iterator->thisentry) : 0;
}
template <class T>
// ---- return a specific linked list entry
T *LinkedList<T>::FindEntry(int pos)
{
    if (pos != -1)    {
        iterator = firstentry;
        if (iterator)    {
            while (pos--)
                iterator = iterator->nextentry;
        }
    }
    return CurrentEntry();
}
```

continued

Linklist.b (continued)

```cpp
template <class T>
// ---- return the first entry in the linked list
T *LinkedList<T>::FirstEntry()
{
    iterator = firstentry;
    return CurrentEntry();
}
template <class T>
// ---- return the last entry in the linked list
T *LinkedList<T>::LastEntry()
{
    iterator = lastentry;
    return CurrentEntry();
}
template <class T>
// ---- return the next entry in the linked list
T *LinkedList<T>::NextEntry()
{
    if (iterator == 0)
        iterator = firstentry;
    else
        iterator = iterator->nextentry;
    return CurrentEntry();
}
template <class T>
// ---- return the previous entry in the linked list
T *LinkedList<T>::PrevEntry()
{
    if (iterator == 0)
        iterator = lastentry;
    else
        iterator = iterator->preventry;
    return CurrentEntry();
}
```

This template definition builds a linked list of objects of any type. After the list is built, the user can navigate it by using the template's member functions, which return pointers to the objects in the list.

There are two templates in the **linklist.h** file. The first one is for the *ListEntry* class, which the *LinkedList* class uses. A using program cannot declare an object of this class. Observe that there is no public constructor. Only a friend of this class template can use it. the *LinkedList* class is its only friend. The *ListEntry* class contains a listed object and pointers to the next and previous objects in the list.

The *LinkedList* template contains the *listhead*: a data structure that includes pointers to the first and last entry in the class and an *iterator* pointer that the class uses to navigate the list. These pointers point to *ListEntry* objects.

There are two private member functions used by the *LinkedList* class to insert and remove *ListEntry* objects from the list. The *LinkedList* class constructs and destroys these *ListEntry* objects.

The *LinkedList* class's public interface consists of a constructor and destructor, member functions to append, insert, and remove objects of the type, and member functions to navigate the list. The following exercises demonstrate this behavior.

A Linked List of Integers

Exercise 11.3 is a program that uses the *LinkedList* class to maintain a list of integers.

Exercise 11.3   *Using a Linked List Template for Integers*

```
#include <iostream.h>
#include "linklist.h"
main()
{
    LinkedList<int> IntList;
    // --- add 10 integers to the linked list
    for (int i = 0; i < 10; i++)
        IntList.AppendEntry(i);
```

continued

Exercise 11.3 *Using a Linked List Template for Integers (continued)*

```
    // --- iterate thru the 10 and remove #5
    int *ip = IntList.FirstEntry();
    while (ip)     {
        cout << *ip << ' ';
        if (*ip == 5)
            IntList.RemoveEntry();
        ip = IntList.NextEntry();
    }   // --- iterate thru what's left
    cout << '\n';
    while ((ip = IntList.NextEntry()) != 0)
        cout << *ip << ' ';
}
```

The program in Exercise 11.3 declares a *LinkedList* object with *int* as the type parameter. Then it adds 10 integers to the list. Next the program uses a *FirstEntry* call and a series of *NextEntry* calls to iterate through the list, displaying each integer as it retrieves it. When it finds the list entry with the value 5, the program calls *RemoveEntry* to remove the entry from the list. When it is at the end, the program iterates through the list a second time, displaying the values to prove that number 5 was removed. Exercise 11.3 displays this output:

```
0 1 2 3 4 5 6 7 8 9
0 1 2 3 4 6 7 8 9
```

A Linked List of Dates

Exercise 11.4 uses the *LinkedList* template to build and maintain a list of *Date* objects. For this exercise you link the program with the *Date* class from Chapter 9.

Exercise 11.4   *Using a Linked List Template for Dates*

```cpp
#include <iostream.h>
#include "linklist.h"
#include "date.h"
main()
{
    LinkedList<Date> DateList;
    Date dt1(12,17,37);
    Date dt2(11,30,38);
    Date dt3(6,24,40);
    Date dt4(10,31,42);
    Date dt5(8,5,44);
    // --- add 5 dates to the linked list
    DateList.AppendEntry(dt1);
    DateList.AppendEntry(dt2);
    DateList.AppendEntry(dt3);
    DateList.AppendEntry(dt4);
    DateList.AppendEntry(dt5);
    // --- iterate thru the dates
    cout << "---Forward---\n";
    Date *dp;
    while ((dp = DateList.NextEntry()) != 0)    {
        dp->display();
        cout << '\n';
    }
    // --- insert a date
    Date dt6(1,29,92);
    DateList.InsertEntry(dt6, 3);
```

continued

Exercise 11.4 *Using a Linked List Template for Dates (continued)*

```
    // --- iterate thru the dates
    cout << "---Backward---\n";
    dp = DateList.LastEntry();
    while (dp != 0)    {
        dp->display();
        cout << '\n';
        dp = DateList.PrevEntry();
    }
}
```

The program in Exercise 11.4 declares a *LinkedList* object with the *Date* type. Then it declares five *Date* objects, which it puts into the list by calling the *AppendEntry* function. The program iterates through the list and displays the *Date* objects. Then it inserts a date by calling the *InsertEntry* function with a *Date* object and the integer parameter 3. The integer parameter specifies that the insertion is to occur before the fourth entry in the list. A zero value would insert the object at the front of the list. Finally, the program iterates through the list in reverse order by calling *LastEntry* and then *PrevEntry* until there are no more entries returned. The exercise displays the dates in reverse order to prove that the insertion worked. Exercise 11.4 displays this output:

```
---Forward---
12/17/37
11/30/38
6/24/40
10/31/42
8/5/44
---Backward---
8/5/44
10/31/42
1/29/92
6/24/40
11/30/38
12/17/37
```

Template Specialization

You can generate a specialized version of a complete class template or of selected member functions of a class template. Specialized templates and functions allow the programmer to define specific behavior related to a particular type. The specialized class or function overrides the class template or template member function when a template object is instantiated by using the specialized type.

Class Template Specialization

Exercise 11.5 illustrates the specializaton of a class template. This exercise defines a class template named *Set*, which has a constructor and a member function named *display*. The *display* function sends the data value of the type being parameterized to the standard *cout* object. Not all types, however, overload the << operator in that way. The *Date* class used in previous exercises is an example. The program in Exercise 11.5, therefore provides a specialized class for instantiation of the *Set* template when the type being parameterized is a *Date*.

Exercise 11.5   *Class Template Specialization*

```
// ex11005.cpp
// class template specialization
#include <iostream.h>
#include "date.h"
template <class T>
class Set    {
    T t;
public:
    Set(T st) : t(st) { }
    void display() { cout << t << '\n'; }
};
// ----- specialized class template
class Set<Date>    {
    Date t;
public:
    Set(Date st) : t(st) { }
    void display() { t.display(); }
};
```

continued

Exercise 11.5   *Class Template Specialization (continued)*

```
main()
{
    Set<int> intset(123);
    Set<Date> dt = Date(1,2,3);
    intset.display();
    dt.display();
}
```

Exercise 11.5 displays these values:

```
123
1/2/3
```

Template Member Function Specialization

The program in Exercise 11.5 specializes the complete *Set* class template even though only the *display* member function changes in the specialization. An alternative approach is to specialize only the member functions that change. Exercise 11.6 modifies the program to eliminate the specialized class template and substitute a specialization of the *display* member function only.

Exercise 11.6   *Template Member Function Specialization*

```
// ex11006.cpp
// template member function specialization
#include <iostream.h>
#include "date.h"

template <class T>
class Set    {
    T t;
public:
    Set(T st) : t(st) { }
    void display();
};
```

continued

Exercise 11.6 *Template Member Function Specialization (continued)*

```
template <class T>
void Set<T>::display()
{
    cout << t << '\n';
}
// ----- specialized class template member function
void Set<Date>::display()
{
    t.display();
}
main()
{
    Set<int> intset(123);
    Set<Date> dt = Date(1,2,3);
    intset.display();
    dt.display();
}
```

Exercise 11.6 displays these values:

```
123
1/2/3
```

N O T E

The member function being specialized cannot be inline in the original template definition.

FUNCTION TEMPLATES

A template can define a parameterized nonmember function. A typical example substitutes templates for the *min* and *max* macros often defined in C. Before considering the function template, consider those C macros:

```
#define min(a,b) ((a)<(b)?(a):(b))
#define max(a,b) ((a)>(b)?(a):(b))
```

These macros have a problem related to side effects. Suppose you call one of the macros this way:

```
a = min(b++, --c);
```

The *min* macro would expand that expression into this:

```
a = (b++) < (--c) ? (b++) : (--c);
```

The side effects occur when either *b* gets incremented twice or *c* gets decremented twice depending on which one is greater. C++ programmers overcome that problem with an inline function as shown here:

```
inline int min(int a, int b)
{
    return (a < b ? a : b);
}
```

There are no side effects, but there is a problem. The *min* function now works with integers only. If your type cannot be converted to a meaningful integral value, then it does not work with the inline *min* function. The apparent solution is to use a function template as shown here:

```
template<class T>
T& min(T& a, T& b)
{
    return (a < b ? a : b);
}
```

This solution isn't perfect either. It won't work unless both objects being compared are of the same type and are either both *const* or non-*const*. But at least now you have one more choice.

Future C++ might allow *const* and non-*const* objects to be used to call the *min* function just shown. This usage would allow you to compare a *const* argument with a non-*const* literal, for example. Some contemporary C++ compilers already permit this usage.

N O T E

Sorting with a Template

The next example of function templates sorts arrays of parameterized types. The Standard C *qsort* function does that by having you provide a call-back function that performs the comparisons of array elements. Using a template, however, is easier as long as the type supports comparisons by overloading relational operators. Immediately following is **quiksort.h**, the definition of the *quicksort* function template.

Quicksort.h

```
// -------- quiksort.h
#ifndef QUIKSORT_H
#define QUIKSORT_H
// ---- function template for quicksort algorithm
template<class T>
inline void swap(T& t1, T& t2)
{
    T hold = t2;
    t2 = t1;
    t1 = hold;
}
```

continued

Quicksort.h (continued)

```cpp
template<class T>
void quicksort(T *array, int hi, int lo = 0)
{
    while (hi > lo)    {
        int i = lo;
        int j = hi;
        //  sort everything higher than median above it
        //  and everything lower below it
        while (i < j)     {
            while (array[++i] < array[lo] && i < j-1)
                ;
            while (array[--j] > array[lo])
                ;
            if (i < j)
                swap(array[j], array[i]);
        }
        swap(array[lo], array[j]);
        // --- sort the set with the fewer number of elements
        if (j - lo > hi - (j+1))     {
            // --- sort the bottom set
            quicksort(array, j, lo);
            lo = j+1;
        }
        else    {
            // --- sort the top set
            quicksort(array, hi, j+1);
            hi = j-1;
        }
    }
}
#endif
```

The template implements the *quicksort* algorithm. It sorts an array of types. Its parameters are the address of the array and the number of elements in the array.

The *quicksort* algorithm divides the array into two parts. First, it arbitrarily selects an element to represent the median value. (This implementation of the algorithm uses the first element in the array for the median value, which, as a guess, is no better or worse than selecting any other element in the array.) Then the algorithm places all elements greater than that value in the upper part and all the lower elements in the lower part. Then it calls itself recursively, once for each of the two parts. When there is only one part left, the array is fully sorted.

Exercise 11.7 is a program that uses the *quicksort* function template to sort integers.

Exercise 11.7 *Using the* **Quicksort** *Function Template*

```
#include <iostream.h>
#include <iomanip.h>
#include <stdlib.h>
#include "quiksort.h"
main()
{
    int dim;
    // --- get the number of integers to sort
    cout << "How many integers?\n";
    cin >> dim;
    // --- build an array of random integers
    int *arrs = new int[dim];
    for (int i = 0; i < dim; i++)
        arrs[i] = rand();
    // --- display the random integers
    cout << "\n----- unsorted -----\n";
    for (i = 0; i < dim; i++)
        cout << setw(8) << arrs[i];
    // --- sort the array
    quicksort(arrs, dim);
    // --- display the sorted integers
    cout << "\n----- sorted -----\n";
    for (i = 0; i < dim; i++)
        cout << setw(8) << arrs[i];
    delete[] arrs;
}
```

The program in Exercise 11.7 builds an array of integers, reading the dimension for the array from the keyboard. It uses the Standard C *rand* function to fill the array with random numbers and displays the numbers in their random sequence. Then it calls the *quicksort* function template to sort the array. Finally, the program displays the array in its new sequence.

SUMMARY

To contemporary C++ templates add *genericity*, an object-oriented feature that was missing in traditional C++ and that many programmers judged to be a major deficiency in the language. Chapter 12 continues the discussion of contemporary C++ by describing exception handling.

CHAPTER 12

Exception Handling

Exception handling is a contemporary C++ feature that lets a program intercept and process exceptional conditions—errors, usually—in an orderly, organized, and consistent manner. In this chapter, you will learn about:

- ❖ Traditional C exception handling
- ❖ Why traditional methods do not work in C++
- ❖ The C++ try/throw/catch idiom
- ❖ Anomalies in C++ exception handling

Exception handling allows one section of a program to sense and dispatch error conditions, and another section to handle them. It is not unusual for one category of code, perhaps the classes and functions in a library, to know how to detect errors without knowing the appropriate handling strategy. It is just as usual for other categories of code to understand how to deal with errors without being able to detect them.

289

For example, a class library function may perform math, detecting overflow, underflow, divide-by-zero, and other exceptional conditions that are the result of user input. Selection of a strategy for handling the exception depends on the application. Some programs write error messages on the console; others display dialog boxes in a graphical user interface; some request the user to enter better data; still others terminate the program. The error could result from a bug in the program or an invalid (and unvalidated) user input. A reusable library function should not presume to know the best exception handling strategy for all applications. On the other hand, an application cannot be expected to detect all possible exceptions.

An example of this relationship is the bounded array class template in Chapter 11. The class detects when an array subscript is out of range by using the *assert* macro, which terminates the program. A more appropriate behavior would be to detect and report the error to the class user and let the user determine how to handle it.

This relationship—that a distant function can report an error to the using program—has implications. Somehow, the detecting function must return control to the handling function through an orderly sequence of function returns. The detecting function can be many function calls deep. An orderly return to the higher level of the handler function requires—at the very least—a coordinated unwinding of the stack.

EXCEPTION HANDLING IN C

Traditional C programs take two approaches to exception handling: They follow each function call with a test for errors; and they use *setjmp* and *longjmp* to intercept error conditions. The first approach, which uses something like *errno* and null or ERROR function return values to report the nature of the error, is reliable but tedious. Programmers tend to avoid or overlook all the possibilities. The *setjmp/longjmp* approach is closer to what C++ exception handling strives for: an orderly and automatic way to unwind the stack to a state that was recorded at a specified place higher in the function-call hierarchy.

The *setjmp/longjmp* approach is intended to intercept and handle conditions that do not require immediate program termination.

Examples: A programming language translator's syntax checker can be in the depths of a recursive descent parser when it detects a syntax error. The program does not need to terminate. It should simply report the error and find its way back to where it can read the next statement and continue. The program uses *setjmp* to identify that place and *longjmp* to get back to it. Following is a code fragment that represents that process.

```
#include <setjmp.h>
jmp_buf jb;
void Validate()
{
    int err;
    err = setjmp(jb);
    if (err)
        /* An exception has occurred */
        ReportError(err);
    while (getInput())
        parse();
}
// --- parse a line of input
void parse()
{
    /* parse the input */
    /* ... */
    if (error)
        longjmp(jb, ErrorCode);
}
```

The *longjmp* call unwinds the stack to its state as recorded in the *jmp_buf* by the *setjmp* call. The initial *setjmp* call returns zero. The *longjmp* call jumps to a return from the *setjmp* call and causes *setjmp* to seem to return the specified error code, which should be nonzero.

There are anomalies in this scheme, however. And, as you will soon learn, C++ exception handling does not solve all of them. Suppose that the parse function looked like this:

```
void parse()
{
    FILE *fp = fopen(fname, "rt");
    char *cp = malloc(1000);
    /* parse the input */
    /* ... */
    if (error)
        longjmp(jb, ErrorCode);
    free(cp);
    fclose(fp);
}
```

Ignore for the moment that in a real program the function would test for exceptions to the *fopen* and *malloc* calls. The two calls represent resources that the program acquires before and releases after the *longjmp* call. The calls could be in interim functions that are called after the *setjmp* operation and that themselves called the *parse* function. The point is that the *longjmp* call occurs before those resources are released. Therefore, every exception in this program represents two system resources that are lost—a heap segment and a file handle. In the case of the FILE* resource, subsequent attempts to open the same file would fail. If each pass through the system opened a different file—a temporary file with a system-generated file name, for example—the program would fail when the operating system ran out of file handles. Programmers traditionally solve this problem by structuring their programs to avoid it. Either they manage and clean up resources before calling *longjmp* or they do not use *longjmp* where there are interim resources at risk. In the function just shown, the problem is solved by moving the *longjmp* call below the *free* and *fclose* calls. It is not always that simple, however.

Unwinding the stack in a C program involves resetting the stack pointer to where it pointed when *setjmp* is called. The *jmp_buf* stores everything that the program needs to know to do that. This procedure works because the stack contains automatic variables and function return addresses. Resetting the stack pointer essentially discards the automatic variables and forgets about the function return addresses—all of which is correct behavior, because the automatic variables are no longer needed and the interim functions are not to be resumed.

EXCEPTION HANDLING IN C++

Using *longjmp* to unwind the stack in a C++ program does not work, because automatic variables on the stack include objects of classes, and those objects need to execute their destructor functions. Consider this modification to the *parse* function, which is now in a C++ program:

```
void parse()
{
    string str("Parsing now");
    // parse the input
    // ...
    if (error)
        longjmp(jb, ErrorCode);
}
```

Assume that the constructor for the *string* class allocates memory for the string value from the heap. Its destructor returns that memory to the heap. In this program, however, the *string* destructor does not execute because *longjmp* unwinds the stack and jumps to the *setjmp* call before the *str* object goes out of scope. The memory used by the *str* object itself is returned to the stack, but the heap memory pointed to by a pointer in the string is not returned to the heap.

The problem just shown is one that C++ exception handling solves. The unwinding of the stack in the exception handling *throw* operation—the analogue to *longjmp*—includes calls to the destructors of automatic objects. Furthermore, if the *throw* occurs from within the constructor of an automatic object, its destructor is not called, although the destructors of objects embedded in the throwing object are called.

The *try* Block

C++ functions that can sense and recover from errors execute from within a *try* block that looks like this:

```
try {
    // C++ statements
}
```

Code executing outside any *try* block cannot detect or handle exceptions. *Try* blocks may be nested. The *try* block typically calls other functions that are able to detect exceptions.

The *catch* Exception Handler

A *try* block is followed by a *catch* exception handler with a parameter list as shown here:

```
try {
    // C++ statements
}
catch(int err) {
    // error-handling code
}
```

There can be multiple *catch* handlers with different parameter lists.

```
try {
    // C++ statements
}
catch(int err) {
    // error-handling code
}
catch(char *msg) {
    // error-handling code with char *
}
```

The *catch* handler is identified by the type in its parameter list. The parameter in the *catch* parameter list does not have to be named. If the parameter is named, it declares an object with that name, and the exception-detection code can pass a value in the parameter. If the parameter is unnamed, the exception-detection code can jump to the *catch* exception handler merely by naming the type.

The *throw* Statement

To detect an exception and jump to a *catch* handler, a C++ function issues the *throw* statement with a data type that matches the parameter list of the proper *catch* handler:

```
throw "An error has occurred";
```

This *throw* statement would jump to the *catch* exception handler function that has the *char** parameter list.

The *throw* statement unwinds the stack, cleaning up all objects declared within the *try* block by calling their destructors. Next, *throw* calls the matching *catch* handler, passing the parameter object.

The *try/throw/catch* Sequence

Exercise 12.1 begins to bring it all together:

Exercise 12.1 *Throwing and Catching an Exception*

```
#include <iostream.h>
void foo();
class Bummer {}; // an exception to be thrown
main()
{
    // --- the try block
    try {
        cout << "\ncalling foo";
        foo();
        cout << "\nreturn from foo";
    }
```

continued

Exercise 12.1 *Throwing and Catching an Exception (continued)*

```
    // --- catch exception handler
    catch(Bummer)   {
        // error-handling code
        cout << "\ncatching Bummer";
    }
    cout << "\ndone";
}
// --- program function
void foo()
{
    int error = 1;
    // C++ statements to do stuff
    if (error)    {
        cout << "\nthrowing Bummer";
        throw Bummer();
    }
}
```

Exercise 12.1 displays this output:

```
calling foo
throwing Bummer
catching Bummer
done
```

In Exercise 12.1, the program enters a *try* block, which means that functions called directly or indirectly from within the *try* block can throw exceptions. In other words, the *foo* function can throw exceptions and so can any function called by *foo*, and so on.

The *catch* exception handler function immediately following the *try* block is the only handler in this example. It catches exceptions that are thrown with a *Bummer* parameter. *Bummer* is a class set up specifically to identify the exception.

Catch handlers and their matching *throw* statements can have a parameter of any type. For example:

```
catch(ErrorCode ec) { ... }
// ...
throw ErrorCode(123);
```

This example assumes that there is a class named *ErrorCode* that can be constructed with an integer parameter list. The *throw* statement builds a temporary object of type *ErrorCode* and initializes the object with the value given in the *throw* statement. The parameter may be an automatic variable within the block that uses *throw*, even if the *catch* uses a reference, as shown here:

```
void bar()
{
    try {
        foo();
    }
    catch(ErrorCode& ec)    {
        // ...
    }
}
// ...
void foo()
{
    // ...
    if (error) {
        ErrorCode dt(234);
        throw dt;
    }
}
```

The *throw* statement builds a temporary *ErrorCode* object to pass to the *catch* handler. The automatic *ErrorCode* object in the *foo* function is allowed to go out of scope. The temporary *ErrorCode* object is not destroyed until the *catch* handler completes processing.

When a *try* block has more than one *catch* handler, a *throw* executes the one that matches the parameter list. That handler is the only one to execute unless it throws an exception to execute a different *catch* handler. When the executing *catch* handler exits, the program proceeds with the code following the last *catch* handler. Exercise 12.2 demonstrates this behavior.

Exercise 12.2   *Multiple catch Handlers*

```
#include <iostream.h>
void foo();
class Bummer {}; // an exception to be thrown
class Dumber {}; // an exception to be thrown
main()
{
    // --- the try block
    try {
        cout << "\ncalling foo";
        foo();
        cout << "\nreturn from foo";
    }
    // --- catch exception handler
    catch(Bummer)   {
        // error-handling code
        cout << "\ncatching Bummer";
    }
    catch(Dumber)   {
        // error-handling code
        cout << "\ncatching Dumber";
    }
    cout << "\ndone";
}
// --- program function
void foo()
{
    int error = 1;
    // C++ statements to do stuff
    if (error)   {
        cout << "\nthrowing Dumber";
        throw Dumber();
    }
}
```

Exercise 12.2 displays this output:

```
calling foo
throwing Dumber
catching Dumber
done
```

Exception Specification

You can specify the exceptions that a function may throw when you declare the function, as shown here:

```
void f() throw(Dumber, Killer)
{
    // C++ statements
    if (err1)
        throw Dumber();
    if (err2)
        throw(Killer());
}
```

The exception specification is part of the function's signature. You must include it in the prototype and in the function's definition header block. Otherwise, the compiler reports a type mismatch when it encounters the second declaration of the function.

N O T E

The Microsoft Visual C++ 2.0 compiler does not implement exception specifications in the function declaration block.

Unexpected Exceptions

If a function includes an exception specification as shown above and if the function throws an exception not given in the specification, the exception is passed to a system function named *unexpected*. The *unexpected* function calls the latest function named as an argument in a call to the *set_unexpected* function, which returns its current setting. A function with no exception specification can throw any exception.

Catch-all Exception Handlers

A *catch* handler with ellipses for a parameter list, shown next, catches all uncaught exceptions:

```
catch(...)  {
    // error-handling code
}
```

In a group of catches associated with a *try* block, the catch-all handler must appear last. Exercise 12.3 demonstrates the catch-all handler.

Exercise 12.3   A Catch-all Handler

```
#include <iostream.h>
void foo();
class Bummer {}; // an exception to be thrown
class Dumber {}; // an exception to be thrown
class Killer {}; // an exception to be thrown
```

continued

Exercise 12.3   *A Catch-all Handler (continued)*

```
main()
{
    // --- the try block
    try {
        cout << "\ncalling foo";
        foo();
        cout << "\nreturn from foo";
    }
    // --- catch exception handler
    catch(Bummer) {
        // error-handling code
        cout << "\ncatching Bummer";
    }
    catch(Dumber) {
        // error-handling code
        cout << "\ncatching Dumber";
    }
    catch(...) {
        // catching leftovers
        cout << "\ncatching Killer";
    }
    cout << "\ndone";
}
// --- program function
void foo()
{
    int error = 1;
    // C++ statements to do stuff
    if (error) {
        cout << "\nthrowing Killer";
        throw Killer();
    }
}
```

The catch-all handler in Exercise 12.3 catches the *Killer* exception because none of the other *catch* handlers has a matching *Killer* parameter list. Exercise 12.3 displays this output:

```
calling foo
throwing Killer
catching Killer
done
```

Throwing an Exception from a Handler

You can code a *throw* with no operand in a *catch* handler or in a function called by one. The *throw* with no operand rethrows the original exception. Exercise 12.4 demonstrates this behavior.

Exercise 12.4   *Rethrowing Exceptions*

```
#include <iostream.h>
void foo();
class Bummer {}; // an exception to be thrown
main()
{
    // --- the try block
    try  {
        // --- an inner try block
        try   {
            cout << "\ncalling foo";
            foo();
        }
        catch(...)   {
            cout << "\nrethrowing Bummer";
            throw;    // rethrow the exception
        }
    }
    // --- catch exception handler
    catch(Bummer)   {
        // error-handling code
        cout << "\ncatching Bummer";
    }
    cout << "\ndone";
}
```

continued

Exercise 12.4   *Rethrowing Exceptions (continued)*

```
// --- program function
void foo()
{
    int error = 1;
    // C++ statements to do stuff
    if (error)    {
        cout << "\nthrowing Bummer";
```

Exercise 12.4 displays this output:

```
calling foo
throwing Bummer
rethrowing Bummer
catching Bummer
done
```

Uncaught Exceptions

An uncaught exception is one for which there is no *catch* handler specified or one thrown by a destructor that is executing as the result of another throw. Such an exception causes the *terminate* function to be called, which calls *abort* to terminate the program. Exercise 12.5 illustrates this behavior.

Exercise 12.5   *Uncaught Exceptions*

```
#include <iostream.h>
void foo();
class Bummer {}; // an exception to be thrown
class Killer {}; // an exception to be thrown
main()
{
    // --- the try block
    try  {
 cout << "\ncalling foo";
        foo();
    }
    // --- catch exception handler
    catch(Bummer)   {
        // error-handling code
        cout << "\ncatching Bummer";
    }
    cout << "\ndone";
}
// --- program function
void foo()
{
    int error = 1;
    // C++ statements to do stuff
    if (error)    {
        cout << "\nthrowing Killer\n";
        throw Killer();
    }
}
```

Exercise 12.5 displays this output:

```
calling foo
throwing Killer
Abnormal program termination
```

N O T E

The last part of the output depends on what the compiler's *abort* function displays before it terminates the program. The Microsoft Visual C++ compiler aborts the program before displaying the first two messages.

You can specify a function for *terminate* to call by calling the *set_terminate* function, which returns its current value. Exercise 12.6 demonstrates that usage.

Exercise 12.6 *Catching Uncaught Exceptions*

```
#include <iostream.h>
#include <stdlib.h>
#include <except.h>
class Bummer {}; // an exception to be thrown
class Killer {}; // an exception to be thrown
// --- to catch uncaught exceptions
void terminator_2()
{
    cout << "catching the uncaught\n";
    exit(-1);
}
main()
{
    set_terminate(&terminator_2);
    // --- the try block
    try {
        cout << "throwing Killer\n";
        throw Killer();
    }
    // --- catch exception handler
    catch(Bummer)   {
        // error-handling code
        cout << "\ncatching Bummer";
    }
    cout << "\ndone";
}
```

Exercise 12.6 displays this output:

```
throwing Killer
catching the uncaught
```

NOTE

Microsoft Visual C++ 2.0 uses the file name **EH.H** instead of **EXCEPT.H** for the header that declares *set_terminate*. The program on the companion diskette includes a compile-time conditional directive to change the included header name.

SELECTING AMONG THROWN EXCEPTIONS

To review: A *try* block is followed by one or more *catch* handlers, which are distinguished by their parameter lists. You must decide in your design how to differentiate the exceptions. You might code only one *catch* handler with an *int* parameter and let the value of the parameter determine the error type. This approach, illustrated next, makes the unlikely assumption that you have control of all the *throws* in all the functions in all the libraries that you use.

```
catch(int exception_code)
{
    switch (exception_code)  {
        case 0:
            // process code 0
            break;
        case 1:
            // process code 1
            break;
        // ....
    }
}
```

Throwing intrinsic types is not the best approach. If all libraries threw *ints*, for example, the *catch* handlers would become a hodgepodge of collisions and conflicts. No doubt conventions will emerge. One possibility uses class definitions to distinguish exceptions and categories of exceptions. A *throw* with a publicly derived class as its parameter is caught by a *catch* handler with the base class as its parameter. Consider this example:

```
class FileError {
public:
    virtual void HandleException() = 0;
};
class Locked : public FileError {
public:
    void HandleException();
};
class NotFound : public FileError {
public:
    void HandleException();
};
void bar()
{
    try {
        foo();
    }
    catch(FileError& fe)   {
        fe.HandleException();
    }
}
void foo()
{
    // ...
    if (file_locked)
        throw NotFound();
}
```

FileError is a public virtual base class. Its derived classes are *NotFound* and *Locked.* The only *catch* handler for this category of exception is the one with the *FileError* reference parameter. It does not know which of the exceptions was thrown, but it calls the *HandleException* pure virtual function, which automatically calls the proper function in the derived class.

This approach is only one of many that you can use. Instead of classes, you can use enumerated types and have switches in the *catch* handlers. Publishers of libraries will document the conventions that they use to throw exceptions, and your *catch* handlers will use those conventions, perhaps using several different conventions in one application. Eventually standards will emerge. Chapter 15 discusses the exception handling conventions being considered for the Standard C++ library.

EXCEPTIONS AND UNRELEASED RESOURCES

Recall the discussion at the beginning of this chapter about the *setjmp/longjmp* anomaly with unreleased resources. C++ exception handling does not solve that problem. Consider this condition:

```
void foo()
{
    string *str = new string("Hello, Dolly");
    // ...
    if (file_locked)
        throw NotFound();
    delete str;
}
```

The *string* object is allocated from the heap by the *new* operator. If the exception is thrown, the *delete* operation is not performed. In this case, there are two complications. The memory allocated on the heap for the *string* object is not released, and its destructor is not called, which means that the memory that its constructor allocated for the *string* data is lost as well.

The same problem exists with dangling open file handles, unclosed screen windows, and other such unresolved system resources. If the program just shown seems easy to fix, remember that the *throw* could occur from within a library function far into a stack of nested function calls.

Programming idioms have been suggested that address this problem, and programmers must consider them. Dr. Stroustrup suggests that all such resources can be managed from within automatic instances of resource-management classes. Their destructors would release everything as the *throw* unwinds the stack. Another approach is to make all dynamic heap pointers and file and window handles global so that the *catch* handler could clean everything up. These methods sound cumbersome, however, and they work only if all the functions in all the libraries cooperate.

SUMMARY

Exception handling is a valuable addition to C++. The next chapter discusses a new casting mechanism and run-time type information, two new features in contemporary C++.

CHAPTER 13

Casts and Runtime Type Information

New-style casts and runtime type information (RTTI) are innovations of the ANSI/ISO committee. Inasmuch as both features are implemented in current Borland and MetaWare C++ compilers, their discussion is included here in Part II of the book, which addresses contemporary C++. The exercises in this chapter work only with the Borland and MetaWare compilers as of the fall of 1994, and the exercises employ those particular implementations, which could change depending on the whims of the committee and the interpretation of the specification. As other compilers add the new ANSI/ISO features—which should happen well within the life of this edition—you can test these exercises with them. You will learn:

❖   New-style casts
❖   Runtime type information

311

NEW-STYLE CASTS

New-style casts replace traditional C and C++ typecast notation, providing safer notation that reflects the design of polymorphic class hierarchies and that you can readily find in code by using text searching tools such as **grep**. The old-style casts are still supported by the language, but their use is discouraged and they will gradually disappear as new programs replace old ones.

In a perfect universe, programs would would need no casts at all, and the framers of the language would like to have eliminated them altogether. Research shows, however, that many idioms require them, particularly in systems programming. The old-style cast is known to be unsafe, error-prone, difficult to spot when we read programs, and more difficult to ferret out in large bodies of source code text. New-style casts are an attempt by the committee to improve the casting situation.

There are four new casting operators. Each one returns an object converted according to the rules of the operator. They use this syntax:

```
cast_operator <type> (object)
```

The *cast_operator* is one of the following: *dynamic_cast*, *static_cast*, *reinterpret_cast*, and *const_cast*. The *type* argument is the type being cast to. The *object* argument is the object being cast from.

dynamic_cast

The *dynamic_cast* operator casts a base class reference or pointer to a derived class reference or pointer. You can use it only when the base class has virtual functions. It provides a way to determine at run-time whether a base class reference or pointer refers to an object of a specified derived class or to an object of a class derived from the specified class. Exercise 13.1 illustrates casting pointers with the *dynamic_cast* operator.

***Exercise 13.1   dynamic_cast** to Pointer*

```
#include <iostream.h>
class Control {
public:
        virtual void foo() {}
};
class TextBox : public Control { };
class EditBox : public TextBox { };
class Button  : public Control { };
void Paint(Control *cp)
{
        TextBox *ctl = dynamic_cast<TextBox*>(cp);
        if (ctl != 0)
                cout << "cp and ctl -> TextBox" << '\n';
        else
                cout << "cp -> nonTextBox" << '\n';
}
main()
{
        // --- instantiate and paint Control
        Control ct;
        Paint(&ct);
        // --- instantiate and paint Button
        Button bt;
        Paint(&bt);
        // --- instantiate and paint TextBox
        TextBox tb;
        Paint(&tb);
        // --- instantiate and paint EditBox
        EditBox eb;
        Paint(&eb);
}
```

The *dynamic_cast* operator provides a form of runtime type identification (not to be confused with RTTI, discussed later). A program can determine at runtime which of several known derived types a base class reference or pointer refers to. This feature supports idioms that virtual functions might not. The *Paint* function in the example knows that a derived *TextBox* class has requirements not shared by all classes derived from the base *Control* class. Rather than burden all classes derived from *Control* with empty virtual functions to emulate those unique to *TextBox*, the design casts the object's base pointer to point to *TextBox* object. If the object is neither a *TextBox* nor of a class derived from *TextBox*, the cast returns a zero value, and the program knows not to call functions that are unique to *TextBox*es.

Exercise 13.1 displays this output:

```
cp -> nonTextBox
cp -> nonTextBox
cp & ctl -> TextBox
cp & ctl -> TextBox
```

If you use references rather than pointers, *dynamic_cast* throws a *bad_cast* exception if the target is not of the specified class,, as shown in Exercise 13.2.

Exercise 13.2   *dynamic_cast* to Reference

```
#include <iostream.h>
#include <typeinfo.h>
class Control {
public:
        virtual void foo() {}
};
class TextBox : public Control { };
class EditBox : public TextBox { };
class Button  : public Control { };
```

continued

Exercise 13.2 ***dynamic_cast*** *to Reference (continued)*

```
void Paint(Control& cr)
{
        try     {
                TextBox& ctl = dynamic_cast<TextBox&>(cr);
                cout << "cr & ctl refer to TextBox" << '\n';
        }
        catch(Bad_cast)         {
                cout << "cr refers to nonTextBox" << '\n';
        }
}
main()
{
        // --- instantiate and paint Control
        Control ct;
        Paint(ct);
        // --- instantiate and paint Button
        Button bt;
        Paint(bt);
        // --- instantiate and paint TextBox
        TextBox tb;
        Paint(tb);
        // --- instantiate and paint EditBox
        EditBox eb;
        Paint(eb);
}
```

Exercise 13.2 displays this output.

```
cr refers to nonTextBox
cr refers to nonTextBox
cr & ctl refer to TextBox
cr & ctl refer to TextBox
```

static_cast

Unlike *dynamic_cast*, the *static_cast* operator makes no runtime check and is not restricted to base and derived classes in the same polymorphic class hierarchy. You can use *static_cast* to invoke implicit conversions between types that are not in the same hierarchy. Type-checking is static—that is, the compiler checks to ensure that the conversion is valid. Assuming that you did not subvert the type system with an old-style cast to coerce an invalid address into a pointer or initialize a pointer with zero, *static_cast* is a reasonably safe type-casting mechanism. Exercise 13.3 compares *static_cast* with old-style casts.

Exercise 13.3   static_cast

```
#include <iostream.h>
class B {
        int i;
public:
        // --- conversion constructor
        B(int a) : i(a)         {.}
        void display()  { cout << i; }
};
main()
{
        // --- old-style cast int to B
        B bobj1 = (B)123;
        bobj1.display();
        cout << '/';
        // --- constructor notation
        B bobj2 = B(456);
        bobj2.display();
        cout << '/';
        // --- static_cast
        B bobj3 = static_cast<B>(789);
        bobj3.display();
}
```

Exercise 13.3 displays this output:

123/456/789

If you are casting from a base to a derived type—which is not always a safe conversion—*static_cast* assumes that its argument is an object of (or pointer or reference to an object of) the base class *within an object of the derived class*. The cast can result in a different, possibly invalid address. Consider this code:

```
class C : public A, public B { /* ... */ };
B *bp;
C *cp = static_cast<C*>(bp);
```

If the *bp* pointer does in fact point to an object of type *C*, the cast works correctly. If it points to an object of type *B*, the cast makes the conversion, but the effective address is less than the address of the *B* object with the difference representing the size of the *B* class. This address is incorrect.

Similarly, if the pointer points to an object of the base class, using the derived class pointer to dereference members of the nonexisting derived class object causes unpredictable behavior.

If you are unsure about the safety of the cast, use *dynamic_cast* and check the result.

If you are casting from a derived to a base type, which is safe, *static_cast* assumes that its argument is a valid object of the derived class or a pointer or reference to an object of the derived class.

reinterpret_cast

The *reinterpret_cast* operator replaces most other uses of the old-style cast except those in which you are casting away *const*ness (discussed next). The *reinterpret_cast* operator converts pointers to other pointer types, numbers to pointers, and pointers to numbers. You should know what you are doing when you use *reinterpret_cast*, just as you should when you use old-style casts. That is not to say that you should never use *reinterpret_cast*. There are times when nothing else will do. Exercise 13.4 demonstrates a simple memory allocator that returns the address of a 100-character buffer as a *void* pointer. The *main* function assigns the return to a *char* pointer. Under the conversion rules of C++ (and unlike those of C), you cannot implicitly convert void* to char*, so a cast is needed. Rather than use an old-style cast, the exercise uses *reinterpret_cast*.

Exercise 13.4   reinterpret_cast

```
#include <iostream.h>
#include <string.h>
void *getmem()
{
        static char buf[100];
        return buf;
}
main()
{
        char *cp = reinterpret_cast<char*>(getmem());
        strcpy(cp, "Hello, Woody");
        cout << cp;
}
```

Exercise 13.4 displays this output:

```
Hello, Woody
```

const_cast

The three cast operators just discussed respect *const*ness. That is, you cannot use them to cast away the *const*ness of an object. For that, use the *const_cast* operator. Its type argument must match the type of the object argument except for the *const* and *volatile* keywords.

When would you want to cast away *const*ness? Class designs should take into consideration users who declares a *const* object of the type. They do that by declaring as *const* any member functions that do not modify any of the object's data member values. Those functions are accessible through *const* objects. Other functions are not. Some classes, however, have data members that contribute to the management rather than the purpose of the objects. They manipulate hidden data that the user is unconcerned about, and they must do so for all objects, regardless of *const*ness.

For example, suppose that there is a global counter that represents some number of actions taken against an object of the class, *const* or otherwise. Exercise 13.5 demonstrates such a program.

Exercise 13.5   *Using the **const_cast** Operator.*

```
#include <iostream.h>
class A {
    int val;
    int rptct;  // number of times the object is reported
public:
    A(int v) : val(v), rptct(0) { }
    ~A()
    { cout << val << " was reported " << rptct << " times."; }
    void report() const;
};
void A::report() const
{
    const_cast<A*>(this)->rptct++;
    cout << val << '\n';
}
int main()
{
    const A a(123);
    a.report();
    a.report();
    a.report();
    return 0;
}
```

Exercise 13.5 displays this output:

```
123
123
123
123 was reported 3 times.
```

If the declaration of the *A::report()* member function was not *const*, the using program could not use the function for *const* objects of the class. The function itself needs to increment the *rptct* data member, which it normally could not do from a *const* member function. *Const* functions cannot change data values. To cast away the constness of the object for that one operation, the function uses the *const_cast* operator to cast the *this* pointer to a pointer to a non*const* object of the class.

Future C++ provides the *mutable* keyword to specify class members that are never *const* even when a *const* object of the class is instantiated. Chapter 14 discusses the *mutable* keyword.

N O T E

RUNTIME TYPE INFORMATION (RTTI)

The *typeid* operator supports the new C++ runtime type information feature. Given an expression or a type as an argument, the operator returns a reference to a system-maintained object of type *Type_info*, which identifies the type of the argument. There are only a few things that you can do with the *Type_info* object reference. You can compare it to another *Type_info* object for equality or inequality. You can initialize a *Type_info* pointer variable with its address. You cannot assign or copy a *Type_info* object or pass it as a function argument. You can call the member function *Type_info::name()* to get a pointer to the type's name. You can call the member function *Type_info::before()* to get a zero or one integer that represents the order of the type in relation to another type. Exercise 13.6 demonstrates some of the *typeid* operator's behavior.

Exercise 13.6 *The **typeid** Operator*

```
#include <iostreams.h>
#include <typeinfo.h>
class Control { };
main()
{
    // --- display name of type
    Control ct;
    cout << '\n' << typeid(ct).name();
    // --- compare typeids and display type of expression
    int counter = 123;
    if (typeid(counter) != typeid(1.23))
            cout << "\ncounter is not a " << typeid(1.23).name();
}
```

Exercise 13.6 displays this output:

```
Control
counter is not a double
```

NOTE

The ANSI/ISO February 1994 working paper and Dr. Stroustrup's The Design and Evolution of C++ imply that when you compare the return values of *typeid* operators with like base class pointers or references as arguments, the comparisons are not equal if the compared pointers or references do not point or refer to the same class in the hierarchy. The Borland implementation does not work this way. Instead, the *typeid* operator returns the type of the declared pointer or reference rather than what it points or refers to.

How would you use *typeid*? What purpose is gained by determining the specific type of an object? The *dynamic_cast* operator is more flexible in one way and less so in another. It tells you that an object is of a specified class or of a class derived from the specified class. But for you to be able to use it, there must be an object of the class already instantiated, and the specified class needs at least one virtual member function. Furthermore, *dynamic_cast* does not work with instrinsic types. The *typeid* operator works with instantiated objects, pointers to objects, intrinsic type names, class names, and expressions.

Consider a persistent object database manager. It scans the database files and constructs memory objects from data values that it finds. How does it determine which constructors to call? RTTI can provide that intelligence. If the first component of a persistent object record is the class name (or, better yet, a subscript into an array of class names), the program can use RTTI to select the constructor. Consider this example, in which the database scanner retrieves the class name of the next object and calls the *DisplayObject* function. In this example, there are only three classes recorded in the database.

```
void DisplayObject(char *cname)
{
    if (strcmp(cname, typeid(Employee).name())==0) {
        Employee empl;
        empl.Display();
    }
    else if (strcmp(cname, typeid(Department).name())==0) {
        Department dept;
        dept.Display();
    }
    else if (strcmp(cname, typeid(Project).name())==0) {
        Project proj;
        proj.Display();
    }
}
```

The example assumes that the database manager knows how to construct each object when the file pointer is positioned just past the type identifier in the record. This technique assumes that the scanner program knows about all the classes in the database and is similar to one that I use in the *Parody* II object database manager in *C++ Database Development*, 2nd Edition.

SUMMARY

This chapter completes the tutorial exercises. Chapter 14 begins Part III of Teach Yourself C++, which discusses future C++, the language that has not yet been implemented.

TEACH YOURSELF C++

PART III
Future C++

CHAPTER 14

ANSI/ISO Language Innovations

The ANSI/ISO committee took advantage of its standardization charter to introduce modifications to the C++ language definition that enhance the language in ways proposed by committee members. This policy is different from that of the ANSI/ISO C standardization committee, which decided to only codify existing practice and resolve ambiguities and contradictions among existing translator implementations.

The C++ committee's changes are innovations. In most cases the changes implement features that committee members admired in other languages, features that they view as deficiencies in traditional C++, or simply features that they've always wanted in a programming language. Not all the proposals were accepted, and not all the new features are defined as originally proposed. A great deal of thought and discussion has been invested in each of them, and consequently the committee feels that future C++ is the best definition of C++ possible today.

I call the ANSI/ISO innovations *future* C++ because most of them are not available in contemporary compilers. The one that is, *namespaces*, is implemented in only one commercial compiler and is relatively untried. Its details could change as experience with the feature reveals its strengths and weaknesses. That potential also exists with the unimplemented future C++ language changes discussed in this chapter and the next.

Most future C++ changes consist of language additions that should not affect existing code. Old programs should still compile with newer compilers as long as the old code does not coincidentally use any of the new keywords as identifiers. As you will learn, there is one potential exception: A change under consideration could alter the scope of identifiers declared within *for* statements. You will learn about:

- ❖ Namespaces
- ❖ The *bool* intrinsic type
- ❖ Digraphs and operator keywords
- ❖ The *mutable* keyword
- ❖ Declarations in conditions and *for* statements
- ❖ Templates

NAMESPACES

Namespaces have represented a problem in C and C++ since the language's inception in the early 1970s. In an interview in *Dr. Dobb's Journal* in 1989, Dennis Ritchie, the designer of C, addressed the namespace problem, saying that the ANSI/ISO X3J11 C standardization committee introduced "...a convention that helps, but it certainly didn't solve the real problem."

Here is the problem: External, global identifiers are in scope throughout a program. They are visible to all object modules in the application program, in third-party class and function libraries, and in the compiler's system libraries. When two variables in global scope have the same identifier, the linker generates an error. Programmers avoid such name collisions in their own code by assigning unique identifiers to each variable. Under Standard C (applying the convention mentioned by Dr. Ritchie), the compiler system prefixes its internal global identifiers with underscore characters, and programmers are told to avoid that usage to avoid conflicts. Third-party library publishers addressed their part of the problem with mnemonic prefixes to global identifiers. This strategy attempts to avoid conflicts with other libraries, but it is unsuccessful when two publishers use the same prefix. The problem is that the language had no built-in mechanism with which a library publisher could stake out a so-called namespace of its own—one that would insulate its global identifiers from those of other libraries being linked into the same program.

Programmers using multiple libraries with coincidental name collisions had three choices: Get the source code to the libraries and modify and recompile them; convince one of the publishers to rename identifiers and republish its library; or choose not to use one of the offending libraries. Often none of the three choices was available.

The C++ committee approached this problem by introducing *namespaces*, a feature wherein identifiers declared within a defined block are associated with the block's *namespace* identifier. All references from outside the block to the global identifers declared in the block must, in one way or another, qualify the global identifier reference with the *namespace* identifier. Publishers of libraries specify the *namespace* identifiers for the libraries' global identifiers. This feature is no more effective than using prefixes—two library publishers could conceivably and unwittingly use the same *namespace* identifier. Identifiers, however, tend to be longer than the typical two- or three-character prefixes and stand a better chance of being unique.

The *namespace* Definition

You define a *namespace* by surrounding all the associated code with a *namespace* block as shown here:

```
namespace MyLibrary  {
    int counter;
    class Date { /* ... */ };
    // ...
}
```

References from within the *MyLibrary namespace*'s enclosing braces to the *counter* variable, *Date* class, and members of the *Date* class do not need to be qualified. References to those identifiers from outside the braces must be qualified with the *MyLibrary* identifier.

Library builders assign *namespaces* to their libraries and place the class definitions and function prototypes in *namespace* definitions in the header files. This usage is shown here:

```
// --- wincls.h
namespace WindowClasses {
    class Window  { /* ... */ };
    class Desktop { /* ... */ };
    unsigned int OpenWindowCount;
}
```

The example shows how a library uses a *namespace* definition. You can similarly group your program's declarations within specific *namespaces* by using the same conventions.

Library users include the library header files and specify which names they intend to use from the *namespaces*. There are three ways for a program to qualify the reference to an identifier that is declared in a different *namespace* than the reference: Explicit *namespace* qualification; the *using* declaration; and the *using* directive.

Explicit *namespace* Qualification

To explicitly qualify an identifier with its *namespace*, you use the :: scope resolution operator as shown here:

```
namespace MyLibrary {
    int counter;
    // ...
}
main()
{
    MyLibrary::counter++;
}
```

Other identifiers named *counter* could be declared in other *namespaces* and would not collide with the usage in the example.

The *using* Declaration

A *using* declaration specifies that all the identifiers in the *namespace* are available to the program within the scope of the *using* declaration. The following example uses the **wincls.h** file shown above:

```
#include "wincls.h"
using namespace WindowClasses;
// ...
```

All the identifiers in the *namespace* are now available to the program without further qualification. Unlike the *using* directive, described next, the *using* declaration does not place the names in the local scope. Instead, it makes all the *namespace's* identifiers available to the program in the context of their own outer scope. This is not always and not usually what you want. The library in question will no doubt consist of many unknown identifiers that need to be hidden within the *namespace*. That is what *namespaces* are for. The principal use of *using* declarations is to support standard library interfaces that are well known. It is pointless to require programs to qualify the standard *strcpy* function or the *cout* object with their respective *namespaces*, for example. The header files for those standard libraries should include appropriate *using* declarations. That way, old programs still compile without needing *namespace* qualifiers, and new programs do not need *namespace* qualifications just to use the standard libraries. See Chapter 15 for a discussion of this issue.

The *using* Directive

The *using* directive tells the compiler that you intend to use specific identifiers within a *namespace*. The *using* directive places those specific identifiers in the directive's scope as if they had been declared where the directive appears. Here is an example:

```
#include "wincls.h"
using WindowClasses::Window;
using WindowClasses::Desktop;
// ...
```

The two *using* directives in the example just shown allow the program to use the *Window* and *Desktop* identifiers that are declared in the **wincls.h** header file. At the same time, other identifiers declared in the header file and in the library's object files remain under the protection of the *WindowClasses namespace* definition.

The *namespace* Alias

Most *namespace* identifiers used by third-party libraries are typically of sufficient length so that the *namespace* stands a better chance of being unique and so that it identifies the library to which it belongs. These long identifiers would be cumbersome as qualifiers in the program's code. To support more readable coding styles, the *namespace* feature allows a program to assign an alias to a *namespace* identifier as shown here:

```
namespace SGL = SpiffyGraphicsLibrary;

main()
{
    using SGL::DoShape;
    DoShape(); // calls SpiffyGraphicsLibrary::DoShape()
    // ...
}
```

Namespace aliases combine the terse and readable syntax of the older prefix-qualifying style with the protection of a fully defining *namespace* identifier.

The Global *namespace*

Any identifier declared in global space outside any *namespace* definition is said to be in the *global namespace*. You may still reference global identifiers just as you could in the past. If the identifiers are the same as other identifiers in other *namespaces*, you can reference them by using the :: global scope resolution operator as shown here:

```
int amount;              // global amount
namespace Payroll  {
    int amount;          // Payroll::amount
    // ...
}
main()
{
    using Payroll::amount;
    amount++;    // increments Payroll::amount
    ::amount++; // increments global amount
}
```

Unnamed *namespace* Definitions

An unnamed *namespace* definition omits the *namespace* identifier. The compiler generates an internal identifier that is unique throughout the program. Identifiers declared within an unnamed *namespace* definition are available only within the translation unit within which they are declared. Here is an example:

```
namespace {
    int counter;
}
main()
{
    counter++;
}
```

The *main* function can reference the *counter* variable declared within the unnamed *namespace*. So can any other function in the same translation unit. Functions in other translation units in the same program cannot reference the *counter* variable. This usage can replace the *static* storage class specification for variables declared outside functions.

Namespaces Summarized

Namespaces are a complex but useful new feature. You can nest *namespaces* and contrive all kinds of interesting, surprising resolutions by mixing and using *namespaces*. I recommend a close reading of Dr. Stroustrup's *The Design and Evolution of C++*, Chapter 17, for a detailed discussion of the more arcane aspects of this feature and for an historical perspective of its development.

To date, the *namespace* feature is implemented in only one MS-DOS compiler, the MetaWare C++ compiler. The committee has defined specific *namespaces* for all Standard Library functions and classes.

THE *bool* INTRINSIC TYPE

Many C++ designers have implemented a Boolean data type. These types have been as simple as macros and as complex as class definitions complete with conversion constructors and overloaded operators. Following are two typical simple Boolean types:

```
// --- bool as a typedef
typedef unsigned char bool;
const bool true = 1;
const bool false = 0;

// --- bool as an enum
enum bool { false, true };
```

These simple Boolean types do not bind their objects strictly to the defined true and false values, and they do not accurately compare when the true values are allowed to be other than the defined *true* constant. Programmers have often designed complete Boolean data types and implemented them as C++ classes to provide the correct behavior.

The ANSI/ISO committee has added a Boolean data type to the language. There are three new keywords: *bool, true,* and *false.* They implement an intrinsic Boolean type that behaves properly when initialized by, assigned from, or compared with integers. Following is a typical usage, which resembles the usage of the classes that programmers designed.

```
main()
{
    bool isdone = false;
    while (!isdone)    {
        // ...
        isdone = true;
    }
}
```

The differences between the committee's new type and the classes that programmers designed are that the names are fixed—there was no standard, and programmers often used Bool, BOOL, Boolean, and so on—and that the program does not need to include a class definition. The *bool* data type is now intrinsic to the C++ language. You can assign and compare integer values to and with *bool* variables. The *bool* variable always maintains its Boolean state and compares correctly with integer values with respect to its true/false state. You can use the postfix and prefix increment operators to set *bool* variables to *true*, although the draft working paper deprecates this practice.

N O T E
The ANSI/ISO standard deprecates many traditional coding conventions that the C++ language supports but that are better expressed with new features. One example is the old-style cast, which is deprecated in favor of new-style casts described in Chapter 13. Another example is the declaration of static variables in the global *namespace,* which the committee deprecates in favor of the unnamed *namespace* convention described earlier in this chapter. It is interesting to observe that in the case of the *bool* type and its increment operator, the committee deprecates part of a feature that the committee itself invented.

OPERATOR KEYWORDS, DIGRAPHS, AND TRIGRAPHS

Not all international character sets include all the C++ operator characters. The eight-bit ASCII values assigned to those characters in the English language are used by special symbols in the alphabets of other languages. As a result, international keyboards might not include all the C++ operator characters. The C committee addressed this problem by providing *trigraphs*—three-character sequences consisting of common characters from the international character set and that substitute for the missing operators. Table 14.1 lists the C trigraphs.

Table 14.1   C Language Trigraphs

Trigraph	Operator
??=	#
??(	[
??/	\
??)	]
??'	^
??<	{
??!	|
??>	}
??-	~

The C++ committee decided to adopt what it considered to be more readable *digraphs* as alternatives for some of the C trigraphs. Table 14.2 lists the C++ digraphs.

Table 14.2   C++ Language Digraphs

Digraph	Operator
%%	#
<:	[
:>	]
<%	{
%>	}

The C++ committee substituted keywords for the remaining trigraphs and assigned other keywords for operators formed from ASCII characters not addressed by the C trigraphs. Table 14.3 lists the C++ operator keywords.

Table 14.3 C++ Operator Keywords

Keyword	Operator
and	&&
and_eq	&=
bitand	&
bitor		
compl	~
not	!
or	||
or_eq	|=
xor	^
xor_eq	^=
not_eq	!=

The following three program fragments compare conventional C++ with the trigraphs of Standard C and the digraphs and keywords of Standard C++. It should be apparent which alternative is more readable.

```
// --- conventional C++
#include <iostream.h>
main()
{
    int a, b, x[20];
    // ...
    if (a || b)
        x[3] |= 5^2;
}
```

```
// --- Standard C Trigraphs
??=include <iostream.h>
main()
??<
    int a, b, x??(20??);
    // ...
    if (a ??!??! b)
        x??(3??) ??!= 5 ??' 2;
??>


// --- Standard C++ Digraphs and Operator Keywords
%%include <iostream.h>
main()
<%
    int a, b, x<:20:>;
    // ...
    if (a or b)
        x<:3:> or_eq 5 xor 2;
%>
```

mutable CLASS DATA MEMBERS

In Chapter 13, Exercise 13.5 illustrates how the *const_cast* operator can override *const*ness when a class member function needs to modify data members in *const* and non*const* objects. Future C++ adds the *mutable* keyword to qualify class data members. A member function can modify a *mutable* data member even when the instantiated class object is *const*. The following code fragment shows how Exercise 13.5 can be changed to use the new *mutable* keyword.

```
class A {
    mutable int rptct;  // number of times the object is reported
public:
    // ...
    void report() const;
};
void A::report() const
{
    rptct++;  // mutable: OK to modify even for const object
    cout << val << '\n';
}
```

DECLARATIONS IN CONDITIONS AND *for* STATEMENTS

As you learned in Chapter 2, Exercise 2.3, traditional C++ allows you to declare a variable within the controlling expression of a *for* statement:

```
// --- traditional C++
void foo()
{
    for (int ctr = 0; ctr < 20; ctr++)   {
       // ctr is in scope
    }
    // ctr is still in scope
}
```

The committee is considering limiting the scope of variables declared in *for* statements to the *for* statement itself instead of the block in which the *for* statement appears. Dr. Stroustrup treats the existing rule as an oversight, wishing that he had made a special case for the scope of variables declared within *for* statements.

No decision has been made at this time, and the working paper of February 1994 reflects the traditional C++ rule. The change, if approved, might have unfortunate consequences. Many programs exist that use an idiom similar to this one:

```
for (int ctr = 0; ctr < 20; ctr++)   {
    // ...
    break;
}
if (ctr < 20)
    // --- break was executed before loop completed
```

The new rule would prevent such programs from compiling. On the other hand, the existing rule prevents the following idiom, which many programmers would like to use:

```
for (int ctr = 0; ctr < 20; ctr++)   {
    // ...
}
for (int ctr = 0; ctr < 20; ctr++)   {
    // ...
}
```

Future C++ adds the ability to declare variables within the conditional expression of an *if* statement as shown here:

```
if ((Wnd *newwnd = OpenWindow()) != 0)  {
    // newwnd is in scope
}
// newwnd is not in scope
```

In this case, the feature is intentionally defined so that the scope of the declared variable is limited to the *if* statement, as the example shows.

TEMPLATES

Future C++ defines many subtle and complex changes to the way that templates are implemented and used. Contemporary C++ implementations vary somewhat in several small, hidden details of implementation. For example, some contemporary implementations require template function definitions to be in header files. Others put the template function definitions in .c files. According to Dr. Stroustrup's *The Design and Evolution of C++*, neither approach is optimal. The header file approach, which most MS-DOS compilers use, causes performance problems. The .c file approach makes the functions difficult for the compiler to instantiate because it does not know where they are. Dr. Stroustrup blames the implementations on the failure of *The Annotated C++ Reference Manual* (ARM) to provide guidance to implementors. He recommends a complex, multistep solution involving a repository. The committee's working paper says that any such solution requires a "model for compilation of templates" and does not provide further guidance to implementors. It is anticipated that the final standard definition will provide this guidance.

Future C++ allows class templates to define default template arguments—that is, the template declaration or definition can specify a default type for the class arguments of a template, as shown here:

```
template<class T = char>
class String {
    // ...
};
```

Programs can instantiate objects of the template with specified types as usual, or they can allow the compiler to substitute the default type by not specifying a type, as shown here:

```
void foo()
{
    String MyStr;    // same as String<char> MyStr;
}
```

The February 1994 working paper specifies that empty template argument lists must include the <> notation as shown here:

```
String MyStr<>;
```

However, subsequent committee deliberations modified that position to permit the usage shown above wherein the <> may be omitted. This decision had far-reaching effects on the C++ Standard Library definition. Several standard class libraries defined in the 1994 working paper have been modified to be implemented as class templates with default argument types. For example, the *string* and *iostream* types will now be defined as templates having *char* as their default argument. This convention allows the definition of string and stream objects made from *wchar_t* types, supporting international wide character sets.

SUMMARY

This chapter discussed C++ language changes that are being considered by the committee. Most of them are not implemented in current compilers, but it is generally understood that they will eventually be approved and implemented. As such, they constitute the language side of future C++. The other side of future C++ is found in the proposed standard library, and Chapter 15 discusses that subject.

CHAPTER 15

The Standard C++ Library

Future C++ includes a standard class library as part of the standard definition. In Chapter 10 you learned about input/output streams—the only de facto library standard that traditional C++ contributes to the C++ Standard library. For years, *iostream* classes were the only common library denominator among C++ compilers. Most compilers included *complex*, *string*, and various container and utility classes, but their implementations were unique to the compilers.

The committee's February 1994 working paper identifies utility classes for managing complex numbers, character strings, bit masks, bit strings, and dynamic arrays of objects and pointers. Since that publication, several proposals have affected the form that such libraries are likely to take. First, the committee approved changes to the way templates work, making possible different and, it is presumed, better implementations of the proposed library classes. Second, a package called the Standard Template Library was submitted to be included in the standard. Most, if not all, of the accepted Standard library classes could be implemented as derivatives of Standard Template Library class templates, and that approach is perceived to be superior to the one already accepted by the committee and published in the working paper.

It is not clear to what extent the public interfaces to the standard library classes will change from those published in the working paper. Probably the *string* class interface will remain fundamentally as is, encapsulating the *wstring* class as a specialized class template. Just as probably, the *float_complex, double_complex,* and *long_double_complex* classes will be encapsulated as a single *complex* class template and the interface will change. Without a crystal ball, however, we have no way of knowing just what form the final class library will take, and the committee shows no inclination to restrain itself from making changes at will and whim. Consequently, this chapter is restricted to subjects common to all parts of the library and discusses the Standard Template Library in general terms. For a detailed discussion and a full implementation of the Standard library as it was defined in the February 1994 working paper (and subsequently overtaken by events), read *The Draft Standard C++ Library,* by P.J. Plauger.

In this chapter you will learn about:

❖ The Standard C library
❖ Library headers and namespaces
❖ Library exceptions
❖ The Standard Template Library

THE STANDARD C LIBRARY

Because Standard C++ incorporates Standard C, all the functions of the Standard C library are included. You can include the Standard C headers and call the Standard C functions as always.

Namespaces

Future C++ circumscribes the Standard C Libraries in its own *namespace,* but programmers do not, as a rule, need to concern themselves with those details. All the Standard C library public interface identifiers are specified in *using* directives to permit programs to reference them without qualification. See the discussion, "Library Namespaces," later in this chapter.

Keywords

Use of Standard C headers in a C++ compiler involves some changes to the headers. For example, *wchar_t* is declared in several headers (**stddef.h**, **stdlib.h**, and **wchar.h**) in Standard C. But *wchar_t* is a keyword and an intrinsic type in Standard C++, so the declaration must be omitted from those headers. Similarly, the operator alternative keywords (*and, and_eq,* and so on) discussed in Chapter 14 are no longer declared as macros in **iso646.h**.

Function Prototypes

Several functions defined in the Standard C library must be changed and overloaded in Standard C++ to permit the caller to pass *const* and non-*const* arguments. These changes are needed because *const* and non-*const* arguments represent distinct types in C++, and distinct types in argument lists define overloaded functions. Following is one example:

```
// --- Standard C prototype
    char* strchr(const char* s, int c);

// --- Standard C++ prototypes
const char* strchr(const char* s, int c);
    char* strchr(      char* s, int c);
```

These changes are transparent from the programmer's viewpoint except that you must be careful not to mix header files from older C-only compilers with those of C++ compilers or combined C and C++ development environments.

Memory Allocation

The Standard C memory allocation functions—*calloc, malloc, realloc,* and *free*— are available in Standard C++, but they do not use the *new* and *delete* operators and might not be compatible if you mix C and C++ memory allocation conventions.

The *exit* Function

In addition to what the Standard C *exit* function does, the Standard C++ *exit* function calls destructors for all *static* class objects.

LIBRARY HEADERS

Future C++ significantly changes the conventions for including Standard C and C++ library headers in programs. First, the *#include* statement does not have to provide a valid file name. An implementation is free to use any means to convert the name specified by the *#include* statement into any file name format recognized by the operating system. This rule acknowledges that not all operating systems have compatible file-naming conventions.

Second, future C++ changes the conventional header names that you specify in the *#include* statement, eliminating the .h suffixes and prefixing the Standard C header names with the character *c*.

 This change does not necessarily change the file names themselves. Remember that an implementation can convert what you specify into an actual file name or, optionally, implement the header internally within the compiler, eliminating the header file altogether.

N O T E

Table 15.1 lists the headers identified in the working paper (omitting the ones that are in question because of pending changes).

Table 15.1 Future C++ Header Names

C Headers	C++ Headers
<cassert>	<defines>
<cctype>	<exception>
<cerrno>	<fstream>
<cfloat>	<iomanip>
<ciso646>	<ios>
<climits>	<iostream>
<clocale>	<istream>
<cmath>	<new>
<csetjmp>	<ostream>
<csignal>	<sstream>
<cstdarg>	<stdexcept>
<cstddef>	<streambuf>
<cstdio>	<string>
<cstdlib>	<strstream>
<cstring>	<typeinfo>
<ctime>	
<cwchar>	
<cwctype>	

LIBRARY NAMESPACES

The C and C++ headers each specify a *namespace* definition, placing their declarations into the standard systemwide *std namespace*. If you include the new headers, you must qualify references to the functions and variables declared in those headers with the *std* namespace, either through explicit *namespace* qualification or with *using* declarations or directives. The following code fragment illustrates this usage.

```
#include <cstring>
main()
{
    char msg[20];
    std::strcpy(msg, "hello");  // std:: qualification required
}
```

Alternatively, you can use a *using* directive as shown here:

```
#include <cstring>
using std::strcpy;          // using directive
main()
{
    char msg[20];
    strcpy(msg, "hello");  // qualification not required
}
```

As another alternative, you can use a *using* declaration as shown here:

```
#include <cstring>
using namespace std;       // using declaration
main()
{
    char msg[20];
    strcpy(msg, "hello");  // qualification not required
}
```

There are corresponding C headers for the 18 Standard C library headers with traditional names such as **assert.h**, **ctype.h**, and so on. Those headers include the new headers (**cassert**, **cctype**, etc.) and provide *using* declarations for the public interface function names of the libraries, as shown in this example:

```
// --- string.h (example, not the real thing)
#include <cstring>
using std::strcpy;
// etc...
```

A program can then include the traditional **string.h** header and use all its global identifiers without qualification as shown here:

```
#include <string.h>
main()
{
    char msg[20];
    strcpy(msg, "hello");  // qualification not required
}
```

So, despite the committee's innovations, everything is back where it started with respect to Standard C headers from the programmer's perspective.

But how about the C++ headers? The exercises in this book include traditional C++ headers such as **iostream.h**, **iomanip.h**, and **new.h**, and contemporary C++ headers such as **typeinfo.h**. What do the new header and namespace conventions do to them? As of this writing, no one outside the committee knows. A great number of existing programs include those file names and expect the identifiers declared in the headers to be in the (apparently) global namespace and scope. Programmers are not likely to warm up to the idea that they have to code *std::cout* where before they coded *cout*. Even if the committee does not mandate traditional headers that provide appropriate *using* directives, compiler vendors will probably provide them. And if the vendors do not, programmers will certainly write the traditional headers themselves and post them publicly for all to use.

LIBRARY EXCEPTIONS

The committee has tried to define a standard mechanism for exceptions thrown by Standard C++ library classes. The mechanism is documented in the February 1994 working paper, but many of the details are under discussion and have changed. More changes are likely.

The objective is sound. Exception handling is a powerful tool, defined by Ellis and Stroustrup in *The Annotated Reference Manual* and refined and accepted by the committee. It is natural to use it in the Standard C++ library, and the committee needs to define a solid and consistent method for throwing exceptions. If the committee builds a reliable, intuitive exception handling model, programmers will adopt it for use in their own designs. In *The Draft*

Standard C++ Library, P.J. Plauger says about exception handling, "...the Standard C++ library has a moral obligation to set a good example."

The example it will set is still being defined. Its essence, however, is as follows:

- ❖ Exceptions thrown will be objects of classes.
- ❖ Exception classes are derived from a common base.
- ❖ The base class supports polymorphic members that describe the exception to the run-time system.

Remember from Chapter 12 that a *throw* with a publicly derived class as its parameter is caught by a *catch* handler with the base class as its parameter. The committee defined a preliminary hierarchy of exception classes based on that behavior and published the hierarchy in the February 1994 working paper. The definition is still under way and has already changed significantly since its first publication. Figure 15.1 illustrates its configuration at the time of this writing.

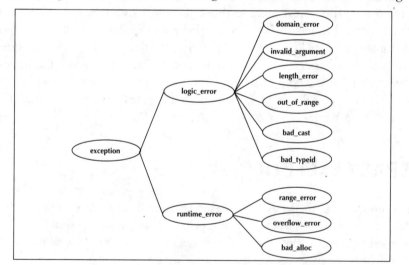

Figure 15.1   *Standard C++ Exception Hierarchy*

A third class derived from *exception* is named *ios::failure* and is used by the stream input/output class libraries.

N O T E

It is generally agreed that programmers should follow the Standard C++ library example and model their own exceptions after this hierarchy (or, more precisely, the formal one after it is published). You should throw objects of these exceptions where appropriate or throw objects derived from the most appropriate of these exceptions depending on the requirements of your application. Table 15.2 lists the standard exceptions and explains their purpose.

Table 15.2 Standard C++ Exception Classes

Exception Class	Purpose
exception	The top-level base class from which all exceptions are derived.
logic_error	A base class that represents programming errors that violate logical conditions that should be detectable before the program runs.
domain_error	A base class for exceptions that report violations of a precondition. [1]
invalid_argument	A base class for exceptions that report invalid argument values passed to a function.
length_error	A base class for exceptions that report attempts to create objects greater than the largest possible object.
out_of_range	A base class for exceptions that report out-of-range argument values.
bad_cast	Thrown by the *dynamic_cast* operator to report bad casts of reference objects.
bad_typeid	Thrown for a null pointer argument to the *typeid* operator.
runtime_error	A base class that represents errors that are detectable only after the program is running.
range_error	A base class for exceptions that report violations of a postcondition. [2]
overflow_error	A base class for exceptions that report arithmetic overflow.
bad_alloc	A base class for exceptions that report failures to allocate memory.

[1] A *precondition* is one that exists before an operation is carried out. For example, when an operation cannot proceed because something in the system related to the operation's domain is not in a state required to support the operation, the program throws an exception derived from *domain_error*.

[2] A *postcondition* is one that exists as the result of an operation. For example, when an operation causes an invalid data condition to occur, the program throws an exception derived from *range_error*.

The *exception* class defines several member functions that derived classes can override. Their details are still being hammered out, but one that seems sure to survive is the *what* function, which returns a pointer to an implementation-dependent string that identifies the exception. The following code example (which compiles and runs with any of the supported contemporary C++ compilers) implements a simple version of the *exception* class to illustrate how a future C++ program can derive exception classes from the future C++ Standard library *exception* class:

```
#include <iostream.h>
// --- class exception (minimally implemented here)
// --- would be provided by the compiler
class exception {
    char *wh;
protected:
    exception(char* w) : wh(w) { }
public:
    const char *what() const
        { return wh; }
};
// --- a user-defined exception class
class Bummer : public exception {
public:
    Bummer() : exception("Bummer") { }
};
main()
{
    try {
        throw Bummer();
    }
    catch(exception& ex)    {
        cout << ex.what();
    }
}
```

The program just shown would display the message "Bummer" on the screen from the *catch* handler. Remember that the program is an example of how properly derived exception classes might work. The details will be more clearly understood when the committee publishes more current specifications. For example, the *exception* constructor and the *what* function will probably use the Standard C++ *string* type instead of character arrays.

THE STANDARD TEMPLATE LIBRARY

The Standard Template Library (STL) was developed at Hewlett-Packard Laboratories and accepted in 1994 as an addition to the Standard C++ library. The breadth of the scope of STL caused committee members to reconsider Standard library container classes that they had already accepted and published in the working paper. Most container-type data structures can be implemented with STL class templates. The bounded array and linked-list templates of Chapter 11 are examples. STL replaces both of them. This discussion provides an overview of STL's underlying concepts. When implementations eventually are available, STL exercises will be appropriate for the advanced C++ student. It's a big subject—perhaps worth a book of its own.

STL is a library of container class templates and algorithmic function templates. Remember from Chapter 11 that templates define generic container classes with which you manage sets of data objects. The containers are unconcerned about the details of the objects they contain, and the objects are unconcerned about the details of containment.

STL Rationale

The rationale for STL is found in this observation: Given one set of data types, another set of container types, and a third set of common algorithms to support the containers, the amount of software to be developed with traditional C++ methods is a product of the number of elements in the three sets. If you have integer, Date, and Personnel objects to contain in lists, queues, and stacks, and if you need insert, extract, and sort algorithms for each, then there are 27 (3x3x3) traditional C++ algorithms to develop. With templates, you can define the containers as generic classes and reduce the number to nine algorithms: three algorithms for each of the three containers.

If, however, you design the algorithms themselves as templates that perform generic operations on parameterized containers, then there are only three algorithms. That is the underlying basis for STL.

That argument is a simplification of the STL rationale, but it hints at larger advantages, ones that cannot be ignored. If class template containers are sufficiently generic, then they can support any user-defined data type that meets their requirements with respect to operator overloading and behavior. You can contain any data type within any kind of supported container without having to develop custom container code. Furthermore, if the algorithms are sufficiently generic, you can use them to process containers of objects of user-defined data types.

You can add containers of your own design by conforming to the rules of STL, and all the existing algorithms will automatically work with the new containers.

Finally, as you add conforming algorithms, you find that they work with all containers and all contained data types—those of the present and those that are not yet designed.

To summarize: If you stick to the rules, you can add to any of the three components that make up STL—the containers, the algorithms, and the contained data types—and all existing components automatically accept the new addition and work seamlessly with it.

The STL Programming Model

STL supports several container types categorized as *sequences* and *associative* containers. Access to containers is managed by a hierarchy of *iterator* objects that resemble C++ pointers. Iterators point to objects in the containers and permit the program to iterate through the containers in various ways.

All the containers have common management member functions defined in their template definitions: insert, erase, begin, end, size, capacity, and so on. Individual containers have member functions that support their unique requirements.

A standard suite of algorithms provides for searching for, copying, reordering, transforming, and performing numeric operations on the objects in the containers. The same algorithm is used to perform a particular operation for all containers of all object types.

As we discuss the container types, remember that they are implemented as templates; the types of objects that they contain are determined by the template arguments given when the program instantiates the containers.

Sequences

A sequence is a container that stores a finite set of objects of the same type in a linear organization. An array of names is a sequence. You would use one of the three sequence types—*vector, list,* or *deque*—for a particular application depending on its retrieval requirements.

Vector

A vector is a sequence that you can access at random. You can append entries to and remove entries from the end of the vector without undue overhead. Insertion and deletion at the beginning or in the middle of the vector take more time because they involve shifting the remaining entries to make room or to close up the deleted object space. A vector is an array of contiguous objects with an instance counter or pointer to indicate the end of the container. Random access is a matter of using a subscript operation.

List

A list is a sequence that you access bidirectionally; it allows you to perform inserts and deletes anywhere without undue performance penalties. Random access is simulated by forward or backward iteration to the target object. A list consists of noncontiguous objects linked together with forward and backward pointers.

Deque

A deque is like a vector except that a deque allows fast inserts and deletes at the beginning as well as the end of the container. Random inserts and deletes take more time.

Associative Containers

Associative containers provide for fast keyed access to the objects in the container. These containers are constructed from key objects and a compare function that the container uses to compare objects. Associative containers consist of *set, multiset, map,* and *multimap* containers. You would use associative containers for large dynamic tables that you can search sequentially or at random. Associative containers use tree structures–rather than contiguous arrays or linked lists–to organize the objects. These structures support fast random retrievals and updates.

Set and Multiset

The set and multiset containers contain objects that are key values. The set container does not permit multiple keys with the same value. The multiset container does permit equal keys.

Map and Multimap

The map and multimap containers contain objects that are key values and associate each key object with another parameterized type object. The map container does not permit multiple keys with the same value. The multimap container does permit equal keys.

Iterators

Iterators provide a common method of access into containers. They resemble and have the semantics of C++ pointers. In fact, when the parameterized type is a built-in C++ type (*int, double*, and so on), the associated iterators are C++ pointers.

Each container type supports one category of iterator depending on the container's requirements. The categories are Input, Output, Forward, Bidirectional, and Random Access. STL defines a hierarchy of iterators as shown in Figure 15.2.

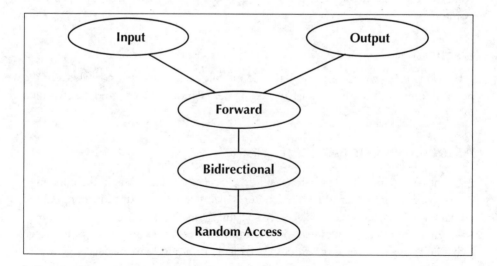

Figure 15.2   *STL Iterator Hierarchy*

Each iterator category has all the properties of those above it in the hierarchy. Those properties specify the behavior that the iterator must exhibit in order to support the container. Iterators are "smart" pointers. They are permitted to have values that represent one of a set of defined states. These states are listed and explained in Table 15.3.

Table 15.3 STL Iterator States

Iterator state	Meaning
singular	The iterator's value does not dereference any object in any container[3].
dereferenceable	The iterator points to a valid object in the container.
past-the-end	The iterator points to the object position past the last object in the container.

[3]The iterator could be uninitialized or set to a logical null value.

Iterators can be initialized, incremented, and decremented, and their bounds can be limited by the current extent of the containers. If you can cause an iterator to be equal to another iterator by incrementing the first, the second iterator is *reachable* from the first. The two iterators are also known to refer to the same container. The two iterators can therefore define a *range* of objects in the container.

Iterators can be set as the result of a search of the container or by subscripted reference into the container. Containers include member functions that return iterators that point to the first object and the past-the-end object position. Iterators are the objects with which STL algorithms work.

Algorithms

Algorithms perform operations on containers by dereferencing iterators. Each algorithm is a function template parameterized on one or more iterator types. Algorithms are the backbone of STL. Table 15.4 lists the standard algorithms provided with STL.

Table 15.4 STL Algorithms

Nonmutating Sequence Operations	Mutating Sequence Operations	Sorting Operations	Generalized Numeric Operations
for_each	copy	sort	accumulate
find	copy_backward	stable_sort	inner_product
find_if	swap	partial_sort	partial_sum
adjacent_find	swap_ranges	partial_sort_copy	adjacent_difference
count	transform	nth_element	
count_if	replace	lower_bound	
mismatch	replace_if	upper_bound	
equal	replace_copy	equal_range	
search	replace_copy_if	binary_search	
	fill	merge	
	fill_n	inplace_merge	
	generate	includes	
	generate_n	set_union	
	remove	set_intersection	
	remove_if	set_difference	
	remove_copy	set_symmetric_difference	
	remove_copy_if	push_heap	
	unique	pop_heap	
	unique_copy	make_heap	
	reverse	sort_heap	
	reverse_copy	min	
	rotate	max	
	rotate_copy	max_element	
	random_shuffle	min_element	
	partition	lexicographical_compare	
	stable_partition	next_permutation	
		prev_permutation	

Algorithms accept iterators as arguments. The iterators tell the algorithm what object or range of objects in a container to operate on. For example, to build and sort a vector container of pseudorandom integers, you could use this program, which has been ported from Exercise 11.7 to future C++:

```
#include <iostream>
#include <iomanip>
#include <cstdlib>
#include "stl"
main()
{
    int dim;
    // --- get the number of integers to sort
    cout << "How many integers?\n";
    cin >> dim;
    // --- a vector of integers
    vector<int> vct;
    // --- insert values into the vector
    for (int i = 0; i < dim; i++)
        vct.insert(vct.end(), rand());
    // --- display the random integers
    cout << "\n----- unsorted -----\n";
    for (i = 0; i < dim; i++)
        cout << setw(8) << vct[i];
    // --- sort the array with the STD sort algorithm
    sort(vct.begin(), vct.end());
    // --- display the sorted integers
    cout << "\n----- sorted -----\n";
    for (i = 0; i < dim; i++)
        cout << setw(8) << vct[i];
}
```

The example program instantiates a vector of integer objects named *vct*. Then it uses the vector template class member function named *insert* to insert random numbers into the vector. It displays the vector's contents, retrieving each of the objects by using the overloaded [] operator. Next, the program uses the STL *sort* algorithm to sort the vector container. The *sort* function accepts a range of objects expressed as a pair of iterators. The second iterator must be reachable from the first. The container *begin* and *end* member functions return iterators that refer to the first object in the container and the *past-the-end* position of the container. This pair constitutes a range that represents the entire container.

Algorithms also accept *predicates*, which are *function object* arguments. A function object is an object that overloads *operator( )* and that you pass to an algorithm as a callback function argument. The algorithm calls the predicate for each object that it processes from the container. In come cases the predicate is a *bool* function that returns *true* or *false* to tell the algorithm whether to select the object. In other cases, the predicate processes the objects that the algorithm finds and returns an object of the type in the container. STL provides a set of standard arithmetic, comparison, and logical function objects that you can use as predicates.

STL Summarized

STL consists of generic containers with iterators and algorithms that operate on those containers through their iterators. STL is almost a different programming model—another paradigm, if you will. It flies in the face of pure object-oriented theory by apparently separating the data from the functions. Algorithms are not bound to classes. They are not methods. They are function templates. Their binding to the data occurs as a function of their parameterized argument types.

The chapter's treatment of STL is by no means an exhaustive study. It should serve, however, as an introduction to the underlying concepts of the library. Once implementations are in place, programmers will begin to use this powerful tool, and virtually all vendor-unique container class libraries can be forgotten.

SUMMARY

Future C++ promises a bigger and richer language. Some of the details are uncertain, and many of the new features are relatively untested. The designers of the Standard are confident that their innovations will work the way they designed them and that the new features solve most of the problems upon which that small society agrees. It remains to be seen whether the complete specification will serve as well the C++ programming community at large.

APPENDIX

C++ Compilers

This appendix discusses MS-DOS C++ compilers that you can use to compile and operate the exercises in this book. The list is not comprehensive, and products are introduced and upgraded regularly. The exercises are tested with Borland, GNU, Microsoft, and Watcom C++. Not all compilers work with all the exercises because not all compilers have implemented all the contemporary and future C++ features.

Borland C++

Borland International, Inc.
100 Borland Way
PO Box 660001
Scotts Valley, CA 95066-0001
(800) 645-4559

Borland C++ is a compiler implementation of C++ that runs on MS-DOS and OS/2 systems. It is the descendent of the very popular Turbo C. Borland C++ comes in many configurations and supports OS/2, Windows, and DOS development and target environments. The 4.1 version for MS-DOS and the 1.5 version for OS/2 support templates, exception handling, new-style casts, and run-time type information. All the exercises in this book work with those compilers.

Comeau C++

> Comeau Computing
>
> 91-34 120th Street
>
> Richmond Hill, NY 11418
>
> (718) 945-0009

Comeau C++ is a CFRONT port, which means that it is an adaptation of the AT&T C++ 2.1 translator to run under MS-DOS and UNIX. The CFRONT program reads your C++ source code and translates it into C code which must be compiled by a C compiler. You need a C compiler to compile the translated output from Comeau C++. The MS-DOS version uses Microsoft C. Developers who want guaranteed CFRONT-compatible code for developing on MS-DOS and other desktop platforms to port to UNIX targets will find Comeau C++ a good choice.

The latest version supports templates and compiles the exercises in this book through Chapter 11.

Computer Innovations C++

> Computer Innovations, Inc.
>
> 980 Shrewsbury Avenue
>
> Tinton Falls, NJ 07724-3003
>
> (908) 542-5920

Computer Innovations C++ is a UNIX implementation of CFRONT that runs on 386/486 UNIX systems. It includes a copy of this book to help programmers get started.

GNU C++

Free Software Foundation, Inc.

675 Mass Avenue

Cambridge, MA 02139

(617) 876-3296

The GNU C++ compiler is distributed by the Free Software Foundation. The compiler is available from numerous Internet sites, on-line services, and CD-ROM distributors. The Free Software Foundation sells a CD-ROM with complete source code and executable versions of the compiler for many platforms. The version of the compiler that I used to test the exercises in this book is modified to work in MS-DOS with a 32-bit DOS extender. The compiler supports templates and works with the exercises through Chapter 11.

The companion diskette to this book includes an executable copy of the GNU C++ compiler. At the end of this appendix are instructions for using the compiler. A file named **COPYING.TYC** on the diskette describe how you can get the source code for the compiler and the DOS extender.

High C/C++

MetaWare Incorporated

2161 Delaware Avenue

Santa Cruz, CA 96060-5706

(408) 429-6382

Version 3.3 of High C++ is the closest to a future C++ compiler that you can get. It supports templates, exception handling, new-style casts, runtime type information, and namespaces. The new version was released in November 1994, too late for me to build exercises for Part III of this book.

High C++ supports development for Windows 3.1 and extended MS-DOS 32-bit applications.

Microsoft Visual C++

Microsoft Corporation
One Microsoft Way
Redmond, WA 98052
(800) 426-9400

Visual C++ 2.0 is a 32-bit compiler intended mainly for development of Windows 3.1, Windows 95, and Windows NT programs. It includes a command-line DOS compiler that compiles contemporary C++ with templates and exception handling and works with the exercises through Chapter 12.

Symantec C++

Symantec Corporation
10201 Torre Avenue
Cupertino, CA 95014
(408) 253-9600

The Symantec C++ compiler supports DOS and Windows development. It descends from Zortech C++, which was the first MS-DOS C++ implementation available commercially.

Watcom C++

Watcom Internationa l Corporation
415 Phillip Street
Waterloo, Ontario
CANADA N2L 3X2
(800) 265-4555

The Watcom compiler is an integrated C++ development environment for DOS, Windows 3.1, Windows NT, and OS/2. New versions include visual development tools. Watcom has long been known for compiling tight, efficient code. Developers often use other compilers for their superior devlopment tools and use Watcom to compile the release version of the software.

Operating Instructions for the GNU C++ Compiler

The GNU C++ compiler on the companion diskette to this book consists of the preprocessor, C++ compiler, assembler, linker, 387 emulator, DOS extender, Standard C library, and *iostream* library. The diskette's installation program installs the compiler along with the exercise source code and batch files to compile the exercises with Borland C++, GNU C++, Microsoft C++, and Watcom C++.

This minimal distribution is sufficient to compile the exercises in this book and to develop MS-DOS 32-bit command line text-mode programs. If GNU C and C++ seem interesting, you should get the complete package on the Free Software Foundation's CD-ROM.

Installation

The installation procedure sets the path and some environment variables that GNU C++ uses. To use the compiler with the exercises in a later session, log into the TYCPP\SOURCE subdirectory and enter this command:

```
setup c:
```

where *c:* is the drive where you installed the companion diskette. That procedure, which is the same one run by the installation procedure, allows you to select one of the supported compilers. You can switch to a different compiler if you have one installed on your computer.

If you want GNU C++ to be a permanent part of your installation, add the following environment variable settings to your **AUTOEXEC.BAT** file. (These examples assume that you installed the diskette onto C:\TYCPP.)

```
SET PATH=C:\TYCPP\GCC\BIN; (followed by the rest of your path)

SET C_INCLUDE_PATH=C:\TYCPP\GCC\INCLUDE
SET CPLUS_INCLUDE_PATH=C:\TYCPP\GCC\INCLUDE
SET LIBRARY_PATH=C:\TYCPP\GCC\LIB
SET GO32=EMU C:\TYCPP\GCC\BIN\EMU387
```

The GO32 environment variable is necessary only if your computer does not have a math coprocessor.

Compiling Programs

The compiler consists of **GCC.EXE**, which is a command-line compiler driver program similar to those available with most compilers. It decides which compiler to run (C or C++) and runs the preprocessor, compiler, assembler, and linker. Because of space limitations the companion diskette does not include the C compiler.

After the program is compiled, the output file is run against the **STRIP.EXE** and **COFF2EXE.EXE** programs to fix it so that you can run it directly from the command line without explicitly invoking the DOS extender.

The companion diskette includes a batch file, **DJGPP.BAT,** that places all the compile commands into one batch command. The **DJGPP.BAT** file assumes that every program links with the *iostream* library. The format for DJGPP is:

```
djgpp <module1> { <module2>.<ext> {<module3>.<ext> {<module4>.<ext>}}}
```

The *module1* parameter is the name of the first .cpp file. That parameter must not have a file extension. The optional other parameters name as many as three additional .cpp files. Those parameters must explicitly provide their extensions.

N O T E

Exercise 2.9 links a C++ module with a C module to demonstrate C and C++ linkage specifications. Inasmuch as the diskette does not include a C compiler, it includes the compiled object module for the C component of Exercise 2.9.

Running Compiled Programs

Compiled programs must be run with the DOS extender, **GO32.EXE**, available in the DOS path. If the target computer does not have a math coprocessor, the file **EMU387** must be included and the GO32 environment variable must be set as follows:

```
SET GO32=EMU <path>EMU387
```

where <path> is the path where GO32 can find the file named **EMU387**.

GLOSSARY

This glossary defines C++ and object-oriented programming terms.

abstract base class

A class definition that is always a base class for other classes to be derived from. No specific objects of the base class are declared by the program. A C++ abstract base class is one that has a pure virtual function, a protected constructor, or a protected destructor.

abstract data type

Also called ADT. A user-defined data type built as a C++ class. The details of implementation are not necessarily a part of the ADT. See also "primitive data type" and "concrete data type."

abstraction

Defining an abstract data type by designing a class.

anonymous object

An internal, temporary object created by the compiler.

argument

The value passed to a function. Its type must match that of the function's corresponding parameter as declared in the function's prototype. See "parameter."

base class

A class from which other classes derive characteristics. All the characteristics of the base are inherited by the derived class. Also called "superclass."

class

A user-defined data type that may consist of data members and member functions.

class hierarchy

A system of base and derived classes.

concrete data type

A user-defined or library data type complete with interface and implementation. The CDT is meant to be instantiated as an object and is not intended solely to be derived from.

constructor

The function executed by the compiler when the program declares an instance of a class. See also "destructor."

data member

A data component of a class. It may be any valid data type including class objects and references.

declaration

As opposed to "definition." A declaration is the statement that declares the format of a type. A declaration reserves no memory.

definition

As opposed to "declaration." A definition is the statement that defines the existence of an object. A definition reserves memory.

derived class

A class that inherits some of its characteristics from a base class. Also called a "subclass."

destructor

The function executed by the compiler when a declared instance of a class goes out of scope. See also "constructor."

encapsulation

The activity of defining a class with its data members and member functions encapsulated into the definition. Encapsulation implies an implementation, which is hidden from the class user, and an interface, which is visible to the class user.

exception

The signal that the run-time system raises (throws) when it senses an error condition. Another part of the program, one that has already run and is higher in the call stack, can intercept (catch) and process the exception.

extraction operator

The overloaded >> operator that reads (extracts) values from an input stream. See also "insertion operator."

free store

The C++ heap. A dynamic memory pool that programs use to allocate and release temporary memory buffers.

friend

A function that has access to the private members of a class but that is not a member function of that class. The class definition declares the function to be a *friend.*

hierarchy

See "class hierarchy."

inheritance

The ability for one class to inherit the characteristics of another. The inherited class is said to be derived from the base class. Also called "subclassing".

implementation

The private members of a class. The implementation defines the details of how the class implements the behavior of the abstract base type. See also "interface."

inline function

A function that the compiler compiles as in-line code every time the function is called.

insertion operator

The overloaded << operator that writes (inserts) values to an output stream. See also "extraction operator."

instantiate

Declare an object of a data type, usually a class.

interface

The public members of a class, which define the class user's interface to the class's data and its behavior. Usually implemented as member functions. See also "implementation."

intrinsic data type

See "primitive data type."

linkage specification

Notation that tells the C++ compiler that a function was or is to be compiled with the linkage conventions of another language.

manipulator

A value that a program sends to a stream to tell the stream to modify one of its modes.

member

A component of a class, either a data member or a member function.

member function

A function component of a class, also called a "method." A member function may be virtual.

message

A message is the invocation of a class's member function in the name of a declared object of the class. The message is said to be sent to the object to tell it to perform its function. The message includes the function call and the arguments that accompany it.

method

A method in C++ is a member function of a class. Programs send messages to objects by invoking methods.

multiple inheritance

The ability for a derived class to inherit the characteristics of more than one base class.

namespace

The logical scope in which names are declared and are unique. Names in an inner namespace can override names in an outer namespace. Code in an inner namespace can reference overridden names by using the scope resolution operator. Two objects in the same namespace cannot have the same name.

object

A declared instance of a data type including standard C++ data types as well as objects of classes.

object database

A collection of persistent objects.

overloaded function

A function that has the same name as one or more other functions but that has a different parameter list. The compiler selects the function to call based on the types and number of arguments in the call.

overloaded operator

A function that executes when a C++ operator is seen in a defined context with respect to a class object.

overriding function

A function in a derived class that has the same name, return type, and parameter list as a function in the base class. The compiler calls the overriding function when the program calls that function in the name of an object of the derived class. If the function in the base class is virtual, the compiler calls the derived class's function even when the call is through a pointer or reference to the base class. See also "pure virtual function."

parameter

The declaration of a data item that a function uses to receive arguments that are passed to the function. This declaration includes the item's type and name and appears in the function's declaration block at the beginning of the function. When the parameter appears in the function's prototype, the parameter's name may be omitted. See "argument" and "prototype."

parameter list

The list of parameter types and names in a function declaration block. Also the same list, which may exclude the names, in a function prototype.

persistence

The ability of an object to succeed its creator and to subsequently exist in space other than the space in which it was created.

persistent object

An object that exhibits persistence.

polymorphism

The ability for methods in a class hierarchy to exhibit different behavior for the same message depending on the type of the object for which the method is invoked and without regard to the class type of the reference to the object.

primitive data type

A data type known to the compiler. Primitive data types in C++ are *char, int, float, double,* and *pointer.* The integer types may be further qualified as *long, short,* and *unsigned.* All types may be organized into arrays of like types and structures and unions of varying types. Also called *intrinsic data types.*

private class members

Members of a class for which access is granted only to the class's member functions and to *friend* functions of the class.

protected class members

Members of a class that are private except to member functions of publicly derived classes.

prototype

The definition of a function's name, return type, and parameter list.

public class members

Members of a class to which access is granted to all functions within the scope of an object of the class.

pure virtual function

A virtual function in a base class that must have a matching function in a derived class. A program may not declare an instance of a class that has a pure virtual function. A program may not declare an instance of a derived class if that derived class has not provided an overriding function for each pure virtual function in the base.

reference

A variable name that is an alias for another variable.

stream

A category of character-oriented data files or devices in which the data characters exist in an input or output stream.

subclass

See "derived class."

subclassing

See "inheritance."

superclass

See "base class."

this

A pointer that exists in all nonstatic member functions. The *this* pointer is a pointer to an object of the class. It points to the object for which the function is being executed.

translation unit

One independently compiled source code unit consisting of the C++ source file and all included headers.

type

The type of a program constant or variable, which can be of a primitive or an abstract data type.

type conversion

The conversion of one type to another. The compiler has built-in type conversions, and a class may define its own conversions for converting from an object of the class to another type and from another type to an object of the class.

type-safe linkage

A technique that ensures that functions and function calls in separately compiled program modules use consistent parameter lists.

virtual function

A member function in a class from which other classes may be derived. If the derived class has a function with the same name and parameter list, the derived class's function is always executed for objects of the derived class. See also "pure virtual function" and "overriding function."

BIBLIOGRAPHY

Cargill, Tom, *C++ Programming Style*, 1992, Addison-Wesley

Coplien, James O., *Advanced C++ Programming Styles and Idioms*, 1992, Addison-Wesley

Dewhurst, Stephen C., and Stark, Kathy T., *Programming in C++*, 1989, Prentice Hall

Dlugosz, John M., Computer Language Magazine, August 1988, "The Secret of Reference Variables"

Ellis, Margaret A. and Stroustrup, Bjarne, *The Annotated C++ Reference Manual*, 1990, Addison-Wesley

Koenig, Andrew, editor, *Working Paper for Draft Proposed International Standard for Information Systems—Programming Language C++*, 1994, ANSI Document Number X3J16/94-0027

Lippman, Stanley B., *C++ Primer*, 1989, Addison-Wesley

Murray, Robert B., *C++ Strategies and Tactics*, 1993, Addison-Wesley

Myers, Scott, *Effective C++*, Addison-Wesley

Pennello, Tom, *Dr. Dobb's Journal*, August 1994, "C++ Namespaces"

Plauger, P.J., *The Standard C Library*, 1992, Prentice Hall, Inc.

Plauger, P.J., *The Draft Standard C++ Library*, 1995, Prentice Hall, Inc.

Stepanov, Alexander and Lee, Meng, *The Standard Template Library*, 1994, ANSI Document Number X3J16/94-0095

Stevens, Al, *C++ Database Development 2nd Edition*, 1994, MIS Press

Stroustrup, Bjarne, *The C++ Programming Language Second Edition*, 1991, Addison-Wesley

Stroustrup, Bjarne, *The Design and Evolution of C++*, 1994, Addison-Wesley

Terribile, Mark A., *Practical C++*, 1994, McGraw-Hill, Inc.

Vilot, Michael J., *An Introduction to the STL*, 1994, ObjectCraft, Inc.

Wiener, Richard S. and Pinson, Lewis J., *An Introduction to Object-Oriented Programming and C++*, 1988, Addison-Wesley

INDEX

DISKETTE INSTALLATION INSTRUCTIONS

1. To install the exercises and the GNU C++ compiler, insert the companion diskette in a disk drive and enter this command:

   ```
   a:install a: c:
   ```

   where a: is the diskette drive and c: is the destination drive.

2. The installation procedure installs the files in a subdirectory named C:\TYCPP. If the subdirectory already exists, the procedure does not proceed. If you need to change the subdirectory name, modify INSTALL.BAT on the diskette.

3. You will need approximately 3 MB on your destination drive.

4. If you do not want to use GNU C++, enter this command:

   ```
   deltree c:\tycpp\gcc
   ```

This measure recovers approximately 2.8 MB of disk space. Note that you need at least a 386 to run the GNU compiler. Some traditional C++ compilers will run on a 286. All contemporary C++ compilers require at least a 386 and 4 MB of extended memory.

RUNNING THE EXERCISES

The installation procedure displays a menu that allows you to select which compiler you are going to use. The procedure does the setup for the GNU compiler as explained in the Appendix, but, if you choose to use the Borland, Microsoft, or Watcom compiler, the procedure assumes that you have installed the compiler and that the path and environment variables are correct.

After selecting a compiler, you will be at the DOS prompt in the subdirectory \TYCPP\SOURCE. Compile and test the exercises for each chapter individually with these commands:

```
CHAPcc
(where cc is the chapter number, 01, 02, and so on)
```

If you see error messages, they probably indicate that your compiler is not properly installed. Some compilers issue a warning with every exercise about the *main* function not returning a value. You can ignore those warnings.

```
EXccxxx
(where cc is the chapter number and xxx is the exercise
number)
```

For example, Exercise 2.3 would be run as EX02003. If you are unsure, do this command to see what executable files are in the subdirectory.

```
dir *.exe
```

It is a good idea to delete all the executable files after you have finished with each chapter.